The Impact of the Media

Michael Welker | Jürgen von Hagen | John Witte, Jr.
Stephen Pickard (Eds.)

The Impact of the Media

on Character Formation, Ethical Education,
and the Communication of Values
in Late Modern Pluralistic Societies

WIPF & STOCK · Eugene, Oregon

Wipf and Stock Publishers
199 W 8th Ave, Suite 3
Eugene, OR 97401

The Impact of the Media
On Character Formation, Ethical Education, and the Communication
of Values in Late Modern Pluralistic Societies
By Welker, Michael and von Hagen, Jürgen
Copyright © 2022 Evangelische Verlagsanstalt GmbH All rights reserved.
Softcover ISBN-13: 978-1-6667-8077-2
Hardcover ISBN-13: 978-1-6667-8078-9
Publication date 5/23/2023
Previously published by Evangelische Verlagsanstalt GmbH, 2022

Table of Contents

Acknowledgments 7

Preface to the Series 9

Michael Welker and Jürgen von Hagen
Introduction 13

Part One: Media and Values

Günter Thomas
**The Texture of Values in the Media of Media Society:
Preliminary Observations** 23

Part Two: Media, Economics, and Ethics

Jürgen von Hagen and Matthias Vollbracht
Media Economics: Overview and Recent Developments 49

Günter Thomas
**Clicks, Likes, and Cookies: The Trading of Active and Possible
Attention in Media-Saturated Societies** 77

Katrin Gülden Le Maire
Are Social Networks Media? 105
The Problematic Financial Classification as Communication
Services Companies

Part Three: Media, Values, and Crises

Nick Couldry
Datafied Media and the Silent Derangement of Ethics 121

Julia Sonnevend and Olivia Steiert
**Seeing a Crisis Through Media: Narrating the Coronavirus
Pandemic in the Early Twenty-First Century** 137

Bert Olivier
Contemporary Media and the Crisis of Values 151

Part Four: Ethical Potentials and Problems in Media Communication

James Mairata
Why Moral Agency Is Crucial to Mainstream Cinema 169

Lizette Rabe
Trolls and Bullies: A South African Case Study of Cyber-Misogyny and the Media 179

Bodo Hombach
"Attitude" Can Damage Attitude When Journalists Abuse Their Power 207

Contributors 213

Acknowledgments

A consultation leading to this volume had been planned to take place at the Forschungszentrum Internationale und Interdisziplinäre Theologie (FIIT) at the University of Heidelberg in 2020. Due to the COVID-19 pandemic, however, the consultation had to be canceled. We are grateful to the McDonald Agape Foundation for the generous support of this publication.

Jürgen von Hagen, Michael Welker, John Witte Jr., Stephen Pickard

Preface to the Series

Five hundred years ago, Protestant reformer Martin Luther argued that "three estates" (drei Stände) lie at the foundation of a just and orderly society—marital families, religious communities, and political authorities. Parents in the home; pastors in the church; magistrates in the state—these, said Luther, are the three authorities whom God appointed to represent divine justice and mercy in the world, to protect peace and liberty in earthly life. Household, church, and state—these are the three institutional pillars on which to build social systems of education and schooling, charity and social welfare, economy and architecture, art and publication. Family, faith, and freedom—these are the three things that people will die for.

In the half millennium since Luther, historians have uncovered various classical and Christian antecedents to these early Protestant views. Numerous later theorists have propounded all manner of variations and applications of this three-estates theory, many increasingly abstracted from Luther's overtly Christian worldview. Early modern covenant theologians, both Christian and Jewish, described the marital, confessional, and political covenants that God calls human beings to form, each directed to interrelated personal and public ends. Social-contract theorists differentiated the three contracts that humans enter as they move from the state of nature to an organized society protective of their natural rights—the marital contract of husband and wife; the government contract of rulers and citizens; and, for some, the religious contracts of preachers and parishioners. Early anthropologists posited three stages of development of civilization—from family-based tribes and clans, to priest-run theocracies, to fully organized states that embraced all three institutions. Sociologists distinguished three main forms of authority in an organized community: "traditional" authority that begins in the home, "charismatic" authority that is exemplified by the church, and "legal" authority that is rooted in the state. Legal historians outlined three stages of development of legal norms—from the habits and rules of the family, to the customs and canons of religion, to the statutes and codes of the state.

Already a century ago, however, scholars in different fields began to flatten out this hierarchical theory of social institutions and to emphasize the foundational role of other social institutions alongside the family, church, and state in shaping private and public life and character. Sociologists like Max Weber and Talcott Parsons emphasized the shaping powers of "technical rationality" exemplified especially in new industry, scientific education, and market economies. Legal scholars like Otto von Gierke and F. W. Maitland emphasized the critical roles of non-state legal associations (*Genossenschaften*) in maintaining a just social, political, and legal order historically and today. Catholic subsidiarity theories of Popes Leo XIII and Pius XI emphasized the essential task of mediating social units between the individual and the state to cater the full range of needs, interests, rights, and duties of individuals. Protestant theories of sphere sovereignty, inspired by Abraham Kuyper, argued that not only churches, states, and families but also the social spheres of art, labor, education, economics, agriculture, recreation, and more should enjoy a level of independence from others, especially an overreaching church or state. Various theories of social or structural pluralism, civil society, voluntary associations, the independent sector, multiculturalism, multinormativity, and other such labels have now come to the fore in the ensuing decades—both liberal and conservative, religious and secular, and featuring all manner of methods and logics.

Pluralism of all sorts is now a commonplace of late modern societies. At minimum, this means a multitude of free and equal individuals and a multitude of groups and institutions, each with very different political, moral, religious, and professional interests and orientations. It includes the sundry associations, interest groups, parties, lobbies, and social movements that often rapidly flourish and fade around a common cause, especially when aided by modern technology and various social media. Some see in this texture of plurality an enormous potential for colorful and creative development and a robust expression of human and cultural freedom. Others see a chaotic individualism and radical relativism, which endangers normative education, moral character formation, and effective cultivation of enduring values or virtues.

Pluralism viewed as vague plurality, however, focuses on only one aspect of late modern societies—the equality of individuals, and their almost unlimited freedom to participate peaceably at any time as a respected voice in the moral reasoning and civil interactions of a society. But this view does not adequately recognize that, beneath the shifting cacophony of social forms and norms that constitute modernity, pluralistic societies have heavy normative codes that shape their individual and collective values and morals, preferences and prejudices.

The sources of much of this normative coding and moral education in late modern pluralistic societies are the deep and powerful social systems that are the pillars of every advanced culture. The most powerful and pervasive of these are the social systems of law, religion, politics, science/academy, market, media, family, education, medicine, and national defense. The actual empirical forms of each of these powerful social systems can and do vary greatly, even in the relatively homogeneous societies of the late modern West. But these deeper social systems in one form or another are structurally essential and often normatively decisive in individual and communal lives.

Every advanced society has a comprehensive legal system of justice and order, religious systems of ritual and doctrine, a family system of procreation and love, an economic system of trade and value, a media system of communication and dissemination of news and information, and an educational system of creation, preservation, and application of knowledge and scientific advance. Many advanced societies also have massive systems of science, technology, health care, and national defense with vast influence over and through all of these other social systems. These pervasive social systems lie at the foundation of modern advanced societies, and they anchor the vast pluralities of associations and social interactions that might happen to exist at any given time.

Each of these social systems has internal value systems, institutionalized rationalities, and normative expectations that together help to shape each individual's morality and character. Each of these social spheres, moreover, has its own professionals and experts who shape and implement its internal structures and processes. The normative network created by these social spheres is often harder to grasp today, since late modern pluralistic societies usually do not bring these different value systems to light under the dominance of just one organization, institution, and power. And this normative network has also become more shifting and fragile, especially since traditional social systems, such as religion and the family, have eroded in their durability and power, and other social systems, such as science, the market, healthcare, defense, and the media, have become more powerful.

The aim of this project on "Character Formation and Ethical Education in Late Modern Pluralistic Societies" is to identify the realities and potentials of these core social systems to provide moral orientation and character formation in our day. What can and should these social spheres, separately and together, do in shaping the moral character of late modern individuals who, by nature, culture, and constitutional norms, are free and equal in dignity and rights? What are and should be the core educational functions and moral responsibilities of each of these social spheres? How can we better understand and better influence the complex interactions among individualism, the normative binding powers of these social systems, and the creativity of civil groups and institutions? How can we map and measure the different hierarchies of values that govern each of these social systems, and that are also interwoven and interconnected in various ways in shaping late modern understandings of the common good? How do we negotiate the boundaries and conflicts between and among these social systems when one encroaches on the other, or imposes its values and rationalities on individuals at the cost of the other social spheres or of the common good? What and where are the intrinsic strengths of each social sphere that should be made more overt in character formation, public education, and the shaping of minds and mentalities?

These are some of the guiding questions at work in this project and in this volume. Our project aims to provide a systematic account of the role of these powerful normative codes operating in the social spheres of law, religion, the family, the market, the media, science and technology, the academy, health care, and defense in the late modern liberal West. Our focus is on selected examples and case studies drawn from Western Europe, North America, South Africa, and Australia, which together provide just enough diversity to test out broader theories of character formation and moral education. Our scholars are drawn from across the academy, with representative voices from the humanities, social sciences, and natural sciences as well as the professions of theology, law, business, medicine, and more. While most of our scholars come from the Protestant and Catholic worlds, our endeavor is to offer comparative insights that will help scholars from any profession or confession. While our laboratory is principally Western liberal societies, the modern forces of globalization will soon make these issues of moral character formation a concern for every culture and region of the world–given the power of global social media, entertainment, and sports; the pervasiveness of global finance, business, trade, and law; and the perennial global worries over food, health care, environmental degradation, and natural disasters.

In this volume, we focus in on the role of the media in shaping character development, ethical education, and the communication of values in late modern pluralistic societies.

Michael Welker, University of Heidelberg
John Witte Jr., Emory University
Jürgen von Hagen, University of Bonn
Stephen Pickard, Charles Sturt University

Introduction

Michael Welker and Jürgen von Hagen

This volume focuses on the role of the media as an important subsystem of modern societies. While "the media" encompasses a very broad range of channels of communication, the authors in this volume mainly deal with media of mass communication, that is, the press, cinema, radio broadcasting, television, and, more recently, the internet and internet-based social platforms. The authors show how the communication of values through these media is a selective process favoring some values over others and creating ethical biases. This process, in turn, affects the formation of ethical judgment on the part of media consumers and, thereby, character formation.

We have grouped the chapters in this volume into four parts. The first part gives a broad overview of and introduction into the general topic of the volume: In what ways are media relevant for the transmission of values and character formation in late modern pluralistic societies? The second part deals with media economics and their ethical implications. The third part looks at several aspects of the impact of the media on the development and change of ethical values in societies. Finally, the contributions to the fourth part can be regarded as case studies of specific ethical problems in communication through mass media.

Part one offers an introductory overview by the theologian and sociologist Günter Thomas entitled "The Texture of Values in the Media of Media Society: Preliminary Observations." Thomas argues that media society is one of the most accurate labels under which contemporary Western societies operate. Communication media permeate not only the organizations of social subsystems but also everyday life and the most private spaces. The resulting complexity generates many problems for the development of comprehensive media ethics and for any diagnosis of the diversity of value orientations in late modern pluralistic societies.

Thomas describes the manifold places of value preferences in the rich media landscape of contemporary societies with reference to the sociological media theory developed by Niklas Luhmann. Thomas starts with the identification of four types of media: communication media as the basis of all social life; technological dissemination media, which "detach communication from interaction (and) enable communication across space and time"; symbolically generalized exchange media, which are connected with specific societal subsystems, such as economy, politics, law, religion, education; and finally, the media system that emerged in the twentieth century as a relatively independent social subsystem of value sphere.

Thomas then considers ten fields of media ethics, related to the four types of media. He identifies different textures of values in the communication media, in the dissemination media, and in the symbolically generalized communication media, and concludes with a description of the contours of ethics in the media system in general. He argues that the complexity of the media landscape should not lead to the impression that we are only more or less helpless spectators. We should rather understand ourselves and each other as active and responsible navigators, conscious of "a double hermeneutic process": on one hand, we should ask "which initially implicit vision of a good, just, and flourishing life is factually assembled from the sum of one's own value preferences. And which visions are contained in the most effective development trends of media practices." On the other hand, we should critically test what value preferences result from the various media communications—both for one's own life and for community life.

Part two begins with a chapter by Matthias Vollbracht and Jürgen von Hagen entitled "Media Economics: Overview and Recent Developments." Vollbracht and von Hagen build on the paradigm of media markets as two-sided markets. On one hand, media companies sell content to consumers. On the other hand, media companies provide advertisers access to potential buyers of their products. Since this side of the markets is the economically more important one for mass media, media companies must tailor their content to maximize the number of consumers. Traditional mass media are also characterized by very large fixed and very small variable costs leading to a strong tendency of market concentration. The result of these structural characteristics of media markets is that content is chosen according to the principle of the least common denominator, meaning that content, including ethical content, does not reflect the large variety of what people in society like. Instead, it reflects what a large number of people in society find acceptable, and perhaps barely acceptable. The result is a much narrower range of values and ethical communications transmitted through mass media.

The rise of the internet, of social platforms or networks (such as Facebook, YouTube, and Twitter), and, since around 2010, of mobile communications devices has reshaped media markets. Fixed costs have fallen dramatically. Producing media content of good technical quality is now something ordinary citizens can do. As a result, the volume and the diversity of content have increased dramatically. At the same time, the use of cookies and algorithms allows media companies to gather an enormous amount of information about the preferences and living patterns of individual consumers. This, in turn, is of great economic value to advertisers, as it allows them to design customer-specific advertising and thus increase the likelihood of advertising that results in purchases of their products. Vollbracht and von Hagen end their chapter with a discussion of the implications this has for the transmission of values and character formation.

One of the important aspects of this new media world is that consumers are constantly bombarded with new information that they cannot possibly pay equal attention to all the time. In other words, consumer attention has become a scarce commodity in this new world. Günter Thomas, in "Clicks, Likes, and Cookies: The Trading of Active and Possible Attention in Media-Saturated Societies," looks at the implications of this new market characteristic. He states that in the new media society, human attention is a very much contested cultural property and resource. He argues that Christian churches are called to be places where the crucial cultural resource of attention is regenerated, redirected, and invested outside the contemporary economy of attention. He sets out with reflections on the difference between natural and cultural resources and sees the need for regeneration in both spheres. He describes a shift in the cultural economy of attention that occurred during the past decades, and several academic endeavors to deal constructively with this shift.

It is crucial to differentiate attention from mere awareness, and to distinguish between self-reflexive attention, perceptive attention, communicative attention, and, finally, accumulated attention. Thomas outlines several influential communication theories and their treatments of attention as a resource and raises the question why attention is a limited resource and in need of being regenerated. He describes six processes that he regards as exploitation of attention through mass media and concludes with a focus on religious and theological reflections and the place of the church in the struggle for attention.

The huge market power that social networks like Facebook and Twitter enjoy in the new media world has led to the question how such companies should be regulated. Katrin Gülden Le Maire considers that question in her chapter entitled "Are Social Networks Media? The Problematic Financial Classification as Media Service Companies." She begins with an overview of the development of print and audiovisual broadcasting and their emergence as the "fourth power" in modern democracies. News media play an important role in monitoring elected governments and political parties, holding them accountable for their behavior, providing objective and unbiased information to the public, and giving voice to different groups in society. To play this role effectively, journalists must be independent from government and committed to high standards of professionalism and journalistic ethos. Today, social networks give individual citizens and organizations with no such commitments opportunities to distribute and exchange information. At the same time, they have attracted much of the advertising business away from traditional media. Social networks thus undermine the function of the "fourth power" with adverse consequences for democracy.

Gülden Le Maire suggests that social networks should be regarded as part of society's essential infrastructure. Like other types of infrastructure, they could then be treated as natural monopolies and regulated by the government accordingly, in order to curtail their market power.

In part three of this volume, we turn to some aspects of the impact of the media on the development of ethical values. First, Nick Couldry offers a chapter of alarm entitled "Datafied Media and the Silent Derangement of Ethics." He speaks of datafied media to draw attention to the fact that today, "most of our online activities occur in spaces, whether platforms or not, that bear a striking feature: they require those activities, as a very condition of their possibility, to be registered and tracked in ways that *through the resulting data* create economic value for corporations, very often without the actors' full knowledge or consent." Starting with this observation, Couldry wants to understand how datafied media affect the conditions of character formation (he uses the German term *Bildung*) in contemporary societies.

Learning from neo-Aristotelian reflections on *Bildung* as a process of being initiated into an inherited historical trajectory of reasoning and thinking ethically about the world, he ponders the relevance of historically shaped evolution of personalities in the interaction among human beings and asks what happens when a huge and rapid growth of partly autonomous artificial intelligence and machine learning systems driven by the economic imperatives of the data industries replace lively polyindividual interaction among human beings. He fears the vanishing of the impacts of history and tradition and the loss of human control of individual and communal developments, and he speaks of the deep conflict between human goals and system goals with a high impact on ethical development and flourishing.

His main concern is what he calls the death of communicative symmetry, a symmetry that he sees naturally given in face-to-face social interaction. But he also warns against alarmist reactions to this development. It will be the task of ethical reflexivity and the cultivation of a media-critical ethics to rise to this challenge.

In the second chapter of this part, Julia Sonnevend and Olivia Steiert present a recent example of "Seeing a Crisis through Media: Narrating the Coronavirus Pandemic in the Early Twenty-First Century." They argue that this crisis offers a unique lens through which to look at the role of media in contemporary social life, revealing what we see and what we do not see with the help of the media. They set out with reflections on what it means to construct an event and on the complex roles of journalists in this process. Journalists not only inform, investigate, analyze, but also mobilize people, promote minority rights, amplify important voices and issues, enhance solidarity, support a diversity of views, and thus provide models for democratically governed spaces.

In all this, journalists shape complex worldviews and provide us with often-shifting mythological figures and stances toward them. Thus, journalists create ritual accesses in opening windows onto the world. This powerful activity not only opens central and broad perspectives on reality but also can block and close crucial insights, not only by intended or unintended misinformation. What are reliable facts and what is fake news? When do powerful visual presentations trigger constructive emotions, and when do they elicit a false sense of enjoyment or fear? The authors speak of the drama of misinformation and underscore the extreme importance of raising reliable truth claims and simultaneously putting them to critical tests.

"Contemporary Media and the Crisis of Values" is the title of Bert Olivier's contribution, the third chapter in this part. Inspired by Renata Salecl's work, it starts with a focus on the immense abundance of choices that contemporary societies and cultures in the West present to their members, not only in the consumer markets. It also points out a lack of willingness to clearly differentiate between choices directed at persons and at goods. This goes hand in hand with an avoidance of the investment of feeling and emotional involvement.

Like other contributions in this book, Olivier's bemoans a weakening or even a loss of intense person-to-person communication and the connected axiological alienation through mediating technology. He quotes many personal witnesses who state how the excessive use of a personal iPhone, BlackBerry, laptop, or iPad led to an obsession to look at a screen, to a hyperconnectivity. He emphasizes the important role of schools and universities in strengthening the powers of *Bildung*. His conclusion is that the "technologization" of knowledge and values has dislocated the conditions of the possibility of "transindividuation" that is indispensable for the maintenance and renewal of disciplines of all kinds.

The praise of aesthetic delight and the cultivation of desire come as antidotes to this gloomy picture of contemporary cultures. In his longing for genuine interpersonal connection, Olivier draws on classic voices such as those of Martin Heidegger and Saint Augustine, but also on contemporary positions such as those Jacques Lacan and Jean-Luc Nancy.

The contributions in part four of this volume present case studies of ethical problems connected with communication through mass media. In "Why Moral Agency Is Crucial to Mainstream Cinema," James Mairata considers the importance of morality in the storytelling of mainstream movies. Cinematic storytelling remains an important part of the culture of Western societies, and the main producers—the Hollywood studios—are today controlled by the world's largest media giants. In a historical review, Mairata shows that, from the beginning, movies were regarded as important channels transporting ethical norms. He shows that a standard form of what is a cinematic story has developed early in the history of the industry. Moral instruction, such as the need for the good to fight the evil, is an important part of that form. Such instruction is part and purpose of all storytelling, as Mairata shows with historical examples going back to the ancient cave drawings of Lascaux, France.

Mairata suggests that moral agency in modern movies can be of both the Humean (playing to emotions) and the Kantian (playing to rationality) kind. Narratives are shaped in ways that try to maximize audience engagement. Audiences are encouraged to predict what will happen next as a story develops. In this process, they develop and correct their own moral judgments about what they see happening on the screen.

Lizette Rabe, in "Trolls and Bullies: A South African Case Study of Cyber Misogyny and the Media," uses the example of women working in South African media to illustrate how women are systematically discriminated against in South African society, which is, therefore, very far from delivering on its official values of fairness and gender equality. Rabe builds her case on two theoretical approaches, feminism and media hegemony theory. She shows how female journalists find themselves exposed to harassment, physical and online threats, and abuses to an extent that male journalists do not experience. South African institutions whose mission it is to protect women against such pressures fail to do so. Despite official declarations affirming the opposite, women in South Africa and, more generally, the Global South, often find themselves sidelined and subjugated to violence and unjust treatment. In view of this problem, Rabe calls for new thinking about women and their position in late modern, pluralistic societies.

The last chapter of this volume is a speech delivered by the eminent German journalist Bodo Hombach at a meeting of TV journalists some years ago. Hombach speaks of the need for high ethical standards of professional journalists, particularly in media that view themselves as serving the general public, such as German public television, and he outlines the content of such standards. He argues that as the "fourth estate"—or "fourth power," as others in this volume refer to it—in democratic societies, mass media derive their legitimacy from high-quality journalism. To assure such high quality, journalists must be willing to constantly criticize their own arguments and hypotheses and to tolerate that their hypotheses fail and require change in light of new facts. Good journalists must also keep a distance from the things they report and not become involved in causes. The promise of journalism, Hombach reminds his audience, is the promise not to be manipulated. There is a real danger, as he sees it, that journalism becomes intentional, aiming at persuasion instead of objective information. Journalists must not give up the claim to objectivity, faithfulness to facts, neutrality, and the search for the truth in order to fulfill their role in democratic and pluralistic societies.

In sum, the contributions to this volume offer a wide range of theoretical, empirical, and practical arguments on the role of the media on character formation, ethical education, and the transmission of values in our societies. They show that the media are indeed an important subsystem impacting ethical development. Technological changes and the development of new types of channels for communication have brought dramatic changes in the media environment of our societies, and this transformation has had important effects on the volume and quality of content citizens are exposed to. High standards of professional ethics of producers operating in this new environment are necessary to ensure that the media contribute to strengthening the moral foundations of our societies rather than to their downfall.

Part One:
Media and Values

The Texture of Values in the Media of Media Society: Preliminary Observations

Günter Thomas

Introduction

Among the many labels under which contemporary Western societies operate, that of media society is undoubtedly one of the most accurate.[1] Not only the liberal societies of the West, but also the societies of the global South and the societies of Asia are inconceivable without the manifold use of modern communication media. They permeate not only the organizations of social subsystems, but also everyday life and the most private spaces. No human being and no human society is conceivable without communication and media. The *animal symbolicum* is also a *homo medialis*, a creator of media through which social life in its diachronic and synchronic dimensions is not only made possible but constantly reshaped.[2]

However, it is also the ubiquity of communication media that obscures the contingencies, alternatives, and value preferences in media creation. Communication media are both objects of moral evaluations and means of transmitting and disseminating moral orientations of humans. Since the early development of societies, religions have been concerned with the problem of communication with transcendent realities. Therefore, religions themselves are laboratories for the development of media and for means of their control.[3] Under these conditions, every

---

[1] On the concept of media society, see Kurt Imhof et al., eds., *Mediengesellschaft. Strukturen, Merkmale, Entwicklungsdynamiken* (Wiesbaden: Springer, 2004), especially section 1, pp. 33–155; Manfred Fassler, "Informations- und Mediengesellschaft," in *Soziologische Gesellschaftsbegriffe. Konzepte moderner Zeitdiagnosen*, ed. Georg Kneer et al. (Munich: Wilhelm Fink Verlag, 1997), 332–60.

[2] Ernst Cassierer, *An Essay on Man: An Introduction to a Philosophy of Human Culture* (New York: Anchor Books, 1944).

[3] On the side of religious studies, see Rainer Neu, *Das Mediale: die Suche nach der Einheit der Religionen in der Religionswissenschaft* (Stuttgart: Kohlhammer, 2010); in relation to Christianity, see Peter G. Horsfield, *From Jesus to the Internet: A History of Christianity and Media* (Chichester: Wiley Blackwell, 2015). From the field of media studies, see Knut

concept of being human, of society, and of spiritual life contains an implicit vision of the place and function of communication and media.

In addition, there is the difficulty that the concept of the medium not only is used in an almost inflationary manner, but also can be determined in many different ways. In the broad fields of communication studies and media studies, a wide variety of philosophical and social-scientific theories are at work. Thus, philosophical and often also latent religious traditions are sources for media and communication ethics.

The systemic necessity of media communication entails that its organizations are closely interwoven with other subsystems. Given the centrality of communication and media use, it is not surprising that their regulation is not left to moral practice but is often embedded in legal formations. Because of the materiality of communication, significant resources are required to create media. Thus, communication and media become a matter of economic calculation and control. Since modern democracies depend on free communication processes and access to media, both "old" and "new" media are highly contested in the political space of civil society. When technological progress enables far-reaching observation of communication and processing of the data generated, the moral implications of such an "omniscient" authority become an intensely debated topic. At the same time, the extent to which media communication can and must replace communication in physical presence, at least for a limited period of time—even in education, religion, and law—became apparent during the COVID pandemic.

Against the backdrop of each of these richly structured and powerful social practices, media ethics has both strong descriptive and normative branches. The complexity of communication and media practices then leads to two insights for ethical observation: First, any ethical reflection on the values in the enactments of media society is embedded in a broader social theory and anthropology. Without a theoretical toolkit, the subject matter does not become sufficiently clear. Second, there is no comprehensive media ethics for all communication processes in which media play a role. For this reason, the field of media ethics is highly differentiated and, at the same time, isolated from other fields of ethics.[4] Because of this com-

---

Lundby, ed. *Religion across Media: From Early Antiquity to Late Modernity* (New York: Peter Lang, 2013).

[4] For an overview, see Lee Wilkins and Clifford G. Christians, eds., *The Routledge Handbook of Mass Media Ethics*, 2nd ed. (New York: Routledge, 2020); Mark Fackler and Robert S. Fortner, eds., *The Handbook of Global Communication and Media Ethics* (Chichester: Wiley-Blackwell, 2011); Stephen Ward, ed., *Handbook of Global Media Ethics* (Cham: Springer, 2019); George Cheney et al., eds., *The Handbook of Communication Ethics*, 1st ed. (London: Routledge, 2010); oriented toward media organizations and media practitioners, Christian Schicha and Carsten Brosda, eds., *Handbuch Medienethik* (Wiesbaden: VS Verlag für Sozialwissenschaften, 2010); and Christian Schicha, *Medienethik. Grundlagen–*

plexity and, ultimately, the associated diversity of value orientations, we should speak of a texture of values.

As already mentioned, the ubiquity of the media creates the impression of an infinite number of lack of alternatives. Nevertheless, a variety of values are operationally effective in the execution of media communication. What is the understanding of values in the analyses offered in this essay? The concept of value is not tied to what is called in moral philosophy *Wertethik* (ethics of values).[5]

In this context, values are regarded as preferences of orientation that shape perception and communication, that is, action and experience, and are ultimately fed by visions of common and individual life. Values are orientation directives for human action, directives of shaping oneself and one's world.[6] The preferences are widely anchored in narratively mediated broader conceptions of life, such as those cultivated by religions and concise worldviews. These value orientations can be present in different ways. The place of their presence is then also, but not only, the consciousness of the morally acting human. Values can be sedimented, deeply embedded, and thus largely invisible in routines and habits. Rarely are they found in formulated sets of rules. They may be manifested in procedures as well as in complex decisions. Not to be forgotten is the embedding and operational effectiveness in organizations, which at their core consist of decisions as final elements. Likewise, it should not be forgotten that, especially in the complex structure of late-modern media societies, many value decisions are manifested in legally valid determinations and laws. These references serve as a reminder that values can be not only close to consciousness, but also downright distant from it. The problem cannot be avoided that value orientations in a media society always remain dependent on processes of interpretation, and thus cannot escape a relativity of meaning. Knowing this, however, does not relieve us of the obligation to analyze the places where values are set and to question the value setting itself in a self-critical way.

The aim of the following considerations is to show the places of value preferences in the dense network of media communication of modern societies. Where are values sedimented in factual decisions? In which decisions can preferences be seen and shaped differently? Such a differentiated development is necessary both to see shifts in the media landscape and not to persist in sweeping

---

Anwendungen–Ressourcen (Munich: UVK Verlag, 2019. The overwhelming majority of contributions to media ethics are devoted to an ethic of the press seen through the eyes of the journalist; in short, they offer professional ethics.

[5] See Eike Bohlken, "Wertethik," in *Handbuch Ethik*, ed. Marcus Düwell (Stuttgart: Weimar Metzler, 2002), 108–21, at 118 f. for connections.

[6] See Werner Stegmaier, *Philosophie der Orientierung* (Berlin: De Gruyter, 2008), 569–80; Christian Krijnen, "Wert," in Düwell, *Handbuch Ethik*, 527–33.

gestures of indignation. Only when the specific decisions are seen can factual decisions be confirmed in terms of value or criticized in terms of alternatives.

The following uses Niklas Luhmann's sociological media theory as a basis for cartography.[7] His theory has the advantage that it takes communication as a fundamental social process as its basis and can thus combine social theory and media theory. At the same time, it works with a differentiated set of instruments of various media, which are related to each other in dynamic development processes.

Analytical Instruments

Four Types of Media

In order to understand the present media society and its development, it is necessary to distinguish among four different types of media.

1. Communication media (M1) are the basis of social life: language, vocal utterances, gestures, smells, smoke, but also more sophisticated media, such as narratives, architectural symbols, rituals, and patterns of dress. Communication media, often analyzed in other theories as signs or symbols, are tied to interaction in specific spaces and at specific times. Communication media are tied to interaction in physical co-presence because they require shared space and perception. Even at this level of physical co-presence, communication is often multimedia: words, the pace of speech, spatial arrangements, perfume, and body postures. The necessary binding of attention results mostly already from the binding of the body in the shared space.[8]

2. Technological dissemination media (M2) enable communication across space and time. They detach communication from interaction. As real-time media, dissemination media may be more likely to bridge space; as storage media, they are more likely to bridge time. Dissemination media require their own substrate that is both medial and material. Writing in general and, in particular, forms such as letters, books, the telegraph, the radio, the telephone, the newspaper, televi-

---

[7] Niklas Luhmann, "Veränderungen im System gesellschaftlicher Kommunikation und die Massenmedien," in Niklas Luhmann, ed., *Soziologische Aufklärung*, vol. 3, *Soziales System, Gesellschaft, Organisation* (Opladen: Westdeutscher, 1981), 309–20; Niklas Luhmann, *The Reality of the Mass Media* (Cambridge: Polity Press, 2000); and Niklas Luhmann, *Die Gesellschaft der Gesellschaft* (Frankfurt am Main: Suhrkamp, 1997), chap. 2, 190–412.

[8] On the material nature of all media, see Birgit Meyer, ed., *Aesthetic Formations: Media, Religion, and the Senses* (New York: Palgrave Macmillan, 2009); and, with a focus on religious communication, Birgit Meyer et al., "The Origin and Mission of Material Religion," *Religion* 40 (2010): 207–11.

sion, the cinema, and, finally, the computer, the internet, and, not least, the cell phone fall into this category. But rituals fixed in sequence as repeatable performances were also powerful dissemination media in the early empires (for example, the imperial cult). Liturgically arranged religious services are among the elementary dissemination media. Every medium of dissemination is part of a specific media dispositif that combines technology, space, time, and subject position.[9]

All dissemination media depend on the existence of communication media (M1). They extend and they limit at the same time the use of communication media. The invention of paper and printing, the development of "electric" media starting with the telegraph, and finally the audiovisual media–television, film, and internet–mark momentous upheavals of technology, communication, and, thus, social design. Movies, sitcoms, and series consist of complex multimedia packages of communication media that can be stored, streamed, and traded in the dissemination medium.[10]

3. Symbolically generalized exchange media (M3) are essential for the function of modern functionally differentiated societies.[11] They have evolved for most social subsystems. If something is communicated through the specific medium of the respective subsystem, be it economy, education, politics, law, or family, the communication is accepted with a high probability. This is true even if it is deemed inappropriate outside the subsystem or social sphere. Power in the political sphere, money in the economic sphere, or love in the sphere of intimacy are prime examples. The different media logics can be visualized by means of a simple test question: Who is allowed to touch human bodies in which subsystem? The answer to this question points to the different ways of dealing with the body in the respective subsystems.

4. It was only through dynamic developments in technology and politics in the nineteenth century that the media system (M4) then emerged in the twentieth

---

[9] For the origin of the term in the philosophy of Michael Foucault and its further development see Ivo Ritzer and Peter W. Schuulze, eds., *Mediale Dispositive* (Wiesbaden: Springer, 2018).

[10] For lucid elaborations of both M1 and M2 as media in philosophical perspectives, see Mike Sandbothe and Ludwig Nagl, eds., *Systematische Medienphilosophie* (Berlin: Akademie Verlag, 2005). That media history can be told only in multiple perspectives is shown by Michael Bailey, *Narrating Media History* (London: Routledge, 2009). Marshall Poe, *A History of Communications: Media and Society from the Evolution of Speech to the Internet* (Cambridge: Cambridge University Press, 2011). Poe distinguishes among *homo loquens* (age of speech), *homo scriptor* (age of manuscripts), *homo lector* (age of print), *homo videns* (age of audiovisual media), and *homo somnians* (age of the internet).

[11] Niklas Luhmann, *Theory of Society*, 2 vols. (Stanford, CA: Stanford University Press, 2012); Jürgen Habermas, *The Theory of Communicative Action*, vol. 2: *Lifeworld and System: A Critique of Functionalist Reason* (Boston: Beacon, 1984).

century as a relatively independent social subsystem or value sphere (Max Weber).[12] The media system functions according to its own code, its own rationality (along with law, politics, religion, sports, etc.) and has a unique function for society. In this sense, the media system is often considered a fourth power alongside the three powers of the state (executive, legislative, and judicial). An efficient media system makes use of a variety of communication (M1) and dissemination (M2) media and uses actuality as its guiding principle of selectivity with respect to the "world outside" of it. However, not every use of dissemination media in the lifeworld or in other subsystems, such as reading the Bible in church or using movies in school or fax machines in university offices, can be considered part of the media system. At the same time, only this systematic approach allows one to analyze the influence of the media system on other subsystems, such as law, education, sports, religion, politics, and medicine.

Three Positions

In order to recognize the decisions or the locations of value in the media society, it is necessary to briefly visualize the three positions in each communication process. For a long time, communication theory coined a simple model of sender-message-receiver. Even if there are good reasons for putting a question mark over the idea of transmitting an identical message, it is nevertheless helpful to distinguish hermeneutically and analytically between three positions: a communicating entity, the message, and an entity receiving the message. However, it should not be overlooked that in many communication processes, a person or an organization can occupy both the producing and the receiving position.

Ten Fields of Media Ethics

At the risk of creating the impression of an overly schematic approach, the four types of media and, in the case of the first three media, the three positions in the communication process are cross-tabulated here. This results in ten fields, each of which raises questions of media ethics.

---

[12] Luhmann, *The Reality of the Mass Media*; Luhmann, *Veränderungen im System gesellschaftlicher Kommunikation und die Massenmedien*.

	Fields of media ethics	
Position of production in communication media	Communication media (M1)	Position of reception in communication media
Position of production in dissemination media	Dissemination media (M2)	Position of reception in dissemination media
Position of production in symbolically generalized media	Symbolically generalized media (M3)	Position of reception in symbolic generalized media
	Media system (M4) in intersystemic resonances	

This approach to four different, yet closely related, types of media has several merits. It connects the classical field of sign theory, in this case of communication media, with the so-called mass media. In addition, with the symbolically generalized communication media, the inner dynamics of organizations can be taken into account. Finally, the thematization of the media system as a social subsystem makes it possible to take an analytical look at the sometimes almost symbiotic and sometimes conflictual relationships with other subsystems.

The Texture of Values in the Media of Communication

The Position of Production in Communication Media

On the side of the producing entity, the first ethical question is whether to communicate at all.[13] What is not allowed to be discussed in a society or in an organization—what is kept silent? Which topics are taboo? Which issues are kept silent to such an extent that silence itself becomes a telling sign? Contrary to the widespread view that one must be able to discuss everything, it is an insight that has proven itself in social life: in view of the limits of understanding and empathy, it may be necessary to remain silent about facts and events. Trauma research points in this direction, but the social phenomenon of tact also thrives on balancing talk and silence in a context-sensitive way. The limits of what can be said are undoubtedly often also the protective limits of humanity. Beyond false taboos, the value of silence must be highly regarded in view of the phenomenon of shame and respect, even in a media society. If democracy and human freedom are valued, the boundaries of what can be said must not be drawn too narrowly. However, the high

---

[13] Niklas Luhmann and Peter Fuchs, *Reden und Schweigen* (Frankfurt am Main: Suhrkamp, 1989).

good of freedom of expression must be set apart from hate speech in favor of civility in society.[14]

From a social point of view, answering the question of who the speakers actually are reveals who has the power of interpretation in the given sociality. Whoever is entitled to speak has some power assigned to him or her. This assignment of power is also empowering the communicating person—in whatever communication medium she or he is attempting to communicate in. Even everyone who plays a musical instrument or practices other forms of artistic communication can perceives this empowerment is a "valuable" part of their own existence.

Media of Communication

The media of communication differ strikingly in terms of precision or vagueness, sensuous materiality, and the capacity for reflexivity in which the medium can become a subject in the medium itself. Consequential value decisions concern the maintenance or deterioration of an abundance, indeed a richness, of the media of communication in a society. Are the various arts promoted as complex communication media in addition to language? Does a society preserve the expressive media of the arts in music, in architecture, in dance and theater? Which media are used for which diplomatic challenge? How sensitive the choice of the medium of communication can be is shown by how highly controversial in religions is the choice of the media to be used in the central cult or worship. Is dance a religious medium? The question of the role of emotions vis-à-vis discursive reason, which is so crucial for political philosophy, is not only, but essentially, a question about the media of communication. In a political demonstration, the bodies of the demonstrators themselves become a powerful medium that is, on one hand, very close to the emotions but, on the other hand, allows neither complex nor discursively mediated communication.[15] Many theological debates, from Christology to questions of the Lord's Supper, are often media questions.

---

[14] For a subtle analysis of interaction systems and their use of media, see André Kieserling, *Kommunikation unter Anwesenden. Studien über Interaktionssysteme* (Frankfurt am Main: Suhrkamp, 1999).

[15] The body as medium of communication is highlighted in communication theories related to rituals, particularly those referring to the French sociologist Emile Durkheim. See Jeffrey C. Alexander, *Durkheimian Sociology: Cultural Studies* (Cambridge: Cambridge University Press, 1988); and Günter Thomas, "Communication," in *Theorizing Rituals: Issues, Topics, Approaches, Concepts*, ed. Jens Kreinath (Leiden: Brill, 2006), 321–43; drawing inexplicitly from this tradition, Judith Butler, *Notes toward a Performative Theory of Assembly* (Cambridge, MA: Harvard University Press, 2015).

Not only in religious communication, but in all communication, the choice of the most basic medium of communication itself contains a metacommunicative message. Value preferences are always embedded in the routines of choosing the medium of communication. An appreciation can be communicated in the materiality of the medium (flowers, wine bottles, vouchers, duration of attention, etc.). Media preferences can have grown historically and at the same time be subject to historical change.

From the earliest times of humankind to the present day, architecture has been a highly effective material medium of communication that deeply shapes everyday life because it creates atmospheres. Architecture indisputably embodies and communicates value preferences that extend into worldviews and visions of what it means to be human.[16]

An issue that has been intensively discussed up to the present concerns the distinction between fictional and nonfictional communication through corresponding frames of communication. Especially the medium of language allows the telling or performing of stories, which are able to captivate the imagination. The debate between Plato and Aristotle concerning the effect of the theater and the stories performed and received there sheds light on the seductive or relieving potential of stories even to the present. While Plato, starting from a mimetic process of reception, considers the moral degrees of freedom of fictional communication as dangerous, Aristotle, in his model of catharsis, is convinced of the purifying power of theater. These opposing positions regarding the effects of fictional communication radiate to the presence on the ethical reflection of media effects.

The Position of the Reception of Communication Media

On the recipient side of communication media, a plethora of ethical choices can be found. To use an expression of Chicago literary scholar Wayne Booth, the decision at hand in many contexts is, "Which company do we keep?"[17] Which communications should one expose oneself to, which ones should one avoid? In which communications does one want to be involved? Visions of what is considered a good

---

[16] In this respect, an instructive classic is Erwin Panofsky, *Gothic Architecture and Scholasticism: An Inquiry into Analogy, Arts, Philosophy and Religion in the Middle Ages* (New York: New American Library, 1957); for contemporary debates, see, for example, Christian Illies, *Bauen mit Sinn. Schritte zu einer Philosophie der Architektur* (Wiesbaden: Springer, 2019); Henriette Steiner and Maximilian Sternberg, eds., *Phenomenologies of the City: Studies in the History and Philosophy of Architecture* (Farnham: Ashgate, 2015).

[17] Wayne C. Booth, *The Company We Keep: An Ethics of Fiction* (Berkeley: University of California Press, 1988).

life are in fact inscribed in the topics and media types of the communication offers in specific communication media. The freedom of choice in the matter of communication media, which is not to be underestimated, aims at a threefold choice—the choice of coupling to the stream of messages, the choice of the medium, and, last but not least, the choice of the topic. On the side of the recipient of messages in communication media, however, there are not only rights but also duties. In many social forms, the coexistence of humans also implies a duty to communicate, to share, and to be curious. The idea of the responsible citizen in democracy contains the obligation to inform oneself and to familiarize oneself in a basic way with the political there and now. An ethics of responsibility in communication concerns these diverse communicative environments in which we live. Self-respect and self-responsibility are essential aspects of this reception-oriented ethics of responsibility.

The Position of Production in Dissemination Media

Dissemination media allow producers of communications to transcend space and time. This means a potential increase in addressees and thus at least a potential increase in power and influence.

Specifically, the invention of writing in conjunction with early storage media marks the evolution toward more complex societies. As the ancient debates about written and oral form show, writing also opens up the development of more sophisticated forms of rationality and allows us to escape the binding power of charisma. The invention of printing intensifies the question of who in society has the freedom, competence, and power to communicate using dissemination media. As countless examples of the banning of dissemination media up to the present show (for example, the shutting down of the internet, the banning of newspapers and radio stations, etc.), elementary rights of freedom are at issue here, and at the same time a not inconsiderable power of influence to be exercised responsibly.

It is the ability to transcend spaces of interaction that makes new visions of universality possible.[18] The space of reason can be imagined as the space of the reading community. Dissemination media allow imagined communities to be generated, so that, for example, the combination of a particular language and the

---

[18] The most current version of this vision is the hope with respect to a global civil society. See Jodi Dean et al., eds., *Reformatting Politics: Information Technology and Global Civil Society* (New York: Routledge, 2006); also Marita Sturken et al., *Technological Visions: The Hopes and Fears That Shape New Technologies* (Philadelphia: Temple University Press, 2004); and Lina Dencik, *Media and Global Civil Society* (Basingstoke: Palgrave Macmillan, 2012). The background imagination of this hope is the philosophy of Jürgen Habermas and the idea of a communicative reason.

imagination of the community of readers of the early newspaper can promote the imagined community of the nation.[19]

The possible anonymity of the recipients has a repercussive effect on the communication itself. How limitless is the freedom of individuals and communities to make their opinions known, not only in small spaces of interaction but also in larger anonymous publics? This question is not new, but it has become an extremely pressing one in the context of so-called social media. It is not only about the right to freedom of expression. Dissemination media, by their reach, increase the demands on the responsibility of producers. Until the special possibilities of the internet and the new media, this responsibility was realized primarily through professional ethics of so-called gate-keepers (editors, trained journalists, publishers, etc.).[20] The new social media bypass these filters and require everyone to adopt a reflected ethic of communication beyond simple standards of etiquette. Social media, such as Facebook, Twitter, Instagram, make it unmistakably clear how important an ethic of "saying" is as part of an ethic of communication. Contrary to the utopias associated with the emergence of the internet, recent years have shown that what is said or published in the broadcast media can also shatter cultural atmospheres and destroy any fair coexistence. It is not for nothing that Facebook, for example, is increasingly confronted with demands to control and censor hate speech.

Dissemination Media

All dissemination media have a complex distance-proximity relationship with the dominant communication media of their time. The COVID-19 pandemic period forced a historically unique shift from interaction in physical co-presence to audiovisual digital dissemination media. In this process, the limits and the opportunities of the media transition became abundantly clear: thus, a saving of time and energy is offset by a loss of the multimedia nature of communication media in physical co-presence and a loss of sustaining atmospheres. As seems clear, digital conferencing circuits are not so powerful, especially in the liminal situations of conflict resolution and unleashing creativity.[21] In the coming years, it will be a complex ethical balancing of goods—not least from an ecological point of view—

---

[19] The undisputed classic is Benedict R. Anderson, *Imagined Communities: Reflections on the Origin and Spread of Nationalism* (London: Verso, 1983).

[20] Stephen J. A. Ward, *The Invention of Journalism Ethics: The Path to Objectivity and Beyond* (Montreal: McGill-Queen's University Press, 2004).

[21] See, for example, Birgit Knatz and Stevan Schumacher, *Mediale Dialogkompetenz. Umgang mit schwierigen Gesprächssituationen am Telefon und im Chat* (Berlin: Springer, 2019).

as to which communications should make use of digital dissemination media and which should not. To this end, sophisticated value decisions will have to be made in many organizations.

In this context of choosing a specific dissemination medium, the Canadian media researcher Marshall McLuhan coined the formula "The medium is the message" in the early 1970 s.[22] With it he drew attention to a double selectivity. In an ensemble of alternatives, already in the case of communication media and even more so in the case of dissemination media, the choice of medium has a metacommunicative quality. For example, the choice of the letter instead of the telephone or the SMS (Short Message Service) is itself already a message. The choice of which medium to use to communicate appreciation or to carry out conflict negotiations is a value decision. In addition, the medium itself limits and restricts what is to be communicated. The dissemination medium helps to shape what can be said. In this respect, message and medium cannot be separated but are mutually dependent on each other. This applies not only to communication media but also, to a large extent, to dissemination media.

Especially the combination of high dissemination speed ("real time") and visualization has led in the twentieth century to dissemination media, which in a pointed sense became media of presence, techniques of medial presence enabling intense styles of immersion. Television and the internet are primary examples. A media presence can now substitute or simulate physical presence. So-called media events are made possible by presence technologies that effectively combine a physical presence and a media presence.[23] As a vast, worldwide field of immersion in a virtual media presence, internet-based computer gaming has developed in recent decades. The question of how much of one's life one would like to spend in a fictional counterworld and what "experiences" one would like to have in it is a far-reaching value preference decision for many people.[24]

The question of the substitutability of physical presence by digital presence will also become an ethical question for CO_2-sensitive tourism—with highly ambivalent consequences for tourism-dependent and low-income populations worldwide.

---

[22] Marshall McLuhan, *Understanding Media: The Extensions of Man* (New York: McGraw-Hill, 1964); Rita Watson and Menahem Blondheim, *The Toronto School of Communication Theory: Interpretations, Extensions, Applications* (Toronto: University of Toronto Press, 2007).

[23] Daniel Dayan and Elihu Katz, *Media Events: The Live Broadcasting of History* (Cambridge, MA: Harvard University Press, 1992); Nick Couldry et al., eds., *Media Events in a Global Age* (London: Routledge, 2010); on the political function of media events and the intermingling of types of presence, see Ron Krabill, "Symbiosis:Mass Media and the Truth and Reconciliation Commission of South Africa," *Media, Culture & Society* 23 (2001): 567–85.

[24] Miguel Sicart, *The Ethics of Computer Games* (Cambridge, MA: MIT Press, 2011).

Dissemination media, which can also be repositories of messages, have been fundamental in transforming the memory of societies since ancient times, and libraries are increasingly taking the place of oral storytelling communities, where narratives can gain a new function through the selective combination of archival materials. As recent decades have made clear in the context of Holocaust memory, as eyewitnesses die, efforts can be intensified to record and document memory in dissemination media that can be stored. The living memory of contemporary witnesses then passes over into complex media arrangements.[25]

In the advanced media society, the internet and the cell phone have become the drivers and symbols of a medialization—not to be confused with mediatization—of everyday life. At the core of this is (a) a far-reaching process of substitution, in which interactions in physical co-presence are replaced by dissemination media, and (b) the sheer extent of the penetration of lifeworlds by dissemination media, so that interaction and creativity are buried, and far-reaching new dependencies emerge (for example, in digital payment systems). These developments document value preferences, indeed visions of a good or even better life, which cannot simply be traced back to individual decisions by individual actors. Structural value preferences thus emerge from the sum of seemingly inconsequential microactions.

The technical development and parallel cost reduction of storage media has brought to the fore an ethical question that at first glance seems astonishing: is there a right to be forgotten, that is, to have one's personal information stored on the World Wide Web deleted? This ethical question reaches into the depths of theological anthropology. Without a forgetting and an erasing of traces, there can be no creative and, at the same time, merciful new beginnings in sinister entanglements and corrosive environments. The concern for appropriate remembering is thus supplemented by a concern for forgetting under the new technical-media conditions.[26]

---

[25] Mordechai Neiger et al., *On Media Memory: Collective Memory in a New Media Age* (New York: Palgrave Macmillan, 2011); Andreas Huyssen, "Escape from Amnesia: The Museum as Mass Medium," in *Twilight Memories: Marking Time in a Culture of Amnesia*, ed. Andreas Huyssen (New York: Routledge, 1995), 13–36; Edward Tabor Linenthal, *Preserving Memory: The Struggle to Create America's Holocaust Museum* (New York: Columbia University Press, 1995); James Edward Young and Matthew Baigell, *Holocaust Memorials: The Art of Memory in History* (Munich: Prestel, 1994); Dörte Hein, "Mediale Darstellungen des Holocaust: Zum World Wide Web und zu seiner Disposition als Gedächtnismedium," *Jahrbuch für Kommunikationsgeschichte* 7 (2005): 176–96.

[26] Kate Eichhorn, *The End of Forgetting: Growing Up with Social Media* (Cambridge, MA: Harvard University Press, 2019); Viktor Mayer-Schönberger, *Delete: The Virtue of Forgetting in the Digital Age* (Princeton: Princeton University Press, 2011).

The furor currently sweeping through Western societies for a just, especially racism-sensitive, memory as a modern *damnatio memoriae* leads to a struggle for symbolic-material dissemination media or storage media of memory: street names, building names, monuments, exhibition exhibits as material dissemination media are subjected to a moral test. In these cases, the so-called woke culture thrives on the unexamined and presuppositional assumption that by removing the media of memory in the present, justice is done for the past and the present. This represents a strong, but arguably illusory, valuation.

The Position of Reception in Dissemination Media

The reception of dissemination media occurs without the social binding forces of interaction in physical co-presence. The dissolution of shared space or a shared time requires a high degree of trust not only in the dissemination medium itself but also in the producing position. The increased demands for trust lead to the formation of mutually affirming communities of reception—a process that is a problem-creating solution, since it also leads to self-seclusion in these communities of reception.

On the side of the reception of dissemination media, there is a mostly implicit but sometimes explicit ethic of consumption. In most cases, this ethic of consumption is embedded in a particular lifestyle. In view of a finite budget of time and attention, the actual consumption of media documents a value preference that is closely connected to more comprehensive conceptions of the good life. How much time is spent on media counterworlds, such as computer games, and how much time is spent on friendships, socializing, or outdoor activities? Are the audiovisual counterworlds educational or entertaining and playful? Beyond a classic high-cultural resentment of the media, the ethical question of the future-shaping or future-burying consequences of expansive media consumption must be asked. Initiatives aiming at a radio-telephone asceticism repeatedly draw attention to the psychological dependencies.

Dissemination media as presence techniques lead to a problem described by media scientists more than by philosophical and theological ethicists: audiovisual presence techniques—that is, dissemination media—enable the recipient to become a spectator and witness of spatial distance and simultaneous distress.[27] Me-

---

[27] For the broad discussion, see Susan Sontag, *Regarding the Pain of Others* (New York: Farrar, Straus and Giroux, 2003); Luc Boltanski, *Distant Suffering: Morality, Media and Politics* (Cambridge: Cambridge University Press, 1999); Lilie Chouliaraki, *The Spectatorship of Suffering* (London: SAGE, 2006); Lilie Chouliaraki, "Ordinary Witnessing in Post-Television News: Towards a New Moral Imagination," *Critical Discourse Studies* 7 (2010): 305–19; Paul Frosh, "Telling Presences: Witnessing, Mass Media, and the Imagined Lives

dia presence techniques enormously expand the perception of misery, distress, and violence. However, this happens under the condition of an abstracting superficiality. The audiovisual-technical medial perception is accompanied by a moral perception and sensitization, to which possibilities of action correspond only to an extremely small degree. The position of the recipient is one of powerlessness and passivity, which can often be articulated only in indignation. The perception of need and the addressing of need diverge in a way that is difficult to bridge. If one looks at the volume of donations to various emergency aid programs, this media perception of need must not be viewed only negatively in its consequences. By creating voyeurs of misery, the gap between perceiving need and addressing it can lead not only to mediated acts of help but also to defensiveness, numbing, and the routinization of distance, even to cynical states of consciousness. Insofar as dissemination media can transcend space and time, this medial constellation leads to the undermining of the classical ethical distinction between a "nearest" neighbor and a "farthest" neighbor. A vacillation between moral overconfidence and a sense of powerlessness is often the ethically problematic consequence.[28]

The Producer Position in Symbolically Generalized Communication Media

The value preferences in the context of symbolically generalized communication media are not visible at first glance, yet they are enormously consequential for modern societies. The starting point is the insight that different social subsystems (Niklas Luhmann) operate in late modern societies. The concept of value spheres, coined by Max Weber, reminds us that different value preferences prevail in each of the systems. Art and science differ, as do religion and law or medicine and ed-

---

of Strangers," *Critical Studies in Media Communication* 23 (2006): 265–84; Eline Huiberts and Stijn Joye, "Close, but Not Close Enough? Audience's Reactions to Domesticated Distant Suffering in International News Coverage," *Media, Culture & Society* 40 (2017): 333–47. See also Amy Richards and Jolyon Mitchell, "Journalists as Witnesses to Violence and Suffering," in Fackler and Fortner, *The Handbook of Global Communication and Media Ethics*, 752–73.

[28] By dissolving this operational distinction, new challenges arise for public morality with regard to the selectivity of helping care. The selective attention of the media system takes over the selection function. The person in need who is not reported on "exists" as little as the "distant neighbor." There appears to be no way to escape the recognition of expandable yet always in some way limited spaces of perception and responsibility. See Günter Thomas, "On the Limits of Responsibility," in *Responsibility and the Enhancement of Life*, ed. Günter Thomas and Heike Springhart (Leipzig: Evangelische Verlagsanstalt, 2017), 243–63.

ucation, business and politics. They each operate on the basis of their own guiding distinctions and thus impute to themselves their own reality generated by communication, their own ontology. Not to forget that they also form their own organizations which—and here lies more than one hidden problem—use the services of other organizations of other systems. An exhibition guard in a museum also wants to be paid, a clergyman also wants an employment contract, and a university wants its research to be reported in the media.

The symbolically generalized communication media of the respective systems now also address a problem that has intensified with dissemination media. How can the addressees of the communications be persuaded by dissemination media not only to understand but also to accept the communication offers? Against the background of this question, it becomes understandable why love in the family, truth in science, and money in economics, or even power in politics are such communication media. In other words, the primary symbolically generalized communication media of the subsystems point to why the systems should really care about society.

It is indeed the case that in this complex constellation, a high degree of systemic media responsibility arises for the actors in organizations, and very specific media responsibility is required. Can and should research at universities—for example, in science—be steered by money? Should science go "public," and to what degree, in order not to lose its credibility?[29] Can and should churches, as organizations of the religious system, depend on resonances with the media system? To what extent should schools, which are part of educational communication, rely on aesthetics? How far may and should sport allow itself to be claimed by politics and economics and, thus, also be instrumentalized?[30] May all goods of a society be subjected to an economic logic, that is, to an economic evaluation? All of these are in essence questions about the choice of symbolically generalized communication media. All of these questions are ethical questions, which are part of subsystemic organizational responsibility in the decisions.

What is disputed in today is whether there is a moral continuum that runs through all subsystems, such as alignment with human rights. This debate is intensified in the presence of extensive moralization of all subsystems. Whether these attempts at a supposed control via morality lead to a justice-sensitive further development of all system logics or to a creeping dysfunctionality and a moral ambiguity may be treated as an open question at the moment.

---

[29] This was still a pressing issue during the COVID pandemic, where the media often tended to play academic minority opinions against a broad scientific consensus of insight. For insights into the complexity of mechanisms and motives, see Katharina Fuhrin, *Der prominente Wissenschaftler. Motive für mediale Präsenz* (Wiesbaden: Springer, 2013).

[30] See, for example, Lutz Hafkemeyer, *Die mediale Vermarktung des Sports. Strategien und Institutionen* (Wiesbaden: Deutscher Universitätsverlag, 2003).

Symbolically Generalized Communication Media

The formation of a guiding distinction and also the development of a symbolically generalized code are characteristics of systemic closure, that is, of the development of a subsystem of media. The media system operates along the guiding distinction interesting/uninteresting and uses topicality as a symbolically generalized medium. Topicality can be conceived temporally or—as in the case of many entertainment genres—factually as an anthropological, permanent topicality of topics.

A view of society informed by systems theory has often been accused of advocating an abstract freedom from values and a rather fatalistic view of the social world. But this strictly critical view of the theory overlooks the points at which value-settings can be identified and operative alternatives sought in systemic processes. In the theoretical language of systems theory, it is the distinction between system-specific codes and so-called programs that have to be connected with them. Thus, law can hardly deviate from working with the distinction right/injustice, nor can the media system veer from the distinction between interesting and uninteresting. To a certain extent, these guiding distinctions are unchanging, while the programs that control code application and application consequences are not only subject to historical change but also relatively open to new determinations. What content is to be taught in education, what principles help to promote justice and allow injustice to be identified? What is considered salvation and harm in religion, what can count as transcendence? What may ultimately be considered an alternative view of the world in art? All this is open to ultimately value-determined negotiations.

For the media system of media society, this means that the system cannot escape the basic distinction between interesting and uninteresting, but that implicit and explicit value orientations are certainly present in the so-called programs—for example, when it is necessary to select which current topics and which permanently current topics are taken up and how differentiated information is presented.

How far in the media system, so to speak, behind the guiding distinction interesting/uninteresting the codes of the other subsystems should be reflected in programs often became a pressing question during the COVID-19 pandemic. Are the contributions in the media system obliged to recognize and disseminate scientific truth even in its relative contentiousness? Are they allowed to disseminate statements that clearly contradict scientific findings with regard to the dangerousness of the corona virus or with regard to the precariousness of a vaccination? May they, in order to attract attention, to bundle and then to sell, give the word to conspiracy theorists, virus deniers, and vaccination opponents? May the media spread untruths if they are only sufficiently interesting and attractive? To what extent must even untruth be covered by freedom of speech? These questions and examples show how elementary the value orientations and how fierce the conflicts over these value orientations are in the so-called execution programs.

The Position of Reception in the Symbolically Generalized Communication Media

Two problem areas deserve to be briefly named in this context. In the position of reception, the subsystemic use of symbolically generalized communication media can be strengthened or questioned with one's own value orientations. The recipient position has the value-oriented power of criticism and affirmation. Which expansion of economic communication with money do we oppose? May everything and anything be subjected to a logic of the market? On one hand, the economization and thus the trade with sex must be tagged with more than one question mark. On the other hand, ecological behavior is often regulated not by morality but by financial nudging, as in the trading of CO_2 certificates or the use of government subsidies. May aesthetic incentives promote religious communication, for example through choirs? Is there a limit to what television is allowed to report on and a limit to what may be presented on the internet? Is there a limit to what politics is allowed to regulate in the code of power down to the depths of the lifeworld? All of these are ultimately media questions that are embedded in comprehensive conceptions of being human and of society and that must be subject to critique and affirmation.

On the reception side of symbolically generalized communication media, the question of a value-driven ethics of perception also erupts. Do humans and organizations retain a perceptual sensitivity to worlds outside of systemic-media descriptions? Do humans leave the power of definition of "what is really real" to the media system's view of the world? Do experiences and events have weight and validity only when they are also observed by the media system, when cell phone cameras or television cameras are present? Who gets to determine what has value and validity? The humans and the organizations of the media society live in fact an ethics of perception and valuation, with which they put the truth, reality, and validity claims of media communication into a relationship with their own perceptions and valuations. Here, in the question of what is "really real" and in the question of which value orientations have ultimate valence, a deep dispute between media and religion appears again and again.[31] Who may determine—and tell and present—what is and should be in a comprehensive sense? The decision about who

---

[31] On the notion of "real reality" or ultimate reality, see Clifford Geertz, "Religion as a Cultural System," in *Anthropological Approaches to the Study of Religion*, ed. Michael Banton (London: Tavistock, 1966), 1–46. The competition is highlighted by Jay Newman, *Religion vs. Television: Competitors in Cultural Context* (Westport, CT: Praeger, 1996).

is allowed to do so is basically a media-ethical decision on the recipient position of the symbolically generalized communication media.

Contours of an Ethics of the Media System

The level of the media system probably eludes everyday perception and its evidence gathering, but it is essential for an understanding of the conflicts in media societies. The basic insight, to begin with, is that an independent social subsystem of the media emerged in the course of technical, political, and social developments during the late nineteenth and early twentieth centuries. The media subsystem stands alongside the multiple uses of dissemination media in the various other subsystems or lifeworlds. The fax machine in a court, the computer in the parish office, and the copying machine at the university are all dissemination media, but they do not yet belong to media systems. Nevertheless, the newspaper, large parts of the internet, and radio and television belong to it. Part of the relative independence of the media system is that, like other subsystems, it has developed its own logic of communication, its own coding. Its overall social task is to produce a description of society that can be used for communication. This description must always be an undercomplex one in comparison to the internal views of the subsystems. What humans in the media society know of the world beyond interactive accessibility, they have learned essentially from the communications of the media system. In a variety of ways, with diverse strategies, accesses, and formats, the media system generates a worldview in a double sense: it creates an image of the world and, at the same time, its own worldview. This happens relatively independently of the respective financing modalities, that is, relatively independently of a private or public media system.

For a value-oriented design of society, the following questions are of great importance with regard to the media system: To what extent should the subsystems of society adjust to observation by the media system? How far should they—anticipating the logic of the media system present in the observation by the media system—adjust to the observation structurally, and that means prepare for change? It is obvious and indisputable that sports and politics, for example, have indeed adjusted structurally to the fact of observation by the media system. But to what extent should science and religion, medicine and education adjust to media observation in a structure-forming way, if, for example, untruth is more interesting than truth, if, even in matters of religion, when "the good news is the bad news" (a popular saying among journalists) and, last, education is trying to survive in a tough battle for attention in competition with the media system? Should the legal system actively prepare itself for media observation if deviance is more interesting than conformity to rules, because it generates more billable hours and press conferences?

While the medialization of communication in the lifeworld and organizations seeks to conceptually capture an ever-increasing penetration of everyday life by dissemination media, the concept of mediatization captures the process of anticipatory adaptation of social subsystems to the logic of media observation.[32] The medialization of communication in organizations and the lifeworld is not the same as the mediatization of social subsystems. In the political field, for example, the actions of Greenpeace are designed to be observed by the media. When sporting events are aligned in such a way that they can be optimally exploited by the media, this is a mediatization of sport. When a so-called public theology aligns itself with the attention-focusing and attention-steering of the media system, this can be understood as a mediatization phenomenon that makes the high ambivalence of this process visible. In the case of mediatization of religion, in times of overheated moral markets a theological capacity for differentiation can be buried, distracting from one's own concerns, and feeding an illusion of resonance.[33]

The media's interest in conflict and drama, in heroes and villains, and not least in timely solutions to complex problems can permanently irritate the necessary processes in other subsystems. For a value-sensitive view of society, it is clear that system logics and system performances must not be disrupted in favor of the "common good" and the communal good life. The dispute over the presence of cameras in courtrooms is an indicator of such intersystemic conflicts.

This mediatization can include the adoption of formats (dramatization), processes of personalization of topics, the control of topic clusters, or even visualization and emotionalization.[34]

There is no consensus, even among Western democracies, on the question of whether and to what extent the organization of the media system should be private or public. The ethically consequential difference is likely to be whether the

---

[32] Unfortunately, in most media research, these two processes are treated not separately. See Günter Thomas, "The Mediatization of Religion—as Temptation, Seduction, and Illusion," *Media, Culture & Society* 38 (2016): 37–47. For a broad overview of the research, see Knut Lundby, "Mediatization of Communication," in *Mediatization of Communication*, ed. Knut Lundby (Berlin: DeGruyter Mouton, 2014), 3–35.

[33] The dependency on media attention is one of the blind spots of public theologies. See Heinrich Bedford-Strohm, "Politik und Religion—Öffentliche Theologie," in *Verkündigung und Forschung* 54, no. 2 (2009); Florian Höhne, "Öffentliche Theologie: Begriffsgeschichte und Grundfragen," Leipzig: Evangelische Verlagsanstalt, 2015. On the complexity of public religions and the media, see Knut Lundby, "Public Religion in Mediatized Transformations," in *Institutional Change in the Public Sphere: Views on the Nordic Model*, ed. Jon Rogstad (Warsaw: DeGruyter, 2017), 241–63.

[34] On media formats, see David L. Altheide, "Media Logic, Social Control, and Fear," *Communication Theory* 23 (2013): 223–38; still informative, David L. Altheide and Robert P. Snow, *Media Logic* (Beverly Hills, CA: SAGE, 1979).

organizations of the media system are more willing and able to resist economic or political influence.

At the level of social subsystems, an intersystemic struggle for attention is taking place. Modern media societies are characterized by a strong disproportion between the media system's communication offers and the mobilizable attention of the recipients. In fact, attention resources are clearly limited, while there is an overabundance of communication offers.[35] The resulting fierce competition within the media system extends beyond the system itself. It is a double competition. Sports, religion, politics, and, above all, the education system are in a fierce battle with the media system for human attention. To the extent that this attention can be capitalized on by means of advertising or behavioral data, it is also a struggle for economic resources. Ethically, what is at issue here is which visions of a rich, multidimensional, and, metaphorically speaking, polyphonic life actually prevail in a society at this point.

Many humans perceive the omnipresence of advertising in the background of media-systemic communication both as ultimately disturbing and as a questionable characteristic of a culturally omnipresent capitalist economic form. Correct as this may be, this judgment does not capture the underlying ethical problem and the dynamics within it that are palpable. Media organizations sell the attention tied to their communications offerings to the companies that place advertising. From the consumer's perspective, his or her own attention invested directly in reception (or attention profile captured in data) is a currency used to pay for media products that otherwise could not have been paid for in euros or dollars. Advertising indicates that humans live beyond their economic means, so to speak, in the reception of media products. In a product world increasingly financed by advertising, the question of an ethic of renunciation, limitation, and abstinence therefore arises. How much media consumption is dispensable? What dimensions of life would or could be opened up by less consumption? What are the losses generated by the consumption of technically advanced media?

At first glance, the new social media do not fit easily into the picture of the media system outlined here. Through advanced technology, they enable the reception and production of messages without the classic gatekeepers of the highly professionalized media system. They also seem to notoriously subvert the systemic boundaries between business, media, lifeworld, and private life to the disad-

---

[35] Günter Thomas, "The Cultural Contest for Our Attention: Observations on Media, Property, and Religion," in *Having: Property and Possession in Religious and Social Life*, ed. William Schweiker and Charles Mathewes (Grand Rapids, MI: Eerdmans, 2004), 272–95; Nick Couldry et al., eds., *Media Consumption and Public Engagement beyond the Presumption of Attention* (Basingstoke: Palgrave Macmillan, 2007); with a critical stance toward the so-called new media, Dominic Pettman, *Infinite Distraction: Paying Attention to Social Media* (Cambridge: Polity, 2016).

vantage of the latter. They individualize and socialize intensely in a covariant way. At the same time, they prove the close connection between content and the concrete shape of the dissemination medium (think, for example, of the number of characters, the imagery, the speed of a response, or the dissolution of the boundaries of the public sphere and, last but not least, the "Matthew principle" [that the rich get richer and the poor get poorer] in the aggregation of attention).

For any ethics of media society, however, a different set of facts is relevant. The new possibilities of social media were—if one considers politics, the feuilleton, philosophy, and, not least, the business start-ups of the 2000 s—linked in an unprecedented way to the dream of a universal understanding overcoming all boundaries. These hopes of universal understanding by means of worldwide communication possibilities have proven to be an illusion. The new media may be able to broaden horizons and create communities of solidarity.[36] But they also deepen conflicts, fuel hatred, harden self-enclosing identities in filter bubbles, and help spread fake news. More communication obviously does not automatically lead to more human understanding.

The development of computer capacities, storage media, and the recording of digital communication by humans are leading to an unimagined comprehensive recording of the actions, thoughts, and experiences of humans. "Big Data" marks the possibility of a total recording and ultimately control and evaluation of humans.[37] It ranges from monitoring sleep patterns and current health data to modes of driving, consumer behavior, communication preferences, conversations in the living space, educational careers, travel patterns, and even emotional management through music and moral behavior in everyday situations. Not without reason, knowledgeable interpreters registered that the God attributes of metaphysically oriented theology, such as omniscience, omnipotence, and omnipresence, have been transferred to late modern data management. If one follows this trail of interpretation, then the essentially ethical inquiries of a biblically oriented theology can rightly be reformulated in a technology-critical way. Is the entity processing the data of life characterized by care? Is it a "God" of care and passion? What are the interests behind the collecting frenzy? Is it a promotion of the good life and justice? Is there such a thing as grace, mercy, and forgiveness in the data universe? When viewed in the light of day, Big Data conceals an entirely legal and unfree world that can only be irritated by surprising disruptions. A freedom characterizing humanity, however, is more than a residual indeterminacy and a final

---

[36] For example, Andreas Hepp et al., *Mediale Migranten. Mediatisierung und die kommunikative Vernetzung der Diaspora* (Wiesbaden: Springer, 2011).

[37] Nick Couldry and Ulises A. Mejias, *The Costs of Connection : How Data Is Colonizing Human Life and Appropriating It for Capitalism* (Stanford, CA: Stanford University Press, 2020).

fuzziness in prognostic efforts.[38] It should be obvious that in the capture of existence by data, a value preference and a vision of life is present, against which a purely moral control of the process is no match. In this context, value preferences require translation into legal regulations.

Outlook

The world of media society is not a value-free space. As should have become clear, however, the field of media communication is at the same time an extremely complex structure. In view of the abundance of communication demands and offers, it not only allows but actually forces people to practice value preferences in their decisions. But at the same time, individuals, organizations, and even groups are constantly confronted with an abundance of design decisions and technical developments that have already been made. No one can completely bypass their own entanglement in an already existing texture of value choices and build their own world, so to speak. In all variations of media, from M1 to M4, a navigational space opens up between what is already given—recursively reinforced and strengthened by practices—and possibilities of variation based on one's own alternative value preferences.

From the abundance of factual and conscious communication behavior, a society- and time-related specific texture of value preferences emerges, which constitute something like the style of communication. The comparison of world areas, cultures, subcultures, and small social spaces like families makes visible that there are not only individual but also communal textures.

In order to navigate in this space in such a way that one, as an acting and experiencing person, is not only a driven person but also an active and responsible navigator, a double hermeneutic process is necessary. On one hand, in a synthetic movement, it is necessary to ask which initially implicit vision of a good, just, and flourishing life is factually assembled from the sum of one's own value preferences. And which visions are contained in the most effective development trends of media practices? On the other hand, starting from one's own visions of the good, just, and flourishing life and those explicitly shared with other people, it is also necessary to ask the other way round: what value preferences result for the various media communications—both for one's own life and for community life?

These broader visions of a good, just, and flourishing life are less unfolded in philosophical systems than in stories—whether Christian or those of the media

---

[38] For a rather pessimistic view of the current structural change of the public, see Jürgen Habermas, "Überlegungen und Hypothesen zu einem erneuten Strukturwandel der politischen Öffentlichkeit," in *Ein neuer Strukturwandel der Öffentlichkeit*, ed. Martin Seeliger and Sebstian Sevignani (Baden-Baden: Nomos, 2021), 470–500.

system's storytelling machine.[39] It is this constellation—in which, on one hand, religious communication always engages media (M1 to M4) and, on the other hand, the media system of late modernity claims the power of interpreting life —that makes the relationship between Christian faith and the media system a dynamic and complex one.

---

[39] On the intimate relationship between narrative, media, and myth, drawing on the Greek cultural forms, see Arthur Asa Berger, *Media, Myth, and Society* (New York: Palgrave Pivot, 2013); in a similar vein, yet focusing on the narrative structure of tragedy, Stephanie Alice Baker, *Social Tragedy: The Power of Myth, Ritual, and Emotion in the New Media Ecology* (New York: Palgrave Macmillan, 2014). The comparison of religious and media narratives is representing an external perspective to theological reasoning. Emphasizing for good reasons the internal realism in theological narratives, Francesca Aran Murphy, *God Is Not a Story: Realism Revisited* (Oxford: Oxford University Press, 2007).

Part Two:
Media, Economics, and Ethics

Media Economics: Overview and Recent Developments

Jürgen von Hagen and Matthias Vollbracht

Introduction

The standard economics paradigm of a market is for private goods produced under competitive conditions. Private goods are characterized by rivalry and excludability in consumption: if one person consumes a private good, it cannot be consumed by another person, and other persons can be excluded from its consumption. Rivalry and excludability are necessary for goods to be owned privately and, therefore, to be bought and sold at market prices reflecting consumer preferences and producers' cost conditions. On the production side, the standard paradigm assumes that production technologies exhibit nondecreasing economies of scale, that is, unit production costs do not fall as the volume of production of an individual supplier increases. This is necessary to sustain competition, since, otherwise, large producers could drive small producers out of the market by setting lower prices and yet remain profitable themselves. As a result, no individual producer has market power. An important condition for this to be true is that there are no (or no significant) fixed costs of production. The standard paradigm furthermore assumes that there are neither *consumption* nor *production externalities*, that is, a consumer's demand for a good does not depend on the extent to which it is consumed by others, nor does an individual producer's cost of production depend on the volume of production of other producers. Under such circumstances, competitive markets generate the allocation of scarce resources that is best for society as a whole. Given the distribution of incomes, it is impossible to make any individual better off without making at least one other individual worse off.[1]

Media markets are different from the standard paradigm, because some of these key assumptions do not hold for them. Media are channels of information,

---

[1] This is the essence of the First Welfare Theorem, for example. See Gérard Debreu, *The Theory of Value: An Axiomatic Analysis of Economic Equilibrium* (New Haven: Yale University Press, 1971).

be it news, historical accounts, results of scientific investigations, descriptions of geographical scenery, or the content of drama or comedy, to name just a few. Media are an important part of our lives. In 2018, Germans spent an average of 10.4 hours daily using different kinds of media; more than nine of those hours were spent using audio and audiovisual media.[2] The market for newspapers in Germany had a volume of about 7 billion euros in 2018; the market for broadcasting had a volume of 21 billion euros.[3] There is thus definitely a demand for such information: consumers desire it and are willing, in principle, to pay for it.

Information, however, is a public good rather than a private one. Many individuals can share a piece of information without diminishing its value to the individual consumer. Thus, there is no rivalry in the consumption. Furthermore, it is impossible or at least difficult to exclude consumers from information that is available in a group or society. Public goods either are not provided by markets at all, or are not provided at the level that is best for society. The reason is that individual consumers are not willing to pay prices for them that cover the cost of production. They expect that others will pay for the information so that they can free-ride on it. If all consumers behave that way, none will pay. Therefore, private producers have no incentive to produce the information in the first place. Society will end up being underprovided with information.

Media exist to solve this problem. Commercial media combine the information to be transmitted with private goods that buyers are willing to pay a price for and, therefore, that private producers have an incentive to supply. The most straightforward example is books. Due to its physical characteristics, a book exhibits rivalry in consumption (two individuals may enjoy reading a book together at the same time, but ten will not; one reader can pass on a book to the next, but the next reader has the disadvantage of waiting) and excludability (I can put my books on a shelf and prevent you from reading them). By being put into the physical medium of a book, the information that the consumer desires can be bought and sold in competitive markets.[4] Similarly, movie theaters create rivalry in consumption (depending on the size of the hall) and excludability.

---

[2] Kommission zur Ermittlung der Konzentration im Medienbereich (KEK), *21. Jahresbericht 2018/2019*, 78–79. TV accounted for 234 minutes, radio for 192 minutes, books for 30 minutes, and newspapers and magazines for 23 minutes of the daily media time budget.

[3] Bernd Weidenbach, "Umsätze der Zeitungen in Deutschland bis 2019," Statista.com 1 Sep. 2020, https://de.statista.com/statistik/daten/studie/204864/umfrage/umsaetze-der-zeitungen-in-deutschland-nach-segmenten/; and Landesmedienanstalt Bayern, *Die wirtschaftliche Lage des Rundfunks in Deutschland 2018–19*, https://www.blm.de/aktivitaeten/forschung/wirtschaftliche_lage.cfm, 15.

[4] One may, of course, still argue that competitive book markets do not generate the supply of books philosophers, theologians, or governments consider best for society. But that is a

Things are more complicated with traditional mass media like newspapers, television, and radio. In principle, newspapers exhibit rivalry and excludability like books, but since, as an old German adage has it, "there is nothing more outdated than yesterday's paper," buyers are likely to give a paper away after reading it, and this reduces the number of consumers willing to pay. Seven out of ten readers in Germany share their newspapers with others, and the average newspaper issue has 2.7 readers.[5] Information that is aired can be received by millions of viewers or listeners at the same time; there is neither rivalry nor excludability.[6] Mass media offer predominantly ephemeral information, that is, information that is consumed immediately after its distribution and loses its value to the consumer shortly afterward.[7] This ephemeralness, too, limits consumers' willingness to pay for mass media.

To generate revenues nevertheless, mass media sell space on their pages or air time on their channels, which are private goods, to advertisers who wish to reach the consumers as potential customers of the goods they offer.[8] Media consumers represent a certain worth to advertisers, namely, the expected sales resulting from advertisements, that is, the probability that media consumers will purchase the item advertised times the average revenue generated per consumer. Media firms offer advertisers access to groups of consumers. Advertisers choose the media and the time slots that get them the most lucrative consumers. Commercial media thus operate on *two-sided markets*, providing consumers with de-

---

different question and one that can be addressed by subsidizing "good" or censuring "bad" literature.

[5] BDZV, https://www.bdzv.de/alle-themen/marktdaten/reichweite-und-auflagengroessen.

[6] This is different for pay TV and pay radio, where the information is transmitted through cables.

[7] Kenneth C. Wilbur, "Recent Developments in Mass Media: Digitization and Multitasking," in *Handbook of Media Economics*, vol. 1 A, ed. Simon Andersen, Joel Waldfogel, and David Strömberg (Amsterdam: North-Holland, 2015), chap. 5., at 206. At the time of writing his chapter, Wilbur noted that "while some television series are archived by services like Amazon, Hulu, and Netflix, these series constitute a small fraction of the tens of thousands of hours of new television content created and distributed each year" (ibid.). Since then, markets for streaming services have surged. The top five companies offering video on demand had more than five hundred million subscribers worldwide in 2021. See https://en.wikipedia.org/wiki/List_of_streaming_media_services. The global market volume of video streaming services was close to USD 60 billion in 2021 and is estimated to grow at an annual rate of 20 percent over the next six years: https://www.grandviewresearch.com/industry-analysis/video-streaming-market.

[8] Jan Vosshage, *Kalkulationsmethoden für Medienprodukte* (ebook: Grin Verlag, 2004), estimated that Germany's main newspaper publishing companies, Gruner & Jahr and Springer, received 42 percent and 43 percent of their incomes from advertisement, respectively, compared to 31 percent and 38 percent from subscriptions and sales.

sired information and providing advertisers with valuable access to consumers. Since the attractiveness of media for the advertisers depends on the number and worth of the consumers reached, while the number of consumers depends on the type and amount of advertising they find themselves exposed to, these two markets are interdependent. Media business models need to balance the market incentives and constraints they find on both sides. For example, advertising is not allowed on public TV stations after 8 p.m. in Germany. As a result, private TV stations schedule the most attractive movie and sports programs after 8 p.m, because doing so captures a particularly valuable audience for advertisers. Typically, advertising revenues subsidize subscription prices or prices paid per newspaper copy, and they are the main, if not the only, source of revenues for commercial TV and radio.[9]

Apart from ad financing, other business models can be found in media markets. Magazines, including academic journals, target very specific readerships who are willing to pay for the particular kind of information they offer. They are, therefore, much less dependent on advertising. Some media are heavily subsidized by private sponsors or organizations and provide specialized information together with the dissemination of religious or secular, ideological content. These media include religious radio stations and TV channels, and donation-financed media, such as National Public Radio in the United States. Recently, a number of newspapers, among them the venerable *Guardian* and the *New York Times*, have set up philanthropic branches that can receive tax-deductible contributions and grants from other foundations.[10] The German newspaper *TAZ* argues on its website that everyone should have access to its high-quality journalism and that, therefore, *TAZ* makes it freely accessible. To cover its costs, *TAZ* invites readers to make voluntary contributions. According to the website, a total of 29,111 individuals had pledged contributions of 5 euros and more in June 2021.[11] Nic Newman finds that the percentage of consumers willing to make donations to news organizations is currently still very small, but that there is considerable potential,

---

[9] Ambarish Chandra and Ulrich Kaiser, "Newspapers and Magazines," in Andersen, Waldfogel, and Strömberg, *Handbook of Media Economics*, vol. 1 A, chap. 9, at 409.

[10] Sarah Scire, "Philanthropic Support Is a Small but Growing Revenue Stream for *The Guardian*, Reaching a Record-Breaking GBP 9M Last Year," Nieman Lab, Apr. 4, 2021, https://www.niemanlab.org/2021/04/philanthropic-support-is-a-small-but-growing-revenue-stream-for-the-guardian-reaching-a-record-breaking-9m-last-year/. Scire reports that philanthropic funding has led news organizations to develop and use measures of impact such as responses from international organizations or legislative initiatives triggered by the reporting.

[11] See https://taz.de/!172178/.

especially among those under forty-five years old. Donors value independent journalism and support it for good quality.[12]

Cable TV, satellite radio, and internet-based streaming services, such as Netflix, Amazon Prime Video, and Disney+, technically restrict access to their products. This allows them to rely mostly or entirely on subscriptions. Others, such as Apple Music and Amazon Music, offer their products on a pay-per-use basis, which again allows them to operate without advertising. Since subscription and pay-per-use models turn the information offered into (almost) private goods, we do not consider them in this chapter. Instead, we focus on ad-financed, commercial media, which are the most interesting from an economics perspective.

There are different models of media systems. The classical framework for classifying media systems offered by Fred Siebert and colleagues distinguishes between authoritarian, libertarian, social responsibility, and soviet systems.[13] In authoritarian systems, media are tightly controlled through licensing and censorship, and sometimes even run by governments that use them to solidify political power. In libertarian systems, media are perceived to be the "fourth power" of democratic governance; they exercise and defend citizens' right to freedom of expression and information. In social-responsibility systems, media are regulated and subsidized by the government to ensure the provision of good and correct information to the general public.[14] In today's democratic societies, media systems are typically mixtures of the libertarian and the social-responsibility model, with the former giving more room to commercial media and the latter more room to public enterprises or private enterprises operating under heavy government regulation. Xiaoqun Zhang names the United States, the United Kingdom, Finland, and the Netherlands as examples of libertarian systems, and France, Germany, and Japan as examples of the social-responsibility system.[15] As providers of good-quality information, media can reduce information asymmetries between the government and the people and between different groups of citizens, thus promoting good governance, political accountability, and economic development. To

---

[12] Nic Newman, "Donations and Crowdfunding: An Emerging Opportunity?," Reuters Institute for the Study of Journalism (RISJ), *Digital News Report 2018*, 48–51.

[13] Xiaoqun Zhang, "Global Digital Networks and Global Media Systems: An Economics Perspective," in *A Research Agenda for Media Economics*, ed. Alan B. Albarran (Cheltenham: Edward Elgar, 2019), chap. 4. Zhang refers to Fred Siebert, Theodore Peterson, and Wilbur Schramm, *Four Theories of the Press* (Urbana: University of Illinois Press, 1956). Siebert, Peterson, and Schramm originally used this classification for print media.

[14] This is also the motivation for OECD governments to provide financial assistance to media in fledgling democracies; see Eduardo Gonzáles Cauhapé-Cazaux and Shanthi Kalathil, *Official Development Assistance for Media: Figures and Findings*, Center for International Media Assistance and OECD (Mar. 2015).

[15] Zhang, "Global Digital Networks," 44.

fulfill this role, they need to be independent from both the government and powerful interest groups, and able to reach a broad range of citizens.[16] Simeon Djankov and colleagues report evidence from a cross-country comparison showing that state ownership of mass media is associated with significantly worse performance in a number of important socioeconomic indicators, such as education, life expectancy, child mortality, and nutrition. This finding is compatible with the view that state ownership weakens the role of media as watchdogs over government policies and their outcomes.[17] While the "four theories" approach was applied mainly to national media systems, the development of global digital networks (GDNs), such as Google, Facebook, and YouTube, has led to an erosion of the link between media governance and national boundaries by penetrating what used to be national systems. Some authoritarian systems, such as China, have responded to this development by erecting firewalls that block GDNs from their markets.[18]

In Germany, all households are required to pay a radio and TV tax, called "broadcasting contribution," regardless of whether or not they own a receiver to listen or watch, and regardless of their incomes (only social welfare recipients can be exempted.) The tax is used to finance public radio and TV, which are considered part of the basic services every citizen should have access to.[19] Public broadcasting in Germany is independent from government and has the statutory task of guaranteeing the free and comprehensive formation of opinions in society.[20] This charge includes a commitment to broadcasting cultural programs that represent the entire spectrum of culture and address all parts of society.[21] It was patterned after the BBC, an independent public corporation funded by the UK government with the mission to "provide impartial news and information to help people understand and engage with the world around them, to support learning for people of all ages, to show the most creative highest quality output and services, to reflect, represent, and serve the diverse communities of all of the Kingdom's nations

---

[16] Roumeen Islam, "Into the Looking Glass: What the Media Tell and Why—An Overview," in *The Right to Tell: The Role of Mass Media in Economic Development*, ed. The World Bank (Washington, DC: The World Bank, 2002).

[17] Simeon Djankov et al., "Media Ownership and Prosperity," in The World Bank, *The Right to Tell*, chap. 8.

[18] Zhang, "Global Digital Networks and Global Media Systems," 45, 51.

[19] Curiously, this is called "free" radio and TV in contrast to "pay TV," for which users pay only when they actually consume it.

[20] Anonymous, "Der Kultur- und Bildungsauftrag der öffentlich-rechtlichen und privaten Rundfunkanstalten," *Deutscher Bundestag, Wissenschaftliche Dienste* WD 10 51/06 (2006), 5.

[21] Ibid., 7.

and regions, and to represent the UK, its culture and values to the world."[22] In the United States, the Corporation for Public Broadcasting (CPB), a nonprofit corporation created by the Public Broadcasting Act of 1967, provides financial grants to local public radio and TV stations with a mission to "ensure universal access to non-commercial, high-quality content and telecommunications services."[23]

There is a tradition of government support for newspapers going back to the founders of the United States as a nation. Recognizing the importance of newspapers and other print products as agenda setters in public discourse,[24] as sources of information about the communities that citizens live in, and as watchdogs disciplining government officials, the government used postal rates to subsidize newspapers substantially below cost to facilitate the building up of distribution networks.[25] The U.S. Newspaper Preservation Act of 1970 exempted newspapers from the antitrust regulations prevailing in other industries. In Germany, newspapers and other print products enjoy a lower VAT rate. At the time of this writing, the German federal government is considering subsidizing the distribution of newspapers, a move that some commentators see as a threat to independent

---

[22] Royal Charter of the BBC, https://www.bbc.com/historyofthebbc/research/royal-charter.

[23] Corporation for Public Broadcasting, https://www.cpb.org/aboutcpb.

[24] The agenda-setting theory holds that mass media influence the public's perception of what are the important political issues in current public debates and that, as "gatekeepers," mass media can prevent issues from entering public debate. See Maxwell E. McCombs and Donald L. Shaw, "The Agenda-Setting Function of Mass Media," *Public Opinion Quarterly* 36, no. 2 (1972): 176–87. For a review of related research, see Dietram A. Scheufele, "Agenda-Setting, Priming, and Framing Revisited: Another Look at Cognitive Effects of Political Communication," *Mass Communication and Society* 3, nos. 2–3 (2000): 297–316.

[25] Stephen Waldmann, *The Information Needs of Communities* (Washington, DC: Federal Communication Commission, 2011); Brad A. Greenberg, "A Public Press?," *UCLA Entertainment Law Review* 19, no. 1 (2012): 189–244; Chandra and Kaiser, "Newspapers and Magazines." For example, Germany's Deutschlandradio reports that 90 percent of its total revenues in 2019 came from "broadcasting contributions." (Deutschland Radio, *Ertrags- und Aufwandsrechnung für das Geschäftsjahr 2019*, https://www.deutschlandradio.de/jahresabschluss.242.de.html). Germany's public television channel ZDF reported that 84 percent of its revenues in 2018 came from broadcasting contributions, while 8.5 percent came from advertisements and sponsors. (*ZDF Jahrbuch 2019*, https://www.zdf.de/zdfunternehmen/2019-jahrbuch-finanzen-jahresabschluss-100.html). In contrast, the private media group ProSieben reported that 87 percent of its revenues in 2019 came from advertising. (*ProSieben Sat1 Media SE Geschäftsbericht* 2019, p. 152).

journalism.[26] German antitrust legislation exempts newspapers from the prohibition of vertical price fixing.[27]

In the next section of this chapter, we explain how two-sided mass media markets work and why they tend to be noncompetitive. In the subsequent section, we review some recent developments in media markets related to the introduction of the internet and social media. We show how these developments have impacted competitive conditions, and we discuss their implications for business models and the quality of information that media provide. The final section provides some tentative conclusions with respect to character formation in modern societies.

Economics of Two-Sided Media Markets

Economies of Scale and Market Concentration

A first important feature of media is that their production processes involve large fixed costs and small variable costs.[28] Variable costs are those that change with the number of customers who are supplied with a given piece of information. In the context of newspapers, for example, these are the costs of printing and some of the costs of delivery. Fixed costs are those that have to be borne independently of how many customers are served. Typically, the largest of these is the cost of producing the relevant information or content, such as producing a movie to be aired on TV or maintaining a staff of news journalists producing news.[29] Another large fixed cost is due to the installation of a distribution infrastructure. This may be small in the case of newspapers and local radio, but for nationwide radio and for TV, this type of fixed cost can be very large. Although only rough estimates of cost structures exist, Simon Anderson and Joel Waldfogel conclude that they are large compared to variable costs, and that, therefore, "it's clear that the availability of these media products depends on many others also wanting them."[30] For news-

---

[26] Steffen Grimberg, "Perfekter Tabubruch für unabhängige Zeitungen," *TAZ*, Nov. 21, 2019, p. 18, https://taz.de/Subventionierung-von-Tageszeitungen/!5640063&SuchRahmen=Print/.

[27] Bundesministerium für Wirtschaft und Energie, *Informationen zum Nationalen Kartell- und Wettbewerbsrecht*, https://www.bmwi.de/Redaktion/DE/Downloads/I/informationen-zum-nationalen-kartell-und-wettbewerbsrecht.pdf?__blob=publicationFile&v=4, p. 2.

[28] See Simon P. Anderson and Joel Waldfogel, "Preference Externalities in Media Markets," in Anderson, Waldfogel, and Strömberg, *Handbook of Media Economics*, vol. 1 A.

[29] David Strömberg, "Distributing News and Political Influence," in The World Bank, *The Right to Tell*, chap. 6.

[30] Anderson and Waldfogel, "Preference Externalities in Media Markets."

papers, Ambarish Chandra and Ulrich Kaiser report estimates that fixed costs amount to 40 percent to 50 percent of total production cost.[31] Data from BDZV suggests that for German daily newspapers, fixed costs, also known as first-copy costs, amount to two-thirds of total production cost.[32] For radio and TV, the cost of serving an additional consumer is zero; for newspapers it is almost zero.

The nonrivalry-of-consumption property of information implies that the first copy can be reused infinitely many times by infinitely many consumers without losing its value. Therefore, the more people consume it, the lower is the cost per consumer. That is, media are characterized by large economies of scale resulting in imperfect competition.[33] Large firms achieve lower unit costs and can drive smaller firms out of the market. This cost-driven market concentration is exacerbated by its consequences on the market for advertising. Buyers of advertising space or time prefer media with larger numbers of users because their advertisements reach more potential customers.[34] As a result, large media firms obtain better prices for advertising space or time, which they can use, partially at least, to offer better prices for their users.

The crowding out of small firms by large firms is not the only implication of large fixed costs for competitive conditions. Firms operating in the same market may collude by sharing some of those activities that lead to large fixed costs. In media markets, such collusion often takes the form of sharing the cost of content production. For example, German newspaper and magazine publishing houses, broadcasting corporations, and media groups together own Deutsche Presse Agentur as a joint service producing high-quality journalism.[35] In the United States, Associated Press has its roots in a similar cooperative agreement among different newspapers.[36] Other forms of collusion include the sharing of news and

---

[31] Chandra and Kaiser, "Newspapers and Magazines," 413.

[32] Bundesverband Digitalpublisher und Zeitungsverleger (BDZV), https://www.bdzv.de/alle-themen/marktdaten/umsaetze-und-kosten. This assumes that total production cost consists of the cost of editorial staff, administrative staff, advertising staff, and production cost (*Herstellungskosten*).

[33] Anderson and Waldfogel ("Preference Externalities in Media Markets," 6) estimate that for the *Columbus Dispatch* (Columbus, Ohio, three million inhabitants), the annual fixed cost per potential reader in its geographical market was about 70 percent larger than the annual fixed cost per potential reader of the *New York Times* (New York City, 22 million inhabitants). See also Chandra and Kaiser, "Newspapers and Magazines," 413 ff.

[34] Bruce M. Owen, "Media as Industry: Economic Foundations of Mass Communications," in The World Bank, *The Right to Tell*, chap. 9, at 171.

[35] The dpa group, https://www.dpa.com/en/company/ownership-structure#ownership-structure.

[36] Associated Press (AP), https://www.ap.org/about/our-story/.

formats among newspapers and the sharing of music programs among radio stations.

Competitive conditions and concentration must be considered relative to market size. An important determinant of market size is preference heterogeneity. Media preferences depend strongly on consumers' national, ethnic, language, and cultural communities. Anderson and Waldfogel note that, in the United States, there are stark differences between black and white consumers in preferences over newspaper content and radio and TV programming.[37] For example, radio programs that two-thirds of all black listeners follow attract only 5 percent of the local white listeners. Where two newspapers exist in a market of black and white readers, black readers strongly prefer one of them.[38] Similar stark differences in media preferences are observed between Hispanic and non-Hispanic consumers. Large differences also exist between consumers of different genders and ages. Preferences regarding newspapers and radio stations depend strongly on where consumers live. Most U.S. newspapers and radio stations serve local markets, such as metropolitan areas.

In Germany, there are currently six national daily newspapers with a combined run of 900,000 copies and 308 local and regional newspapers with a combined run of 10.2 million copies.[39] Most of the local ones serve relatively small markets. According to 2012 data, daily print runs varied between 794 and 373,200. One hundred and ninety-five newspapers had print runs below 10,000, forty-one had print runs between 100,000 and 200,000, and ten had print runs exceeding 200,000. Forty-six cities in Germany had two different local newspapers, eleven had three, and only one (Berlin) had four. Taking common ownership structures into account, only twenty-six cities had two different local papers, and only three had three different local papers.[40] Where more than one local paper existed, they were typically local editions of other newspapers. Many local papers were owned by larger publishing groups.

In 2016, only thirty-one German cities with more than 100,000 inhabitants had two or more independent daily newspapers. In 2018, 330 daily newspapers with a combined average daily print run of 15.7 million were published in Germany. Local subscription papers accounted for a total print run of 11.2 million,

---

[37] Anderson and Waldfogel, "Preference Externalities in Media Markets," 7.

[38] Joel Waldfogel, "Who Benefits Whom in Local Television Markets?," *Brookings-Wharton Papers on Urban Affairs* (2004): 257–305, at 258.

[39] Bundesverband Digitalpublisher und Zeitungsverleger (BDZV), https://www.bdzv.de/alle-themen/marktdaten#c33585; Zeitungsmarketinggesellschaft, https://www.die-zeitungen.de/argumente/auflagen.html; Informationsgesellschaft zur Feststellung der Verbreitung von Werbeträgern e.V. (IVW), https://www.ivw.eu/ivw/4-quartal-2020.

[40] "Liste Deutscher Zeitungen," *Wikipedia*, https://de.wikipedia.org/wiki/Liste_deutscher_Zeitungen#Tageszeitungen.

local nonsubscription papers for a total print run of 2.06 million, and national newspapers for a total print run of 960,000. Among the daily subscription papers, the five largest publishing groups had a market share of 46 percent, while the largest ten publishing groups had a market share of 65 percent. There were only five nonsubscription papers nationwide, and the largest one held 80 percent of the market. An increasing number of newspapers use common journalistic and editorial services, resulting in a rising degree of publishing concentration.[41] These data indicate that newspaper markets are strongly regionally fragmented and typically local monopolies or duopolies. Furthermore, common ownership structures across local markets result in a high degree of concentration even at the national level.

The same can be observed in the United States, where only three national newspapers exist. In 2018, there were 1,279 local and regional daily newspapers, down from 1,748 in 1970.[42] Seventy percent of newspapers in the United States were part of newspaper chains.[43] In 2007, the largest four newspaper publishing firms accounted for 29.4 percent of the total market, the largest eight firms for 44.9 percent, and the largest twenty firms for 62.9 percent.[44] Thus, not only are local newspapers typically local monopolies, but even at the national level market concentration is high.

Radio broadcasting in the United States is in an interesting example of the effects of government regulation on media markets.[45] As in TV broadcasting, market entry is limited by the fact that governments regard spectrum as a public property and require licensing as a condition for entry. Government regulation of market entry is deemed necessary to achieve coordination of frequencies across stations and avoid interference. In the early years of the radio industry, federal regulators favored the development of large, national radio networks. As a result, the U.S. market was mainly served at the national level by a small number of networks. Local stations were restricted to relatively small geographical markets. Furthermore, ownership of multiple radio stations was very limited. These restrictions were lifted during the 1980s and 1990s. As a result, market concen-

---

[41] Kommission zur Ermittlung der Konzentration im Medienbereich (KEK), *Sicherung der Meinungsvielfalt im digitalen Zeitalter, Sechster Konzentrationsbericht. Schriftenreihe der Landesmedienanstalten* 132 (Berlin: ALM, 2018), 110–11, 138–39.

[42] Amy Watson, "Number of Daily Newspapers in the US, 1970–2018," Statista.com, Mar. 3, 2020. See also Chandra and Kaiser, "Newspapers and Magazines," 410 ff.

[43] Ibid., 416.

[44] "Market Concentration in the U.S. Newspaper Publishing Industry 2007," https://www.statista.com/statistics/186115/market-concentration-in-the-us-newspaper-publishing-industry/#statisticContainer.

[45] Andrew Sweeting, "Radio," in Anderson, Waldfogel, and Strömberg, *Handbook of Media Economics*, vol. 1 A, chap. 8, 345 ff.

tration increased strongly. In March 1996, the largest station owner in the United States, CBS Radio, owned thirty-nine stations and received 6 percent of the total industry revenues. Five years later, the largest station owner was Clear Channel Communications, with 972 stations. It received 26.2 percent of total industry revenues.[46] In 2019, the company, which is now called iHeartMedia, owned 856 stations serving 160 U.S. markets and earned 29 percent of the total industry revenue.

In Germany, private broadcasting was first allowed in 1987. In terms of viewer shares, Germany's public TV stations, had 93.4 percent of the market in 1987, and private TV stations had 1.5 percent. Ten years later, public stations had only 41.5 percent, and private stations 53.7 percent, while in 2006 the shares were 44.6 percent and 52.8 percent, respectively. Among private TV stations, two groups, RTL and ProSieben, held the lion's shares in 2018, with 23.2 percent and 17.8 percent, respectively,[47] down from 24.3 percent and 21. percent in 2002.[48] In addition to these high degrees of horizontal concentration, there is, as the KEK's *Konzentrationsberichte* show, also a high degree of vertical concentration. Both RTL and ProSieben hold shares in major TV production companies. Furthermore, newspaper publishers have close ties to private TV stations in Germany.

Demand Externalities

We have already noted above that media preferences are very heterogeneous across different groups of society. Two additional features of media preferences are important. One is that media are *experience goods*. These are goods whose value or utility can be known only by experience, that is, by consuming them.[49] Readers, listeners, or viewers must spend some time consuming a certain product before they can tell how well it fits their preferences. This makes the demand for media products inelastic relative to changes in price and quality.

Furthermore, media consumption involves network externalities, especially as regards media transmitting ephemeral information. Consumers like to be informed about the things their friends, colleagues, and peers are informed about. Knowing that the people one relates to read a certain paper or watch the news on a certain TV station makes that paper or station more attractive to the individual

---

[46] Ibid., 350.
[47] KEK, *Sicherung der Meinungsvielfalt im digitalen Zeitalter 6, Konzentrationsbericht. Schriftenreihe der Landesmedienanstalten*, vol. 52 (2018).
[48] KEK, 2, *Konzentrationsbericht* (2004), 88 and 101.
[49] Phillip Nelson, "Information and Consumer Behavior," *Journal of Political Economy* 78 (1970): 311, 329. Experience goods are contrasted with search goods, which are such that the consumer can easily determine their value or utility.

consumer and makes it more difficult to switch to another paper or station without knowing whether and when the others will switch, too. Such network externalities also result in demand hysteresis, adding to the media firm's market power.

Media urgency is the consumer perception that media content loses value if it is not consumed during some upcoming and narrow window of opportunity, because missing it reduces future opportunities.[50] A high degree of media urgency allows media to interrupt content frequently with commercials, because consumers do not want to miss part of the content when they skip over the interruption. This increases the economic value of the audience for advertisers.

Based on that market power, media firms can force their readers, viewers, or listeners to consume information they do not desire—advertisements—as a condition for obtaining what they desire. This is the basis for the two-sided market business model.[51] Furthermore, media can make consumers accept second-best or third-best options, such as formats that do not correspond to what they like best in terms of content.

This power gives rise to preference externalities in media markets and has important implications for market performance. Since consumer preferences are very differentiated, one would expect the content offered by the media firms serving a given market to be very differentiated, too. That is, a very large spectrum of content would be offered by a very large number of small firms. In the presence of fixed costs, however, the number of firms that can exist in a market is limited. Media firms operating in a given market must choose content that attracts a sufficient number of consumers to cover their fixed cost and to generate enough ad revenue. Demand hysteresis implies that consumers are willing to forgo their

---

[50] See Douglas A. Ferguson, "The Obstinate Audience Revisited: The Decline of Network Advertising," in *The Twenty-First Century Media Industry*, ed. John Allen Hendricks (Lanham, MD: Lexington Books, 2011), chap. 4, here at 62–63. Ferguson gives the following example: Before DVRs, streaming services, and cable TV, there were few windows of opportunity to watch feature movies: large theaters, small theaters, network TV, and finally syndicated TV stations playing them late night. To the extent that the pleasure derived from watching a new movie depends on the ability to talk about it with friends and colleagues shortly after its release, that pleasure declines when the opportunity to watch it in a theater is missed, and it declines further when it is missed on network TV.

[51] It is true that some advertising may be viewed as desirable by the consumer, especially local ads in local newspapers or local radio stations. According to BDZV, "Werbung in der Zeitung ist," 81 percent of readers find advertising in local newspapers "credible," 68 percent read it before shopping for things of daily needs, and 62 percent consider it helpful: https://www.bdzv.de/alle-themen/marktdaten/werbemarkt. Generally, however, "advertising is effective when its message cannot be avoided": Ferguson, "The Obstinate Audience Revisited," 61.

most preferred content and to consume second-choice products. The implication is that the number and quality of the products consumers find in a given market depend on the existence of a sufficiently large number of consumers willing to consume these products in that market. Consumers with rare kinds of preferences are unlikely to find what they prefer most. Consumers with average preferences are likely to fare best.

To illustrate the point, we use a number of examples based on Peter Steiner's seminal paper on the issue and adapted from Anderson and Waldfogel.[52] We first consider a local media market in which two groups of consumers, C1 and C2, exist. Initially, we assume that there are two alternative types of content or program that media can transmit, P1 and P2. C1 consumers will use only media that transmit P1, while C2 consumers use only media that transmit P2. For simplicity and without loss of generality, we assume that there is no user charge for media consumption. Furthermore, we assume that all consumers represent the same value to advertisers, and that each media firm can transmit exactly one program. Each firm chooses the program that will generate the most revenue from advertising. For simplicity, again, we let variable costs be zero. Media firms will then enter this market if and only if the revenue they receive from advertising exceeds their fixed costs.

Obviously, no media firm will enter if the ad revenue from either P1 or P2 (that is, from serving either C1 or C2) is not large enough to cover fixed costs. In that case, the market will not be served at all. If entry is possible at all, the market outcome will depend on the relative size of the two populations, C1 and C2. If they are of equal size, at least two firms will enter, one choosing P1 and serving C1, and one choosing P2 and serving C2. Assume that, when k firms serve a given population of size Ci, all firms will have equal shares of that population, C_i/k. If entry is possible for more firms (k>2), half of them will serve C1 and the other half C2.

This leads to an inefficiency: since the information transmitted is freely accessible to each group of consumers, producing and distributing it more than once is a waste of resources. The more firms enter the market, the more resources are spent on fixed costs without generating more benefits to the consumers. This waste of resources generates an incentive for media firms to engage in horizontal integration. Firms serving the same group of customers have an incentive to share the cost of producing content that their consumers appreciate. By a slight extension of the argument, firms serving the same type of consumers in different local markets have an intensive to cooperate and share their fixed cost of content production.

---

[52] Peter O. Steiner, "Program Patterns and Preferences, and the Workability of Competition in Radio Broadcasting," *Quarterly Journal of Economics* 66 (1952): 194–223.

Now suppose that C1 makes up 70 percent of the total population. If the ad revenue from C1 is large enough to cover a media firm's fixed costs, it will enter the market and offer P1. What about the second firm? Since 70/2 is larger than 30 (C2), the second firm entering the market will offer program P1, too, if half of the ad revenue from C1 still covers fixed costs. Sharing the larger of the two submarkets is more profitable to the second firm than entering the other market. Only P1 will be transmitted, and C2 consumers will not be served at all. Waldfogel calls this the (simplest form of the) tyranny of the market: "Majority tastes override minority tastes in a market place with few alternatives."[53] The combination of fixed costs and limited population size results in a market failure. Competition in this setup leads to duplication of programs offered, which is wasteful, since both firms spend resources on their fixed costs.

Note that if the distribution of the consumer population becomes more uneven, wasteful competition increases. If the revenue generated from serving a third of C1 consumers suffices to cover a firm's fixed cost, three firms will enter the market and all three will choose P1, leaving C2 consumers unserved. Government intervention can overcome this inefficiency. If market entry were licensed by the government and allowed to only one firm, the monopolist would generate maximum revenues by offering both programs. Alternatively, the government could set up a public media firm serving one or both types of consumers.

Suppose, now, that the two consumer types have equal shares in the population, but that the value of C1 types to advertisers is two-and-a-half times the value of C2 types. This could be because C1 types have higher incomes, greater wealth, or a greater propensity to spend out of their incomes, perhaps because they are younger. If the half revenue generated from ads exceeds the firms' fixed costs, two firms will choose P1 and none P2. Anderson and Waldfogel call this the "tyranny of the economic majority," or, more colloquially, the "tyranny of the Yuppies."[54] The implication is that advertisers spend more on media targeting consumers that are more valuable to them, and that the number of consumers reached is not all that counts.[55]

Next, assume that there are three programs, P1, P2, and P3. C1 consumers will select the media offering P1, but if P1 is not available, they would select media delivering P3. C2 consumers select media delivering P2, but if P2 is not available,

---

[53] Joel Waldfogel, *The Tyranny of the Market: Why You Can't Always Get What You Want*, (Cambridge, MA: Harvard University Press, 2007), quote from Anderson and Waldfogel, "Preference Externalities in Media Markets," 12.

[54] Anderson and Waldfogel, "Preference Externalities in Media Markets," 14.

[55] Strömberg, "Distributing News and Political Influence," 97, reports an interesting example for this, in which the British *Times* increased its sales by two thirds but lost revenues from advertisement because it lost readers that were particularly valuable to advertisers in the process.

they select media delivering P3. Thus, P3 is the second-best for both, or, as Anderson and Waldfogel call it, the "lowest common denominator." Suppose that ad revenues generated from either P1 or P2 are not enough to cover firms' fixed cost. In that case, there is still a chance that a firm would enter the market and offer P3, as all consumers would use it. This case is easily modified assuming that only some part of each type would consume P3, as long as the sum of those parts is large enough. Mary Jackson Pitts and Lily Zeng describe this outcome for the U.S. TV market as follows: "Through the offering of a little something for everybody, the three broadcast networks secured 90 percent of prime-time television viewership in the 1970 s."[56] The interpretation of this result is ambiguous. In the context of arts and music, it may mean that lower-quality content that appeals to many people, say pop music, has better chances to be distributed than higher-quality content appealing only to a small group of people, say modern opera. In the context of political news and information, it means that mass media tend to avoid issues that concern people of extreme political positions and focus on issues in the middle of the political spectrum.

Assume, again, that both groups represent equal value to advertisers, but one is 70 percent of the total population. A monopoly firm would distribute P3 alone and get the whole market. Two firms entering the market would both distribute P3, since half of the total market revenue exceeds the revenue that can be generated from C2 consumers. In this case, then, the existence of C2 consumers in the market has a negative effect on C1 consumers, since the latter would be served with P1 if they were alone. C2 consumers are positively affected by C1 consumers, since they would not receive any program they like if they were alone. If, however, the revenue that can be generated by serving C2 consumers alone is large enough for a firm to enter the market, the other two firms will choose to offer P1, since 100/3 (the revenue from all offering P3) is smaller than 0.7*100/2 (the revenue each firm gets from serving C1 consumers with P1.) The firm serving C2 consumers would, in this case be indifferent between offering P2 or P3. Thus, both types of consumers can be better off. This is a *market size effect*. Given the distribution of consumer types in the market, all consumers can be better off, if market size—that is, the total number of consumers—increases. Conversely, all consumers can be better off if, for a given market size, fixed costs fall, because more product diversity can be offered.

As explained by Anderson and Waldfogel, this model can be extended to a more realistic case with a richer structure of media preferences. Suppose, again, that there are two types of consumers, C1 and C2. C1 consumers are uniformly distributed over the interval [0,1] such that for consumer C1x, $0 \leq x \leq 1$ is the ideal content type of the media product. If a product x* is offered, the probability that

---

[56] Mary Jackson Pitts and Lily Zeng, "Media Management: The Changing Media Industry and Adaptability," in Hendricks, *The Twenty-First Century Media Industry*, 29.

consumer C1x receives advertisements transmitted together with x* is p(t|x*-x|), where p is a decreasing function of the distance between the consumer's ideal content x and the content offered, x*. The parameter t describes the strength of the consumer's adversity to content differing from his ideal one. If t=0, the consumer is indifferent between different types of content, while even small differences matter for large values of t. Think of consumers having preferences over different types of music ranging from rap to baroque. A consumer liking baroque has a high probability of being reached by ads of a station playing baroque and a small but not zero probability of being reached by ads of a rap station. Similarly, C2 consumers are uniformly distributed over the interval [z, 1+z], 0<z<1. Preferences are thus different but overlap in the interval [z 1]. The larger z is, the less overlap there is, and the more different are the tastes of the two groups. Advertisers are willing to pay c1 to reach C1 consumers and c2<c1 to reach C2 consumers. Thus, C1 consumers represent greater economic value to advertisers.

Suppose that there is a monopoly media firm financed entirely by advertising and able to maximize profits. The firm must choose its location, x*, in the content space [0, 1+z]. A benchmark case is where c2=c1 and the consumers are equally distributed over their respective interval. Then, if a product is offered at all–that is, if ad revenues suffice to cover fixed costs–the monopolist chooses to be right in the middle of the content space, x*=(1+z)/2. Individuals with average preferences in the population are served best. If C2 consumers have no economic value for advertisers, c2=0, the monopolist firm will choose x*=0.5, the average preference of C1 consumers. C2 preferences are irrelevant, and C2 consumers can only receive what is being catered to C1 consumers. If c2 > 0, x* shifts to the right, the more so, the larger is c2. If, however, c2=c1, x* may still be to the left of (1+z)/2, if the mass of C1 consumers is larger than the mass of C2 consumers. Thus, minorities are served less well, and the bias against them increases as the mass of C1 increases relative to C2.

Consider a market served by two media firms, P1 and P2, which assumes that the overall market is large enough to cover twice the fixed costs. We continue to assume that c1>c2. Again, the two firms must choose their location in the content space [0, 1+z]. To keep things simple, we assume that z=1. When the two firms jointly serve the same group of consumers, both get half of the revenue generated by that group.[57]

Without loss of generality, assume that firm P1 serves predominantly C1 consumers and P2 serves predominantly C2 consumers, such that P1 offers x1* and P2 offers x2* and x1*<x2*. Remember that P1 gets half of the revenues generated by consumers located between x1* and x2*. If firm P2 moves a little bit closer to x2*, say, to x2'<x2*, she gains half of the market between x2' and x2* and loses

---

[57] This is an application of the well-known model of locational choice first presented by Harold Hotelling, "Stability in Competition," *Economic Journal* 39 (1929): 41-57.

C2 consumers whose preferences are close to x=2. Some of the consumers P2 gains are C1, the rest C2. Conversely, if P1 moves a bit closer to x2*, she gains some additional C2 consumers and loses C1 consumers. Since C1 consumers are more valuable that C2, the implication is that P2 has an incentive to be further away from the average C2 consumer than P1 is from the average C1 consumer. P2 pushes to the left, and this pushes P1 to the left. In the end, both firms are closer to the middle than they would be if only one group of consumers existed. Both groups are served less well than if they were alone in the market. If the economic value of C1 consumers increases, the incentive for firm P2 to move left rises and, therefore, C2 consumers are worse off.

The take-away from these considerations is that, due to the combination of large fixed costs and preference externalities, media markets are unlikely to generate efficient outcomes. Government regulation can improve market performance.

Media Markets in the Time of the Internet and Social Media

Facts and Trends

The introduction of the internet and the rise of internet-based media, such as search engines, streaming services like YouTube, and—with the start of Facebook in 2004, Twitter in 2006, and WhatsApp in 2009—social media, have brought dramatic changes for media markets.[58] Technological developments like the increasing speed of the internet, the introduction of the iPhone in 2008 with the subsequent spread of smartphones, and of the iPad in 2009, contributed to these changes by facilitating the use of internet-based media on mobile devices.

Toward the end of the 1990s and in the context of the bursting of the "dot-com bubble," a large part of ad spending had already migrated from traditional media, such as newspapers, TV, and broadcasting stations, to new media, such as search engines and social media. The two top players today, Google and Facebook, are predominantly ad-financed. Alphabet's (Google's mother company) ad revenues accounted for 86 percent of its total revenues. For Facebook, ad revenues amounted to 98 percent of total revenues.[59] Digital revenues accounted for 40.7 percent of

---

[58] In 2009, Ben Grossman, one of the leaders in the US media industry, predicted that Twitter would soon fade away and had had its "15 minutes." Susan Smith and John Allen Hendricks, "New Media: New Technology, New Ideas or New Headaches," in Hendricks, *The Twenty-First Century Media Industry*, chap. 1, at 15.

[59] Zhang, "Global Digital Networks and Global Media Systems," 49; subsequent references in text.

total global entertainment and media revenues in 2014. In 2020 it was 57.3 percent, and the 2023 share is projected to be 61.6 percent.[60] Market concentration has increased. In 2017, Alphabet and Facebook together received 62 percent of global online ad revenues, and 25 percent of total media advertising revenues world-wide (Zhang, 51). As the owner of Instagram, Messenger, and WhatsApp, Facebook reaches 84 percent of users in Reuters' *Digital News Report's* (DNR) combined sample of 40 countries, and 57 percent of news consumers alone. Global players channel a large share of media revenues from other countries into their home country, while content flows predominantly from their home countries to other parts of the world. There is thus an important asymmetry in content flows: consumers receive the same information globally, but little information about and from their own neighborhoods (Zhang, 50).

As a result of the migration of ad spending and the fact that more and more consumers get their news online, real ad revenues of U.S. newspapers fell by 80 percent between 2000 and 2018, and the share of advertising revenue in total revenues fell from 82 percent to 57 percent. Total annual circulation of weekday papers in the United States fell by 49 percent, from 55.7 million to 28.6 million, between 2000 and 2018. Early on, most newspapers made content freely available and relied predominantly on ad revenue. After 2010, paywalls were introduced, allowing some user-financed revenue.

The shift in revenues has also produced changes in spending on content production. The total number of newsroom employees in the U.S. newspaper sector fell from 71,640 in 2004 to 37,900 in 2018, a decline by 47 percent. During the same period, newsroom employment in other news-producing industries, including internet publishing and broadcasting and search portals, increased by about 25 percent.[61]

On the consumers' side, the internet has promoted the attitude that news, like other media products, can be had for free. Reuters' *DNR 2017*[62] finds that, in a large sample of national media markets, less than 20 percent of consumers are willing to pay for online news. In Norway, the country with the highest willingness to pay, only 25 percent of consumers will pay for news.[63] Most of those who

---

[60] PwC, *Global Entertainment & Media Outlook 2019–2023*, https://mediaoutlook.pwc.com/dist/assets/pdf/Take-a-Tour-Outlook-2019.pdf, 3.

[61] Pew Research Center, "Newspaper Fact Sheet," https://www.journalism.org/fact-sheet/newspapers/; see also Pew Research Center, "Newsroom Employment at U.S. Newspapers Dropped by 51% between 2008 and 1019," https://www.pewresearch.org/fact-tank/2020/04/20/u-s-newsroom-employment-has-dropped-by-a-quarter-since-2008/ft_2020-04-20_newsroomemployment_02/.

[62] RISJ, *Digital News Report 2017*, https://reutersinstitute.politics.ox.ac.uk/sites/default/files/Digital%20News%20Report%202017%20web_0.pdf.

[63] Richard Fletcher, "Paying for News," *RISJ Digital News Report 2017*, 33 ff.

pay do so to get access on mobile devices or because they get an interesting bundle of print and digital news. Being informed quickly is an important motivation for paying. Most of those who do not pay say that they can get the news they want for free. Across countries, the willingness to pay is negatively correlated with how likely users are to bump into a paywall when trying to access news. In other words, willingness to pay falls as the likelihood to get away with free riding increases.[64] Similarly, across all national markets the proportion of consumers willing to pay for video is less than 30 percent; for audio it is less than 25 percent; for news it is less than 15 percent. Interestingly, younger consumers seem to be more willing to pay.

According to the Reuters DNR, the mix of media use is changing significantly.[65] Print media have declined significantly as a source of news, while social media and news aggregators, such as Google news or Apple news, have grown. While TV is still the dominant source of news for older consumers, the younger seek news online, including in social media and, more recently, messaging apps. About one-third of consumers get their news by direct access to relevant websites, while two-thirds get their news by way of search engines, social media, aggregators, and others. This means that the news they are discovering is brought to them by algorithms of some sort rather than by editors. Reuters finds that algorithms confront users with more news sources and, therefore, more diverse news than they would usually find. However, this does not necessarily imply better quality of information, as algorithms also pick up less reputable sources, such as conspiracy websites. Only 25 percent of consumers think that social media do a good job separating news from fiction, while 40 percent think that news media do. Users feel that the lack of rules and the presence of viral algorithms encourage low-quality and fake news to spread quickly.[66] In contrast, users of news groups on social media typically say that they trust the news they get from these sources. Typical users use a variety of different news sources, including partisan ones, and are active in a variety of groups.[67]

In the pre-internet world, traditional mass media not only transmitted news but also made news by selecting, editing, and putting into context what was published.[68] They thus performed an important role as gatekeepers of news and topics discussed in society, a role that may get lost in the internet world.

---

[64] Ibid., 33–37, 33.
[65] RISJ, *Digital News Report 2017*, 10.
[66] Ibid., 8.
[67] Antonis Kalogeropoulos, "Groups and Private Networks—Time Well Spent?," RISJ, *Digital News Report 2019*, 38–41.
[68] See, for example, the Glasgow Media Group, "Bad News," *Theory and Society* 3, no. 3 (1976): 339–63, JSTOR, www.jstor.org/stable/656969.

Convergence is one important feature of the new environment.[69] It occurs in a variety of dimensions. Providers and distributors are linking up as newspapers offer video, audio, and text on their websites in digital format, and sports events are shown on streaming services, TV networks, telecoms, and social media. Some big players on the internet operate as aggregators of information and content, which they collect from various producers.[70] Regarding access to information, more and more users expect constant connectivity. Former distinctions among TV, cable, satellite, wired, and wireless services are becoming void in this environment. Media professionals have acquired convergence skills, like writing for the web, shooting pictures, and producing videos for websites.[71]

Business models have converged. Amazon was first a book retailer and Apple a manufacturing company. Today, both act as producers and distributors of audio and video content. Disney was first a content factory and now has its own distribution network.[72] Different geographical markets converge as large players like Google, Facebook, Apple, and Amazon are active globally.[73] For example, news consumption used to be connected with reading (newspapers or text on websites). Today, it is possible in markets all over the world to watch news videos or listen to news reports and comments at the same source where news can also be read. Across a sample of forty national markets, 67 percent of survey respondents consume video news weekly.[74] Over 69 percent of respondents use smartphones for news weekly, and these devices encourage the growth of short video content via third-party platforms as well as audio content like podcasts. Those using smartphones are significantly more likely to access news via social networks.[75] Advertising is harder to display on the small screens of these devices, and this difficulty contributes to the financial challenges of many publishers. Content formats designed for print or desktop devices are becoming outdated on smart phones.

Three waves of convergence can be distinguished. The first, between 1999 and 2003, comprised mergers of traditional content business and delivery-focused business—for example, AOL and Time-Warner. However, the expected synergies were not realized. Between 2008 and 2010, the second wave was driven mainly by the goal of realizing economies of scale and scope. The third wave, currently going on, is driven by the aim at ubiquitous connectivity, the use of mobile

---

[69] Smith and Hendricks, "New Media," 16.
[70] Martin Peitz and Markus Reisinger, "The Economics of Internet Media," in Anderson, Waldfogel, and Strömberg, *Handbook of Media Economics*, vol. 1 A, chap. 10, at 447.
[71] Pitts and Zeng, "Media Management," 31.
[72] See Albarran, *A Research Agenda for Media Economics*, 36.
[73] PwC, *Entertainment and Media Outlook 2018-2022*, https://www.pwc.com/ke/en/publications/entertainment-and-media-outlook.html, 4–10.
[74] RISJ, *Digital News Report 2020*, 29.
[75] Ibid., 28.

devices, the need for new sources of revenue growth, and a value shift to platforms that have benefited more from advertising, subscriptions, and transactions. This latest wave has found its most prominent expressions in the creation of encompassing media environments, such as the Apple Ecosystem and the transformation of Facebook into Meta.[76]

First digital video and audio recorders, then the availability of media content on websites and archives, have allowed consumers to avoid commercials by skipping over them in recorded programs. This freedom reduces the potential revenue generated by commercials and induces the development of new advertising strategies. It generates a preference for programming live events, such as sports or talk shows, where skipping over commercials implies missing part of the event.[77] Furthermore, consumers no longer have to watch or listen to the sequence of programs broadcast by TV or radio stations, nor do they have to read newspaper articles day by day in the sequence they are presented by their paper. Instead, they can decide what they wish to consume when.[78] Streaming services reinforce this new approach to time-shifting media consumption, as does the portability of media content on smartphones. The media libraries offered by many TV and radio stations allow both backward shifting (viewing or listening later than the original programming time) and forward shifting, as programs are available in the library prior to the programming time. The possibility of time shifting has reduced *media urgency*. For example, consumers do not have to watch an episode of a TV series at the exact time when it appears on the program. They can now determine for themselves when to consume it.

As a result, the great national audiences that used to gather around TV sets to watch the daily news or the popular soap operas all at the same time have disappeared. The resulting fragmentation of audiences makes it much less predictable for media firms when consumers watch or listen to a certain program, and this reduces the economic value of the audience to the advertiser.[79] At the same time, such fragmentation facilitates targeting advertising to audiences with similar socioeconomic characteristics, such as language, level of education, or income. In

---

[76] See Business Research Methodology, "Apple Ecosystem: Closed and Effective," https://research-methodology.net/apple-ecosystem-closed-effective/; "The Apple Ecosystem," *Apple Magazine*, https://applemagazine.com/the-apple-ecosystem/36702; and "Facebook: Wie wir uns auf Metaverse vorbereiten müssen—bevor es zu spät ist," *Gehaltstest für IngenieurInnen*, https://www.ingenieur.de/technik/fachbereiche/ittk/facebook-metaverse/.

[77] James R. Walker and Robert Bellamy, "DVRs and the Empowered Audience: A Transformative New Media Technology Takes Off," in Hendricks, *The Twenty-First Century Media Industry*, chap. 3, at 46–47, 49–50.

[78] Ibid., 41–57.

[79] Ferguson, "The Obstinate Audience Revisited," 61 ff.

this new environment, audiences need no longer be fed with second- or third-choice content to capture a sufficiently large number of consumers.

New Economics of Media Markets

As explained earlier, traditional economics of media markets was based on the concept of two-sided markets, with media firms offering content to audiences and audiences to advertisers. Large fixed costs of production and distribution implied the need to serve large audiences, leading to second- and third-best programming and a high degree of concentration in the industries.

A first aspect of the new economics of media markets is that fixed costs of production and distribution have fallen dramatically. The internet allows even small firms and individuals to offer content on a global scale. The top four influencers on Instagram, for example—two women and two men—have followers numbering several hundred million people.[80] The top four individuals in terms of followers on Twitter—a former U.S. president and three musicians—counted over one hundred million followers.[81] Technological advancement has reduced the cost of media equipment and made it "smaller, lighter, more user-friendly, and multifunctional."[82] Even small firms can afford such equipment and produce professional-quality output, and even audiences of one can now be served.

Media firms no longer think of audiences as large, amorphous masses of people, but as aggregates of individuals with very different characteristics in terms of age, ethnicity, language, education, lifestyles, work habits, etc. Instead of "broadcasting," where homogeneous content is pushed to large audiences, "multicasting" and "narrowcasting" have become possible, that is, serving smaller audiences with differentiated content according to their preferences.[83] As content diversity increases, so does the likelihood that the first choices of consumers are served.[84] Resources are used more efficiently as the incentive for doubling and tripling of programming is reduced. This is welfare improving. Realizing the changes, advertisers have shifted ad spending to new internet media and digital platforms.[85]

---

[80] Influence Marketing Hub, "Top Instagram Influencers," https://influencermarketinghub.com/top-instagram-influencers/.
[81] Wikipedia, "List of Most-Followed Twitter Accounts," https://en.wikipedia.org/wiki/List_of_most-followed_Twitter_accounts/.
[82] Pitts and Zeng, "Media Management," 31.
[83] Albarran, *A Research Agenda for Media Economics*, 31.
[84] Walker and Bellamy, "DVRs and the Empowered Audience," 51–55.
[85] Albarran, *A Research Agenda for Media Economics*, 30.

With low-cost internet publishing, it is possible to serve audiences with less common preferences, and that includes more extreme parts of the political spectrum and of social attitudes. A large range of partisan opinions is available on websites, blogs, and videos. Social media have reinforced the tendency to spread uncommon views on issues like COVID-19 and vaccination or the trustworthiness of the electoral process. The result has been greater political polarization in many countries around the world. Responding to this development, some traditional media have also focused on stronger and more distinctive opinion as a way of attracting and retaining audiences. Some commentators have increasingly questioned the value of objective news in a world where people have access to news from so many different points of view, while others worry that social media and algorithms are encouraging echo chambers and pushing communities apart.[86]

However, being exposed to a much greater diversity of content and a much broader range of opportunities to consume confronts the consumer with the need to make more and more frequent choices of what to consume. While consumers in the old environment had to take what was offered when it was offered, they now must decide how to allocate their time and attention to one of many different offerings at the time when they choose to consume media. This has given rise to a second, new aspect of media markets: consumer attention has become a scarce commodity, and content providers must compete for it in order to sell it to advertisers. The ability to attract and control the attention of consumers is an important determinant of competitiveness in media markets.

Attention economics suggests that consumers make such choices based on relevance (how important content is for them), resonance (how much they desire it), and engagement (how much they enjoy the actual experience of it). New media offer new modes of experience due to unbundling, nonlinear consumption, and interactivity.[87]

Online and social media allow consumers to interact with content providers and other members of the audience. Social media in particular have torn down the wall previously separating content producers and consumers. The audience is no longer passive. Consumers can provide content and updates, share comments with other users, and express preferences.[88] Interactivity creates opportunities for cost reduction: in the interactive media world, audiences are invited to present their opinions on complex political, social, and even scientific issues, while the presentation of facts, which would require costly research, is pushed to the background. Interactivity is linked to consumer attention and involvement, and this

---

[86] RISJ, *Digital News Report 2020*, 14.
[87] Albarran, *A Research Agenda for Media Economics*, 32.
[88] Ibid., 41.

creates new advertising opportunities for advertisers who wish to target certain segments of the population.[89]

The ability to keep track of individual consumers and provide them with personalized content has become a further important feature of the new market environment. The consumers' use of personal devices enables media firms to learn about their preferences and habits of consumption. In this environment, providing personal data (knowingly or unknowingly) is part of the price the consumer pays for using internet media.[90] The use of data analytics and technology to target consumers according to their media experiences enables them to serve their consumers better, but also to identify specific groups of consumers that are likely to buy specific types of consumption goods.[91] Using cookies to collect such information and algorithms able to process huge amounts of data, firms can learn to predict which type of consumer pays attention to what kind of content and to sell this knowledge to advertisers. While content and advertising in the old environment were largely produced and distributed independently, ads now are matched to the content provided to specific groups of consumers. By counting the clicks generated by an ad, media firms can also measure its effectiveness, which is valuable feedback for the advertiser.[92] At the same time, targeting consumers with the content they are likely to consume is a way to reduce the information overload they would otherwise be exposed to and saves them search time. This is welfare improving.

In the new market environment, firms with access to more data and more content (such as platform companies) have a competitive advantage.[93] Data collection and processing thus has become a new source of fixed costs that induces market concentration. First-party data have become most valuable assets that can be used to predict user behavior.[94] This characteristic of the new environment casts substantial doubt on the idea that media giants like Google or Facebook would lose their dominant position if their platforms were regulated in ways similar to network utilities. Even if other content suppliers were allowed to use the platforms, this would not eliminate the market power resulting from huge amounts of customer data.[95]

---

[89] Pitts and Zeng, "Media Management," 35.
[90] Peitz and Reisinger, "The Economics of Internet Media," 513.
[91] PwC, *Global Entertainment and Media Outlook 2018-2022*, 5-7; *2019-2023*, 3.
[92] Peitz and Reisinger, "The Economics of Internet Media," 448.
[93] RISJ, *Digital News Report 2017*, 17.
[94] PwC, *Perspectives from the Global Entertainment and Media Outlook 2018-2022*, 8, PwC, *Global Entertainment and Media Outlook 2019-2023*, 3.
[95] Dipayan Gosh, "Don't Break Up Facebook—Treat it as a Utility," *Harvard Business Review*, May 30, 2019, https://hbr.org/2019/05/dont-break-up-facebook-treat-it-like-a-utility.

But size is not everything. Success also depends on the ability to build direct relationships, bond with fans, and use data to provide good user experience and loyalty, thus making users attractive for advertisers.[96] There is space for smaller and more focused companies to thrive, too.[97]

Some Conclusions Regarding Character Formation

Do media impact character formation? The question doesn't even seem worth posing. It should be no coincidence that the Lord chose a medium—the Book of books—to speak to his people, to teach them his laws and statues, and, thereby, to form their character. Mercer Schuchardt describes the Protestant Reformation as a "media event," driven by the invention of the Gutenberg printing press and the resulting decline in the cost of printing.[98] The Reformation, with all its impact on the development of the modern world, would have been far less effective and important without this accompanying revolution of media economics.

Media economics suggests that, in the pre-internet world, mass media catered predominantly to audiences with average preferences, staying away from more extreme views and content. The media served a function of gatekeeping relative to the information that reached their audiences and to the interpretation of it, thus strengthening societies' middle ground. Plausibly, the media also catered predominantly to audiences of average moral views and reinforced what seemed ethically acceptable, even if not most preferred, to the majority of people. To the extent that consuming media contributed to character formation, this served to stabilize societies' ethical consensus. To the extent that media workers saw their mission in providing information and content for mature and responsible citizens, they fostered the development of a citizenry corresponding to the ideal of a bourgeois, middle-class democracy.

In the new media world of low-cost publishing and consumer tracking on the internet and social media, this social role of mass media has been largely lost. As smaller audiences can be served, audiences have become fragmented and polarized in terms of political views and social attitudes. To the extent that this carries over to moral views and ethical preferences, media today serve different groups of society with content that confirms and strengthens their moral positions. Character formation no longer draws people to the middle ground. Instead, groups of very diverse and partly antagonistic attitudes can exist in isolated media bubbles, in which their moral views are never questioned but are constantly reaffirmed.

---

[96] PwC, *Global Entertainment and Media Outlook 2019*-2023, 12.
[97] Ibid., 14.
[98] Mercer Schuchardt, "The Reformation as Media Event," *Second Nature*, Oct. 31, 2017, https://secondnaturejournal.com/reformation-media-event-full-essay/.

The United States today seems the most advanced in this direction. Some Christian groups consume media calling for civil war to defend their freedom from wearing masks,[99] while Republican patriots consume media calling for storming the Capitol.[100]

Today's world is impregnated with emotivism (Alasdair MacIntyre[101]) or expressive individualism (Charles Taylor[102])–that is, a general attitude that human beings are defined by their emotions. Ethical discourse has become almost impossible, because there is no generally shared understanding of a foundation of ethics transcending human feelings, aesthetics, and attitudes. The result is that ethical discourse has been relegated to a debate about individual emotions, and emotions are largely fueled by the desire to be recognized.[103] In this world, social media and media serving communities sharing the same feelings enable public hate speech and hate storms that promote disrespect of individuals who do not share the same views, as well as a general disrespect of authority.[104] Of course, pious communities of various religions and philosophies might also build their own bubbles reinforcing their religious and humanistic feelings. It is not clear, however, that this contributes more to the stability of democratic societies.

Finally, low-cost publishing opportunities serving niche groups of consumers have also promoted the view that mainstream news media produce "fake news." To some extent, this is good, because it teaches consumers not to accept news and other content uncritically. But a media environment in which the credibility of news and facts is questioned as a matter of principle teaches consumers that their own opinions take precedence over generally shared information in personal and political decisions, and this undermines democracy.

---

[99] For example, pastor and denomination leader Douglas Wilson's Twitter account or pastor Matthew Trewhellas's YouTube channel.

[100] https://www.youtube.com/watch?v=mh3cbd7niTQ.

[101] Alasdaire MacIntyre, *After Virtue: A Study in Moral Virtue* (London: Duckworth, 1981).

[102] Charles Taylor, *A Secular Age* (Cambridge, MA: Belknap Press, 2007).

[103] Carl R. Trueman, *The Rise and Triumph of the Modern Self: Cultural Amnesia, Expressive Individualism, and the Road to Sexual Revolution* (Wheaton, IL: Crossway, 2020), 56 ff.

[104] Following President Trump's Twitter account before it was closed, it was often appalling how individuals addressed the president of the United States with complete disrespect. See also Jon Ronson, *So You've Been Publicly Shamed* (London: Picador, 2016).

Clicks, Likes, and Cookies: The Trading of Active and Possible Attention in Media-Saturated Societies

Günter Thomas

1. Introduction

Times are changing. They are changing rapidly. In 1972 the first report of the Club of Rome pointed out the limits of growth by describing the limitations of our natural resources as well the increasing pollution of our natural environment.[1] Since 1984 the annual *State of the World* reports of the Worldwatch Institute have provided information about the current trends in the world economy, the global use of scarce resources, and issues concerning a sustainable society.[2] The ecological crisis is a primary topic in almost all societies. Even though the more efficient use of natural resources made great progress during the last decades, all advanced industrial societies still depend heavily on natural resources—in a highly questionable and contested way.

But do we depend only on natural resources like oil, gas, water, coal, wood, and metals? What is the most valuable resource, the most *contested* property of the advanced information society? The most valuable and the scarcest resource of our society saturated by television, internet, and cellphones is *human attention*. Every day, human attention is measured by "click-through-rates" and captured eyeballs, by the number of unique users and Nielsen ratings, and today by the collection of consumer and user data. Human attention is a property over which many forces fight. Billboards, newsstands, instant messages, phone calls, social media, and above all Google wrestle for our attention. This property, attention, is a resource needed by all communication processes in which human beings are involved. Human attention belongs to a subgroup of cultural resources, a little-explored group, but one that is necessary for the flourishing of human life and modern societies. The fact that those institutions and persons who attract and absorb

---

[1] D. L. Meadows et al., *The Limits of Growth: A Report for the Club of Rome's Project on the Predicament of Mankind* (New York: Universe Books, 1972).

[2] L. R. Brown et al, *State of the World: A Worldwatch Institute Report on Progress Toward a Sustainable Society* (New York: W. W. Norton, 1984–).

lots of attention have cultural and often economic power underscores the importance of this cultural resource. Like natural resources, cultural resources can be used or exploited, but unlike many natural resources, cultural resources need to be regenerated and renewed. And in this struggle over the cultural resource of attention, religious communities cannot be silent.

This leads to the theses of my essay: Human attention is a very much contested cultural property and resource.[3] This contest implies processes of having, gaining, and losing, and raises the question of where this resource is regenerated. The Christian churches are called to be places where the crucial cultural resource of attention is regenerated, redirected, and invested outside the contemporary economy of attention. So far, the general theses.

What Are Cultural Resources?

If anything has become apparent during the past three decades, it is the recognition that the way modern societies deal with their natural environments depends not only on the societal power structure, but also on the mindset of people, that is to say, on the complex cultural framework that influences political and economic action.[4] For better or worse, the functioning of society as well as the world of everyday life draws on cultural resources. As every reader of Max Weber's historical studies and Talcott Parsons's theory knows, the development of Western societies is heavily influenced by value systems, motivations, habits, and patterns stemming from certain strands of religious traditions. Specific value systems, latent patterns, an ethos sustaining and reshaping the legal system, and everyday habits of behavior—all are cultural resources that are, for good and bad, at the basis of our individual and communal life. They are used in economic processes, in the legal system, and in the political system. Not only knowledge transmitted and acquired in educational processes but also visions of a shared future and a good life are necessary cultural resources for the development of a society. Such cultural re-

---

[3] For the change of mentality beginning in the nineteenth century, see Jonathan Crary, *Aufmerksamkeit. Wahrnehmung und moderne Kultur* (Frankfurt am Main: Suhrkamp, 2002). Focused on classical media, see Jonathan Beller, *The Cinematic Mode of Production: An Attention Economy and the Society of the Spectacle* (Hanover, NH: University Press of New England, 2006).

[4] This fact comes through occasionally in the *State of the World* reports and lies at the basis of the churches' responses to the ecological crises. For an overview of the religious responses, see Barbara Kohler, "Die Überlebensfähige Gesellschaft angesichts der globalen ökosozialen Krise. Weltmodelle und Überlebenskonzeptionen des Worldwatch Institutes und thematisch verwandter kirchlicher Verlautbarungen," (diss., Heidelberg, 1992).

sources are embedded in cultural institutions and in individual beings who hold up these institutions.[5]

Cultural resources are those "entities" that contribute to economic or political processes as necessary elements but are not the result of such processes. Yet are cultural resources only to be "found," like oil, air, and water? The whole set of cultural resources one can divide into roughly three groups. In one group are those that can be actively produced and built up, like certain skills and forms of knowledge. To the second group belong ethical orientations, habits, and values that need to be inculcated, yet can only be "produced" in quite indirect and complex ways.[6] The third group consists of resources which can only be regenerated or nourished, such as curiosity or attention. Unlike natural resources, these cultural resources are not just "there" in order to be found and used but are themselves the result of cultural processes. Cultural resources in this third group emerge out of systemic and self-referential processes in which they are the "product" as well as the precondition. However, like their "natural" counterpart, they are intrinsically limited, even though they may seem to be unlimited.

Compared to natural resources these cultural resources are invisible properties that become most apparent when they are absent. They come into focus if they become one side of a distinction. Corruption in economic life, sociocultural brutalization, the lack of necessary types of knowledge, a breakdown of the legal system, the extinction of the arts—each of these phenomena can indicate the partial or total exhaustion or absence of cultural resources. And, unlike natural resources, although the very absence of cultural resources might make them "present," they are not easily quantified.

But of greater concern is the fact that many cultural resources need to be regenerated. For example, the basic trust that life is comprehensible, the ability to cope with life in the face of suffering, and the belief in justice—to name just a few—are all constantly being challenged.[7] Nevertheless, they are preconditions, or re-

---

[5] However, the issue of cultural resources should not be fused with the other issue of cultural institutions as it is outlined by William J. Bennet, *The Index of Leading Cultural Indicators: American Society at the End of the 20th Century* (New York: Broadway Books, 1994).

[6] They suffer from a paradox in communication. If, for instance, moral communication is recognized as intentional moral communication, its risk of being rejected rises extremely. These cultural resources can be built up only if they are not intended.

[7] Clifford Geertz's theory of religion, for instance, can be read as an attempt to point out the ways religion helps to preserve and regenerate the cultural resource of knowledge, emotional stability, and ethical orientation—by working "at the limits of ... analytic capacities, at the limits of ... powers of endurance, and at the limits of ... moral insight." See Clifford Geertz, "Religion as a Cultural System," in *The Interpretation of Cultures* (New York: Basic Books, 1973), 87–125, at 100.

sources, for the flourishing of social and individual life. Within this broad range of cultural resources, one that has gone almost unnoticed by many social theorists up to now is human attention—both as an actual and as a possible one.

2. Human Attention—the Current Debate

The topic of human attention is coming to the forefront of the current debate about the international media culture.[8] It seems worthwhile to point out, however, that the issue in some respect is a rather old one. Only if we realize the key aspects of the older debate can we observe the dramatic shift that occurred at the end of the twentieth century.

The goal of catching someone's attention stands at the center of the long rhetorical tradition. Moreover, early on the Roman poet Lucretius reasons in *De rerum naturae* about the need of focused and selective attention (*attentio animi*) in order to gain real insight.[9] The connection between novelty and attention—that is to say, the issue of attracting attention through the novelty of an external stimulus—is also a matter of concern for a number of "classical" philosophers, even though they mention this issue only in passing. Johann G. Fichte, Johann G. Herder, and Jean-Jacques Rousseau are rather critical regarding the value of new insights and events that attract human attention. On the opposite side, David Hume and Gottfried W. Leibniz value novelty as a way to channel people's interest in their philosophical programs. While all these references to attention point out the relation between novelty, individual attention, and successful communication, their peculiar premodern background becomes visible if one analyzes their shortcomings. Just as these philosophers cannot imagine our current overflow of (possibilities for) communication, they also do not envision an absolute scarcity of attention. For similar reasons, the lack of attention is not considered to be a cultural problem but only an individual one.

The shift in the cultural economy of attention that occurred during the past decades has produced a lively debate, which takes as its starting point two recent contributions: Michael Goldhaber's and Georg Franck's idea of an economy of attention.[10] Both share many insights regarding the phenomenon of attention,

---

[8] The present discussion is documented in *Attention Please—Online-Kommunikation und Aufmerksamkeit*, ed. Klaus Beck and Wolfgang Schweiger (Munich: Reinhard Fischer, 2001); and *Ressource Aufmerksamkeit. Ästhetik in der Informationsgesellschaft*, ed. Florian Rötzer (Ruppichteroth: Kunstforum international 148, Jan. 2000), 51–181.

[9] For this and the following historical references, see Niels Werber, "Zweierlei Aufmerksamkeit in Medien, Kunst und Politik," in Rötzer, *Ressource Aufmerksamkeit*, 139–51.

[10] See Georg Franck, *Ökonomie der Aufmerksamkeit. Ein Entwurf* (Munich: Karl Hanser, 1998); "Jenseits von Geld und Information," in Rötzer, *Ressource Aufmerksamkeit*,

even though they differ in important respects. Despite these differences, they both develop this concept of attention in terms of two framing developments in modern society: 1. Economic models and concepts become more and more important for decoding social and cultural processes. 2. Within the overall economy there occurs a further "dematerialization" in the production of value. Goldhaber as well as Franck take as their starting point the overflow of information over against the scarcity of attention. For both, the internet is the paradigm and the latest step in this development.[11] At the same time, both Goldhaber and Franck observe that in any given society, the need for attention is even more widespread than the need for money. Through a reciprocity of expectations, attention becomes something that can be traded: I am longing for attention and can give away attention. At the same time, I know that others are longing for attention and can give it away. Out of this reciprocity and exchange, an economy of attention emerges.

However, Goldhaber and Franck do not stop simply with a view of attention as a rare and highly valued tradable possession. Both move further by claiming that attention becomes a kind of currency that is the basis for the "attention economy." This move from an illuminating metaphor, or even a conceptual model, of an economy of attention to the claim that such an economy exists is a move that is very much debated among economists. While Franck suggests that there exists a "second economy" driven by attention and connected to the classical money economy, Goldhaber makes an even bolder claim.[12] He suggests that the attention economy will eventually replace the currently dominant monetarily based capitalist economy. Goldhaber believes the attention economy will eventually take the place of

---

84-94, also in *Telepolis*, Nov. 9, 1998 (http://www.heise.de/tp/deutsch/special/auf/6313/1.html); "Die neue Währung: Aufmerksamkeit," in *Merkur* 43 (1989): 688-701; "Ein Kampf um Aufmerksamkeit. Zur Organisation von Wissenschaft," in *Merkur* 51 (1997): 72-79; Michael H. Goldhaber, "The Attention Economy and the Net," 2nd draft version of a talk presented at the conference on "Economics of Digital Information," Cambridge, MA, Jan. 23-26, 1997, http://www.well.com/user/mgoldh/AtEcandNet.html; "Kunst und die Aufmerksamkeitsökonomie im wirklichen Raum und im Cyberspace," in Rötzer, *Ressource Aufmerksamkeit*, 78-83. For further developments in favor of a mode of existence and a view back, see Georg Franck, *Vanity Fairs: Another View of the Economy of Attention* (Cham: Springer, 2020).

11 One of the main arguments is that in the World Wide Web, most information is free, and thus money is no longer the main motive for distributing information. Whether this observation can hold true remains to be seen. The crises of the web economy in 2000 and 2001 seem to invalidate this argument. In addition, this observation does not differentiate between relevant information and irrelevant information or, to be more specific, between data and information.

12 However, Franck, in *Ökonomie der Aufmerksamkeit*, p. 51, does claim that attention might become more important than money for the social allocation and rationing of resources.

money as the driving force behind work. The transaction of products will finally be substituted by the transaction of attention.

Without doubt, Goldhaber's strong substitution thesis is itself a questionable product of the attention economy. Not only is such a claim theoretically untenable, it even distracts from observing the powerful links between the money market and attention, an issue I will on touch later. It also diverts scholarly attention away from the crucial issue of an ecology of attention. The other idea, of attention being something like a currency, cannot be rejected wholesale but needs further sociological elaboration and theoretical scrutiny, particularly in the light of Talcott Parsons's theory of "symbolic media of interchange" and Niklas Luhmann's "symbolically generalized media of communication."[13] What seems worthwhile, however, is the distinction between attention as a *resource* and attention as a *property of exchange*. It will be valuable to explore the subtle dynamics between these two manifestations of attention. The following two sections briefly explore this distinction and dynamic between attention as a resource and as a property of exchange.

3. Human Attention as Cultural Resource—Conceptual Clarifications

The public debate over Goldhaber's and Franck's theses clearly indicates the need for further conceptual clarification. The confusion about the concept is intensified in the German discussion, since the German term *Aufmerksamkeit* can mean both awareness and attention. At the moment, I would like to differentiate the following concepts with the help of terminology borrowed from Luhmann.[14]

---

[13] Talcott Parsons, "Social Structure and the Symbolic Media of Interchange," in *Social Systems and the Evolution of Action Theory* (New York: The Free Press 1974), 204–28; Nicklas Luhmann, *Die Gesellschaft der Gesellschaft* (Frankfurt am Main: Suhrkamp, 1997), 316–97. Based on Parsons's and Luhmann's insights, the debate of Franck's and particularly of Goldhaber's proposal suffers from a theoretical confusion that already overshadows Goldhaber's texts: Assuming that attention becomes a kind of currency, a medium of exchange, does *not* necessarily mean that this currency can substitute for money. If, as the critics rightly affirm, attention can never substitute for money, we are left with the question, what is the system attention is the currency of? Thus, the critique from economists does not automatically invalidate the claim that attention is a currency.

[14] For a rather differentiated scheme from the side of a philosophy of mind with leanings toward phenomenology, see Sebastian Watzl, *Structuring Mind: The Nature of Attention and How It Shapes Consciousness* (Oxford: Oxford University Press, 2017). And yet Watzl does not elaborate the media-related issue of an external guidance of subjective attention. For an introduction into the growing field of attention research, see Michael I. Posner,

3.1 Types of Attention

a) *Awareness* is not yet attention, since awareness only requires being awake and conscious with some kind of feeling, an intransitive state that includes the possibility of turning to something. Attention is reached when awareness is combined with a focused intentionality. With this in mind, I would like to differentiate at least three types of attention.[15]

b) Attention can be directed toward the self, in the form of either self-reflection or daydreaming. This *self-reflexive attention* (*As*) does not require a stimulus from the "outside." Therefore, it is not based on irritability but needs selectivity in order to achieve focused intentions. In cases when consciousness, or the cognitive-emotional system, turns to the outside, there are still two options. But both cases involve a highly complex process between the act of focusing attention through the cognitive-emotional system, on one hand, and the attraction of attention by the intended "object," on the other. Due to the autopoietical nature of consciousness, attention can be directed by "internal" processes (intentions) or by outside irritations that mobilize and attract attention.[16]

c) Attention can be used to gain and to process selective perceptions. This type of *perceptive attention* (*Ap*) should not be equated with passivity, since it can be very active in working through pattern recognitions and other forms of searching for and working through information. The binding of *Ap* can occur by natural perception (such as the nonmediated environment present while driving a car or climbing in the mountains) or mediated perception (for example, film, listening to recorded music, etc.).

d) The third type of attention is based not only in awareness but also in perceptive attention. Since it includes the coupling with other cognitive-emotional or even social systems for the purpose of communication, I would like to call it *communicative attention* (*Ac*). Not all attention has to be directed toward communication. This assumption is one of the most common mistakes made in the current debate. But for communication to occur, attention has to be very focused, and therefore this type of attention is easier to work out and understand. This type

---

"Guides to the Study of Attention," in *The Oxford Handbook of Attention*, ed. Kia Nobre and Sabine Kastner (Oxford: Oxford University Press, 2014), 3–7.

[15] For Franck (Ökonomie der Aufmerksamkeit, p. 29), who is at this point more precise than Goldhaber, attention could be translated as "selective perception and goal-oriented processing of information." And yet, the latter seems to be too far-reaching. Active attention is already required in situations in which perception is intensified and has to face the possibility of information. For further information, see among many, Elizabeth A. Styles, *The Psychology of Attention* (Hove, UK: Psychology Press, 2006).

[16] Styles, *The Psychology of Attention*, 215–253.

of binding of attention differs from Ap, since the double contingency of communication makes this process rather risky.

The much-debated case of *accumulated attention*[17] necessitates some kind of reciprocity, either in Ap or Ac or the attribution of attention. However, since the reciprocity of perception almost always leads to communication, accumulated attention is the result of direct or indirect communication that attributes attention.[18] If this accumulation of attention is centered on specific topics and attains some stability over time, it results in the creation of a public.[19]

3.2 Attention as Resource in Communication Theories

But why is human attention so important for modern societies, and in what sense is it a resource? Why is it such a valuable property, and—as I may add—why is its examination so important for the understanding of late modernity and so illuminating for theological reasoning about the church? To answer this question, one has to look back briefly to the shift in scholarly paradigms and how they are connected. Even this brief look at philosophical tradition reveals that attention is a resource because it is—to borrow a rather technical model—a dynamic interface. Research within the great tradition of German idealism focused in many ways on the self, or the human person, and his or her consciousness. The potential of individual reason, the inner life, the "I," the individual subject, and the edification of a personality were at the center of interest. Although in many respects already anticipated by idealists such as Schleiermacher, Herder, and Humboldt, the twentieth century became the century of the linguistic turn. Language, shared symbolic systems, and patterns of discourse became the primary objects of intellectual

---

[17] Naomi Eilan and Christoph Hoerl, eds., *Joint Attention: Communication and Other Minds: Issues in Philosophy and Psychology* (Oxford: Oxford University Press, 2005).

[18] Two examples might illustrate the point. Mount Rushmore is famous not because the mountain realizes that it is the object of perceptive attention of many people, but because people talk about it and communicate about their invested attention, thereby attributing attention. While communicative attention might include a reciprocity of attention between living beings, mediated communication makes it possible that even dead persons can accumulate attention through attribution processes. Many authors became famous only after their death, so they cannot perceive any more in some meaningful sense the communicative attention they attract and receive.

[19] This formal conception of "public" is broader than the enlightenment concept connected to reason and rationality. Yet it allows one to decode the so-called "decay of the public" as a transformation of publics through shifts in style, medium, and topics. See Günter Thomas, "Öffentlichkeit," in *Metzler Lexikon Religion*, vol. 2, ed. Christoph Auffarth, Jutta Bernhard, and Hubert Mohr (Stuttgart: J. B. Metzler, 1999), 586–89.

inquiries. It seems to me that one link between both traditions is the role of human attention. Attention is the interface between objectified sociocultural processes, on one hand, and subjectivity and the whole complex of one's "inner life," on the other. By leaving out the place of attention, modern theories of communication are unable to point out their own presuppositions and are ill equipped to uncover the resources on which communication depends. Let me offer three short sketches instead of elaborated reconstructions.

1) Hans-Georg Gadamer, whose work influenced much philosophical as well as theological hermeneutics, places the question of attention squarely at the center of the hermeneutical experience.[20] The logical structure of openness that characterizes hermeneutical consciousness rests on the priority of the question over against the answer. But why question? This is a question Gadamer never raised. Yet any act of questioning requires the investment of focused attention. In particular an act of questioning is based on highly selective attention that opens a horizon of questioning as the intellectual space within which this question makes sense. Therefore, communicative attention (A_c) is the interface between traditions, texts, and cultural objects, on one hand, and the understanding taking place in the hermeneutical experience of the person, on the other. Any reaching out to traditions and texts requires the delicate resource of attention. Seen in this way, Gadamer's work points toward the immense importance of attention for the whole human project of understanding.

2) In a similar vein, Jürgen Habermas concentrates in his theory of communicative action on the structure of linguistic expressions, their illocutionary power, and their semantic and pragmatic dimensions, which allow interlocutors to differentiate between instrumental, strategic, and communicative actions.[21] How do communicative acts contribute to the creation of interactions based on clearly articulated and negotiated normative claims? In raising such questions, Habermas explicitly rejects the examination of the dispositions leading to such linguistic behavior as merely a task of psychological inquiry. But, in so doing, Habermas cuts himself off from the question of the preconditions, or the cultural resources, required to engage in such communication. Communicative attention seems to be the invisible "condition of possibility" (*Bedingung der Möglichkeit*) for such linguistic engagement. By neglecting the issue of attention, Habermas also loses a valuable tool to analyze the systemic colonization of the life world, since this process could be decoded as an absorption of attention by other systems.

---

[20] Hans-Georg Gadamer, *Truth and Method* (New York: Seabury, 1975), chap. 2.3.c. Gadamer asks for the logical structure of openness that characterizes the hermeneutical consciousness, yet stops at the "question," without further questioning for the requirements for questioning.

[21] See Jürgen Habermas, *Theory of Communicative Action*, vol. 1 (Boston: Beacon Press, 1984), chap. 3.

3) Let me turn briefly to a last example: Niklas Luhmann's theory of communication and of modern society which culminates in the—at first glance rather strange—dictum, "Not persons, only communication can communicate."[22] For Luhmann, society as a texture of autopoietical social systems consists of type-different forms of communication that emerge out of noise, that is to say, the utterances of—among others—psychic systems. Both social and psychic systems operate interdependently and autonomously, yet they are connected by means of coupling. For Luhmann, the person is ultimately placed in the internal environment of society, even though he emphasizes the need for coupling in communication systems. While "viewing communication not as a phenomenon but as a problem," he wants "to ask how communication is possible at all."[23] However, he never concentrates on the vital requirement of such coupling, that is to say, the resource in the environment of attention.[24] Only attention makes understanding possible and enables the operation of communication, which is the unity of information, utterance, and understanding. What Luhmann calls coupling between the human consciousness as a psychic system and the social system happens to take place by means of human attention. While stressing difference, he never elaborates the selective exposure to communication as the construction of difference that operates by means of the selective distribution of attention.

What is the reason for such neglect by leading theorists of communication and language? In short, my hypothesis is that they do not realize the severe imbalance between the overflowing possibilities of communication and the scarce property of attention that characterizes the information society of late modernity. Like theorists of economy during the eighteenth and nineteenth centuries, they just assume that there is enough attention provided for in the communication process. Their theories do not take into account the paradox that actual communication is severely restricted by the overflow of communication, and that this constraint might become an issue in considering the future of modern societies.[25]

---

[22] Luhmann's complex social theory with his communication theory is best accessible in Niklas Luhmann, *Ecological Communication* (Chicago: University of Chicago Press, 1989), chap. 6. See also *Social Systems* (Stanford: Stanford University Press, 1995), chap. 4.

[23] Niklas Luhmann, "The Improbability of Communication," in *Essays on Self-Reference* (New York: Columbia University Press, 1990), 86-98, at 87.

[24] Luhmann clearly sees attention as the necessary requirement for communication, but it does not play a role in his communication theory. For his view on attention, see ibid., 88.

[25] To be more precise, the issue is present in more media-oriented communication theories but not yet appropriately taken up by social theorists or social ethicists. For a remarkable exception, see Orin E. Klapp, *Opening and Closing* (New York: Cambridge University Press, 1978); id., "Meaning Lack in Information Society," *Journal of Communication*

Luhmann does reflect on the improbability of communication, but he does not consider the dynamic that is unleashed in order to bind human attention.

3.3 Regenerating a Scarce Resource

Now I have to turn to the question, why is attention a limited resource, and why does it need to be regenerated? If we look at the whole issue of attention with this concern in mind, two types of scarcity come into view. First, there is the scarcity of awareness, even though the limit can be neither measured nor understood as naturally given.[26] Human beings are finite beings in many respects. Not only in terms of our life span, but also in terms of the limitations of time during a day, a week, or a year that define our natural and cultural rhythms, our attention is limited. All types of attention, even awareness, are limited. At least in terms of time, awareness is not without limits.

The second limitation can be found in the transformation of awareness into attention, as either As, Ap or Ac. If we try to quantify attention in terms of time and persons, the natural limit of any kind of attention is the time of awareness. All types of attention taken together cannot exceed the time of awareness. As we shall see later, communicative attention is the object of social contests, so that the relation between Ap and Ac becomes one of competition. Everyone knows situations where we are exhausted, tired, and no longer able and willing to enter into deep communications, yet where we are still willing to engage in perception. The exhaustion of communicative attention is a clear marker that, even if we are awake and fully conscious, we have embodied minds and are bodily creatures. It should also be noticed that in the case of technologically mediated perception in Ap, and in the case of Ac, *individual* attention becomes the basis of *social* phenomena.

Since the primary location of such attention (As, Ap, Ac) is the individual cognitive-emotional system, the whole topic of attention is primarily dealt with in the field of psychology.[27] But since attention is required for the social process of communication, the psychologically given becomes a social resource and social property. The fact that attention inevitably becomes part of the sociocultural dynamic of having, gaining, and losing is nicely revealed in two linguistic expressions.

---

32 (1982): 56–66; and id., *Overload and Boredom: Essays on the Quality of Life in the Information Society* (New York: Greenwood Press, 1986), especially chaps. 2 and 7.

[26] Compared to premodern times, artificial light as well as legal drugs, such as coffee, tea, and cigarettes, shift the limit.

[27] For an overview of the various theories, see Werner Wirth, "Aufmerksamkeit. Ein Konzept- und Theorieüberblick aus psychologischer Perspektive mit Implikationen für die Kommunikationswissenschaft," in Beck and Schweiger, *Attention Please–Online-Kommunikation und Aufmerksamkeit*, 69–89.

Both point to communicative attention as the basis of social life. In English, you "*pay* attention to," or one might ask, "please give me your attention," indicating that attention is a valuable good like money, even a social currency. In German, you "*donate* attention" (*Aufmerksamkeit schenken*), which clearly implies, on one hand, the idea of giving something freely away by being attentive and, on the other, the idea of receiving a gift—the attention of another person. Since attention is intrinsically a relational phenomenon, it becomes a social phenomenon within the sociocultural dynamic of having, gaining, and losing.[28]

At the end of this section, I turn to the question of why attention needs to be regenerated. However, the topic of regeneration needs to be placed within the broader context of an "ecology of attention."[29] At this point, I can only highlight essential aspects of such an ecology of attention. This wider context makes it apparent that the regeneration of attention has a formal as well as a qualitative side. While awareness can be taken for granted, attention in the form of As, Ap, and Ac cannot be taken for granted. The formal side concerns the bare presence of attention and the balance between the types of attention. Perceptive attention should not supersede communicative attention. In particular, communicative attention depends on individual as well as cultural memory and expectations. Any substantial change in the cultural memory will result in changed expectations. Another formal aspect is the relation between attention that is triggered and attracted primarily through irritations of the cognitive-emotional system, on one hand, and attention that is intentionally "invested" with interests, motivations, curiosity, or formed expectations. If more and more attention depends on external powers to attract attention, the result will be deep shifts in patterns of cultural reproduction. An additional aspect of an ecology of attention is the cultivation of sufficiently focused attention required for the communication of complex subjects, especially those that are not just "fun."[30] An angle I will touch on later is the cultivation of attention through interruption, which allows a process of refocusing.

The more qualitative side of the regeneration of attention takes as its starting point the fact that all attention is bound by something. Attention has to turn to something. Yet to what objects and subjects of perception, to what topics and semantic fields of communication is attention to be turned? Since the degree of necessary selectivity is increasing in our media-saturated society, this question becomes pressing. The binding and management of attention becomes the primary

---

[28] The annual journal *Cultural Machine* in 2012 dedicated a full issue to the topic "Paying Attention" (free access).

[29] See Günter Thomas, *Medien, Ritual, Religion. Zur religiösen Funktion des Fernsehens* (Frankfurt am Main: Suhrkamp, 1998), 631 ff.

[30] One indicator for that claim may be the widespread phenomenon of attention disorders among children. Even though they might be a case for the social construction of diseases, they point to different types of attentions.

social and political steering mechanism of media societies. In a media society, the distribution of bound attention comes to be a discourse of power. It is further qualified by certain semantic realms, certain themes, and communicative practices. Where attention is a scarce resource, any binding of attention is at the same time a potential unbinding of some other attention. The public attention of a given culture can be so absorbed that pressing issues for the flourishing of the communal life remain outside of the focus of attention. In such a case, the regeneration of attention is primarily a refocusing on relevant issues. The selective binding of attention becomes a question of individual and communal responsibility. One crucial issue within the ecology of attention is the possible commodification of attention, which increasingly takes place in an advertisement-driven culture. This process is closely linked to the other problem of a substitution of communicative attention by perceptive attention. When these processes come together in a media society, an exploitation of attention occurs.

4. Audiovisual Media and the Exploitation of Attention

Even though there is a longer tradition of research looking into the interconnection between attention and social life, the trading of actual and possible attention needs a closer analysis.[31]

To see the link between the exploitation of attention through mass media, one has to keep in mind several simultaneous tendencies that characterize late modern information societies:
1. the construction of scarcity of attention by the overflow of possibilities of communication;
2. the substitution of money by attention;
3. the attraction of attention through the physical stimulation of perception;
4. the close link between the management of attention and the collection of data through all kinds of consumer tracking;
5. the threat of invisibility based on inattention; and, eventually; and
6. the problem of forgetting in information and media societies.

---

[31] For the social dimension of attention, see, for instance, Eilan and Hoerl, *Joint Attention: Communication and Other Minds*; and Christopher Mole, *Attention Is Cognitive Unison: An Essay in Philosophical Psychology* (Oxford: Oxford University Press, 2011).

4.1 The Construction of Scarcity

I have already noted that natural as well as cultural resources come to the forefront of attention when they become scarce. In this regard, attention does not differ from clean water and clean air. Scarce resources are the most valuable properties. How is it that attention has become a scarce resource? What makes it one of the most valuable properties of the information society? With the advent of the printing press, the invention of the telegraph, the telephone, radio, and television, not to speak of the internet, societies experienced a dramatic shift in the correspondence of attention and possibilities of communication. Undoubtedly, the amount of leisure time available for people to use outside their everyday work also increased significantly during the past century. But what increased even more are the organized possibilities of communication. Because of the limitations of human attention, not every possibility of communication can be actualized. In Luhmannian terms, the selectivity between an utterance and the following understanding that creates communication as its unity increased sharply. In this regard, the World Wide Web again increases the possibilities of communication almost infinitely: in theory, one can now communicate simultaneously with everyone—a privilege in former times that only the metaphysical Godhead could enjoy. Human attention in today's society is not anymore overabundant than in the past but, relative to possible communication, is rare. This is definitely a new situation that has emerged during modernity. Undoubtedly, this process cannot be perceived merely through the eyes of cultural pessimism. The new situation came along with general education, democracy, and a liberation of cultural productivity. But at the end of this process, we face a strange situation: human attention becomes scarce even for the media system itself, in spite of the fact that the media already take up most of our time outside of work and sleep. The media system itself becomes trapped in a deadly paradox: the more media products there are on the market, the harder it becomes to attract sufficient attention.[32] The only way to "solve" this problem is to amplify it. However, there exists a problem for the broader culture: the sheer amount of time used for the consumption of audiovisual products makes human attention even more scarce for all those groups in civil society who rely on the availability of the time people spend outside work and sleep.

---

[32] See Siegfried J. Schmidt, "Aufmerksamkeit, revisited. Das Mediensystem verstrickt sich in eine mörderische Paradoxie," *Telepolis*, Dec. 22, 2000, http://heise.de/tp/deutsch/special/auf/4543/1.html.

4.2 The Substitution of Money by Attention

This second tendency is manifested in an advertisement-driven media culture, which today still includes the classical TV networks and cable TV networks but also such institutions as Google, Facebook, Instagram, Flickr, and TikTok. We all consume much more mediated communication in the form of newscasts, films, soaps, stock news, and instant messages than we can pay for with money. Only a very few people could afford a newspaper, all the available television programs, and the internet if they were required to pay with cash. What is actually taking place in our society is that more and more of the cost of communication is paid for by advertising. But what does this mean? What we don't pay for with money, we pay for with attention. Attention becomes the "currency" we exchange when we run out of money to get what we want—and we have already run out of money relative to what we get. Television networks, newspapers, and magazine publishers as well as the net portals attract our attention with their offerings and sell it to advertisers, who in turn pay in cash for what we cannot afford. At the very least, then, advertisement-enabled communication is driven by the "currency" of attention. We don't really get these things or services for free, we just pay in another "currency," that is to say, we trade some valuable property.[33] At the moment of this trade, the perceptive or communicative attention is not a resource used for actual perception or communication but becomes a property, or commodity, given away in order to get something beyond these moments of attention. And the rarer the property of attention grows, the more sophisticated become the means to attract it.

To point out these connections is not intended as just one more complaint about the media and their evil influence. One could easily turn the target of observation around: the economization of the cultural sphere—that is to say, the increasing tendency that monetary payment for cultural products is offset, or reduced, by the inclusion of advertising—could also mean that the danger that civil society is weakened by an "attention-drain" may be a result of our drive to consume more than we can pay for with money. By doing this, we engage in a strange kind self-exploitation.[34] But it may also raise questions of social justice,

---

[33] The value of human attention attracted by advertising is at least as much as the amount paid for advertising. But in this case the companies that advertise would still not make money by advertising. Since they advertise because they can make more money by doing it than by not doing it, the amount must be much higher. Written in a popular style, but nevertheless informative, Karen Nelson-Field, *The Attention Economy and How Media Works: Simple Truths for Marketers* (Singapore: Springer, 2020).

[34] For this reason, any media ethics that does not encompass an ethics of consumption, an ethics of imagination and production, and an ethics of distribution falls short of the complexity of the whole communication process. On willingness to be distracted, see Dominic

since people with more money can afford to pay less with attention. Their buying power makes their attention harder to get and therefore more economically valuable.

4.3 Attraction of Attention through the Physical Stimulation of Perception

Politicians, advertiser, hardware producers, and analysts of contemporary culture mostly agree that we are living in a situation of vastly enhanced possibilities to communicate. The cellphone is always at hand, and access to the internet almost always available. This general impression has to be challenged, however. Over against this common-sense view, I would like to state that the widespread use of audiovisual media primarily enhances the possibilities of mediated perception, even possibly at the expense of communication.

How is such a scenario possible? The media, ranging from radio and television to the internet, must capture our attention in order to sell it to advertisers. But given the necessary selectivity on the user's side, this binding becomes more and more difficult. How, then, does it take place? The key to this process is the recognition that most so-called information (including the internet in two or three years) is audiovisual communication. Yet I would like to ask further: Is most audiovisual communication really communication? Drawing on a distinction in communication theory, I have developed in some detail elsewhere the suggestion that television, film, magazines, and the future internet primarily offer not communication but preconfigured spaces of perception.[35] The process of communica-

---

Pettman, *Infinite Distraction: Paying Attention to Social Media* (Cambridge, UK: Polity, 2016).

[35] See Thomas, *Medien, Ritual, Religion*, 434–43. At this point I am drawing on Niklas Luhmann's communication theory. He assumes that communication is the emergent unity of the differentiation of information, utterance, and understanding: 1. information as a selection of meaning out of a horizon of possibilities; 2. an act of utterance as a selection of this information; and 3. understanding as subsequent selection out of a second horizon of meaning that is based on the difference between the information and the utterance. As communication is the emerging unity of this process, no single consciousness can capture or "see" all three aspects. If we look at the process from the perspective of an individual consciousness, an important task is to detect in the stream of perception units that carry the difference between information and utterance. To see someone blink her eyes can be just the perception of a physical behavior, or, seen as an utterance with information, it can be a hint to adjust my tie. Among the various media, some forms carry with them almost automatically this difference between utterance and information. Listening to speech, we are fine tuned to such a difference and expect something other than noise.

tion is always very slow and difficult, while perception can be very fast and deal with high degrees of complexity without decoding it completely. In order to attract our attention for perhaps three to six hours a day, the media system does not primarily offer information and communication, but rather prearranged spaces of perception for experience-like consumption. This has far-reaching consequences for the attraction of attention. While communication binds attention through novelty and relevant themes, perception has other means to achieve this binding. Perception can bind attention through attracting bodies. The use of film techniques to create the effect of speed (think about the movie *Speed*); thematic orientation toward crime and violence and other basic human needs and drives; illusions of closeness—these are all means of attracting and binding bodies through perception. Of course, this observation should not be overgeneralized. But it certainly highlights a paradoxical tendency in the so-called information society: to bind and attract more attention, one has to substitute perception for communication. If the media offered only communication in the strict sense of the word, they could never bind a person's attention for such a long time each day. In light of the distinction developed above, one can see that audiovisual media mobilize perceptive attention, not necessarily communicative attention.

> When we detect the difference between information and utterance, we attribute it to another cognitive-emotional system. Audiovisual media, moving pictures, don't carry with them this difference to such a degree as language.

Human consciousness is most of the time a perceiving consciousness rather than a communicating consciousness. Perception creates a compact unity that does not imply passivity and is not without the making of distinctions. On the contrary, it implies the fast recognition of patterns, movements, and complex forms that tend to be generalized. The differentiating marker of communication over against perception is the recognition of a selectivity, that is to say, the difference between information and utterance, which can be attributed to another self-referential system. Between just looking at a sunset and enjoying it, on one hand, and looking at it and seeing in it a message of a communicating god, on the other hand, there is only a tiny difference: in the latter case, the sun is an utterance carrying information coming from a self-referential godhead, not just a beautiful natural object of perception. Yet perceptions can be treated as communicative utterances. This phenomenon seems to be the basis of conversations with pets and of some mental diseases. But also, the other way around, communicative utterances can be treated as mere perceptions, which is the case in the reception of audiovisual communication with moving pictures: cinema and television.

4.4 The Underlying Connection between Attention and Big Data through Processes of Modalization

The intensive aggregation of personal data associated with modern information-processing techniques, the internet, and social media must be seen in line with the economization of attention—even if this is not so obvious at first glance.[36] The classical advertising industry aggregates and sells current attention to companies that bet on future purchase actions of customers whom advertising addresses. When advertising is effective, it is able to realize current, not just potential, attention investments. For that reason, the cost of advertising depends on the amount and intensity of attention raised in any kind of mediated communication.

On the other hand, the collection of personal preferences in behavior, experience, and communication, which goes under the keyword "Big Data," aims—if the data collection fuels an advertising market, as is the case with Google, for example—at *future* attention behavior. Whoever has the data on people's preferences not only can forecast their future buying behavior but also can process the data into complex behavioral profiles and forecast future attention investments in terms of their relative likelihood. Big Data therefore enables a far-reaching modalization of attention—not only real attention but also possible attention, because future attention allocations stored in data patterns can be traded. It is precisely from the aggregation of past and present "attention actions" that future attention actions can be inferred. The data contain real (!) possibilities of future actions.

With this modalization from reality to real possibility and by means of the storage of these possibilities as probabilities, the attention economy experiences a tremendous expansion. Every "like" predicts future "likes." That these are not speculations is shown by the enormous profits that the relevant companies make from the sale of personal data. And what makes the data so valuable is not simply a need for manipulation, for management and control. What makes it valuable is the high probability of future attention being paid to it—even though people subjectively perceive themselves as free. For example, those who use free or low-cost apps on their cell phones and more or less voluntarily allow access to their own data (address book, connections, audiovisual consumption preferences, material purchase decisions, mobility data, etc.) "pay" not with current advertising consumption but with probable future attention allocation to certain offers and advertisements (in the context of a compact profile that can be created by a sufficient amount of information).

The management of Big Data thus implies a movement (a) from present real attention investment (this is measured, tapped, or given away or traded as a valuable commodity), (b) through possible future attention investment (this is calcu-

---

[36] See, for example, Claudia Roda, ed., *Human Attention in Digital Environments* (Cambridge: Cambridge University Press, 2011).

lated and the calculations are traded), (c) to real future attention investment (to which the buyers of the data will engage).

In terms of moral theory, the collection of data also allows prediction of future behavior—to the exclusion of freedom and responsibility.

4.5 Inattention, Invisibility, and Oblivion

The organizing media system (the classic public or private (Mx), but also platform media such as Twitter, Instagram, Facebook, etc.) contribute to the management— that is, the control and focusing—of public attention. In a polycontextual world where (a) world constructions can observe other world constructions and (b) all attention is finite, inattention becomes observable by other observers. Under conditions of finitude and the pressures of selectivity, inattention is, metaphorically speaking, the shadow of all attention. This is true for individual as well as for all social forms of invested attention. Inattention is invisible to the attention-investing entity itself. It can, however, be seen as inattention from a third party or through temporally displaced self-observation.

If attention is understood as an entitlement, then the inattention that is relegated to invisibility can be morally attributed, precisely as disregard or even as punishment. That inattention is inescapably organized is abundantly clear in the case of major events, such as during a war. Even with enormous expansion of communication, public attention is drawn away from many issues. The media battle for attention then becomes, in many cases observably, a battle against inattention. Without attention—that is, in the invisibility and silence of inattention—communication succumbs.

The perspective, however, can be radically reversed. Without the rejection of any claims for paying attention in late modern media societies, no privacy can exist. Without deliberate and intentional organized inattention, a private life or just moments of privacy and solitude would be unattainable.[37] This raises the question who can decide the value and coding of inattention.

4.6 In/attention and the Organization of Social Forgetting

Modern media (television and movies, postnetwork television, as well as social media) not only steer social attention but also play a crucial role in the construction of social memory. Forgetting is the permanently present other side of not only memory but also social attention management. Only what is communicated on

---

[37] Mark Tunick, *Balancing Privacy and Free Speech: Unwanted Attention in the Age of Social Media* (Abingdon: Routledge, 2015).

the basis of invested attention is not going to be forgotten.[38] Following the lead of Niklas Luhmann's communication theory, Elena Esposito radically reformulates the phenomenon of social memory and social forgetting in the framework of media-based social communication.[39] Memory is not the thematization of the past. Instead, memory is manifest in the recursive operations of communication that permits, in a situation of constant flux, a relative stability in terms of concepts, situations, themes, and stories in current communication processes. Anything that does not remain in active communication is forgotten. Memory becomes media-based access to information. Esposito's provocative thesis holds that memory's task is not one of remembering but of forgetting. Through the management of attention as regulative power, archives (that is, libraries) as institutions of social forgetting can be transformed into communication. The growth of archives by means of the internet makes visible not only the fact of selectivity in investing attention but also the overwhelming power to forget. At the end, two types of forgetting need to be distinguished. First, there is a forgetting that is relative to a second-order observer (a third agent or self-observation). This observer is able, due to some possible access to an archive, to observe the forgetting and hence "knows" what is forgotten. The second type of forgetting can be called "deep forgetting," that is, in principle, unobservable and divested of any human attention. If there is no human second-order observer, human beings cannot even know what they have forgotten.[40]

Let me summarize the argument so far. I started out with the observation that we have today a clear sense of natural resources but still lack an equally developed sense of cultural resources necessary for the flourishing of individual and social life. Then I tried to cast some light on human attention, which I consider to be one of the most valuable properties of our information society, even though it is not yet considered to be a necessary cultural resource by leading communication theorists, and even though few people realize how it is in constant need of regeneration. To comprehend the exploitation of attention in the current media society, I pointed out three concurrent tendencies: first, the construction of scarcity through an overabundance of possibilities to communicate and—for other cultural communication—through the factual absorption of most attention besides work; second, the transformation of attention into a tradable property that can substitute for money; and, third, the increasing tendency to attract attention not by com-

---

[38] Elena Esposito, *Soziales Vergessen. Formen und Medien des Gedächtnisses der Gesellschaft* (Frankfurt am Main: Suhrkamp, 2002).

[39] Niklas Luhmann, *The Reality of the Mass Media* (Cambridge, UK: Polity, 2000); Niklas Luhmann, *Theory of Society*, 2 vols. (Stanford, CA: Stanford University Press, 2012-13).

[40] This constellation of "deep forgetting" is calling for a divine agency who can still observe this human forgetting—in order to bring justice to a world that is otherwise simply forgetting all the unnamed victims of this world.

munication but by perception. These three tendencies absorb, erode, and transform human attention—with far-reaching consequences for our culture. Over the past four decades, the internet and the processing of huge amounts of data have intensified this hunt for attention by modalizing current attention to possible future attention.

But after all these considerations, you might ask, where does religion come into the picture? Why is attention something that should be taken seriously by systematic theology? How should theological reflection react to this situation? These questions I want to address in the following section.

5. Religious Reflection, Theological Reasoning, and the Place of the Church in the Struggle for Attention

Religions in general, past and present, are institutions for the steering of attention —in modern times competing with the media system.[41] How does religion act as a forming power of culture, and how does the Christian church come into play? The first and most important reaction is to move beyond the competition principle. That means that religious reflection should explicate the specific contribution religions make in this situation. And finally, theological reasoning has to give theological reasons for how the Christian church can make a difference at this point in time.[42]

5.1 Beyond the Competition Principle

Without doubt, churches as religious communities operate within a market where there is stiff competition for attention. In many regards, the churches with good reason fight for their share of public and individual attention.[43] Not only com-

---

[41] See Aleida Assmann and Jan Assmann, eds., *Aufmerksamkeiten* (Munich: Wilhelm Fink, 2001).

[42] In doing that, theological reflection and ecclesial practice face a paradox that should be acknowledged but which should not become an obstacle: even the discourse about attention and even the life of the church need attention. Not even the regeneration of attention is free from consuming attention.

[43] The media not only absorb attention that could be directed to other groups of civil society but, in some respects, they even took over functions previously addressed by explicit religious communication. For a short overview of the current debate, see Günter Thomas and Michael Welker, "Einleitung. Religiöse Funktionen des Fernsehens?," in Günter Tho-

pared to medieval times, the churches even in the modern era have lost a considerable amount of mind share and public attention. Many debates about the public role of the Christian churches document this perceived loss of attention. But this is, I want to point out, only one side. On the other side, churches are called to quit lamenting about competition and ask anew what it means to be the church in the current environment. The churches are called to move beyond what I would like to call the "competition principle" and ask what they are in this cultural environment of the twenty-first century and what their contribution to their cultural environments could be.

However, the question "What is the church?" cannot be answered apart from any concrete cultural environment. The mission to which the church is called, the way it becomes a witness of Christ to the world, is tied to a specific time, to a specific cluster of cultures. And this relation of church, culture, and history is characterized by a double contingency: The social and cultural realities of a particular time challenge the church to see itself in a new light, and, at the same time, the church is challenged to contribute to the self-understanding and the flourishing of communal life. Even "resident aliens" interact with the cultural environments they inhabit as "residents."[44] For this reason, I argue that the cultural battle for the property of human attention should be seen as a challenge to ask, what is the church's unique contribution which, at the same time, can be the basis for a critical stance and an engagement in the public debate?[45] What can religious reflection discover in the life of religious communities, given this environment?

5.2 Religions and the Regeneration and Redirection of Attention

What difference does religion make in the fight for attention? At least three elements seem to be worth noting. First, religions use yet also regenerate, reallocate, and qualify attention. As many scholars of religion have elaborated, religious communication interrupts the rhythms of other activities, organizing a qualified

---

mas, *Religiöse Funktionen des Fernsehens? Medien-, kultur- und religionswissenschaftliche Perspektiven* (Opladen: Westdeutscher Verlag, 2000), 9–25.

[44] Stanley Hauerwas and William H. Willimon, *Resident Aliens: Life in the Christian Colony* (Nashville: Abingdon Press, 1989). I agree with Hauerwas to start with drawing a distinction. Yet the ways Christians relate to culture appear to be much more varied if we try to conceptualize these relations in the horizon of trinitarian theology. The absence of any serious trinitarian thinking in matters of culture is something Hauerwas shares with H. R. Niebuhr as well as John Howard Yoder.

[45] To take the existence and contribution of the church as a starting point for reflection does not justify any retreat to the church as an ethical realm. On the contrary, it prepares the church for its mission to "seek the welfare of the city" (Jeremiah 29:7).

"time-out." It decouples itself from other agendas and spheres of attention. The cultural institution of Sabbath and Sunday embody social knowledge. Communal and individual life is best served when it is regularly interrupted to refocus attention. Religious communities give these interruptions the shape of festive celebrations, offer diverse forms of participation, and focus the attention on a commonly shared symbolic network. Ritualized communications combine the novelty of new events in life with the security of expectations provided by repetitions. The regeneration of attention happens in all these forms through a festive and shared deceleration of communication.

Second, this regeneration of attention occurs along with a reallocation of attention. By interpreting life outside the festive "time-out" in light of sacred texts, religions reframe or remap the perception of reality. The appeal to some "real counterreality" challenges the perception of reality together with its allocation of attention. This reallocation of attention stimulates an active interplay between religions and other spheres of culture and allows one to differentiate styles of religiosity.

Finally, depending on the concrete content of its religious symbolism, religious communication also qualifies attention in ways leading to specific dispositions of action. By qualifying attention, such communication encourages specific behavior and shapes everyday life, yet without determining completely certain behavior.

As many past and present religious conflicts vividly show, this process of regenerating, reallocating, and qualifying attention is highly ambiguous. It might be dangerous or life-enhancing—depending on the standpoint of the observer and the observed religious community. Therefore, it is necessary to move on from a general functional perspective about religion to theological reasoning, that is to say, to develop a systematic-theological and Christian perspective on the church's being and place within the current culture.

5.3 Responsibility and Extravagance: The Breaking of the Logic of Attention

Together, this regeneration, reallocation, and qualification of attention within the Christian church follows a specific inner dynamic and is characterized by three elements. The inner dynamic of festive celebration does not consist simply in a turn to self-reference, closure, or introspection; this dynamic is not just the result of decoupling. It is characterized by three processes that are quite precisely spelled out in the Gospel of Matthew 18:12: "For where two or three are gathered in my name, I am there among them." The Christian community comes together with a clear thematic focus on the event and life of Jesus Christ. By doing this, Christians celebrate and recall the qualified attention God paid to them in Jesus

Christ. This active remembrance in word and sacrament implies an active immersion into the canonical memory of Christ.[46] Yet this movement of their attention away from their present changes their present: Christ will be among them through the activity of the Spirit. "I am among them." By Christ's presence, they experience God's attentiveness to their present life. In Christ, God pays positive attention to our life regardless of human attentiveness, and takes up the constant human search for attention and the ongoing need to pay attention to receive attention. What is called justification by faith is, among other things, a precise interruption and reorganization of one's own economy of attention.

By gathering in Christ's name, Christians try to see their reality and their involvement in the economy of attention from God's perspective. A critical observer might see there nothing but one of Gödel's strange loops—people trying to see the world from the inside as it would be possible to see it from the outside. Critics, the non-Christian as well as the theological, might see nothing but the construction of a Christian world following the mechanisms Nelson Goodman described: composition and decomposition, a specific weighting, ordering, some deletion and supplementation as well as deformation.[47] Still, Christians hope and believe that God uses their constructions to make himself present. For this reason, faith in God becomes a serious matter of truly perceiving, interpreting, and evaluating the world in God's perspective.

The qualification and reallocation of attention from God's perspective is influenced by three elements: faith, love, and hope.[48] All three elements move the church's attention beyond its own boundaries. The reception or realization of God's attention in faith leads to a widening of human attention, temporally, socially, and in terms of its content orientation. Attention is widened in terms of time by the confrontation with the canonical memory of Christ and the perspective on what Christians hope for this world. Attention is widened in its social dimension, insofar as those gathered in Christ's name become part of the universal body of Christ, which spans times and nations, and participate in the mission of

---

[46] Michael Welker, "Resurrection and Eternal Life: The Canonic Memory of the Resurrected Christ, His Reality, and his Glory," in John Polkinghorne and Michael Welker, *The End of the World and the Ends of God: Science and Eschatology in Dialogue* (Harrisburg, PA: Trinity Press International, 2000), 279-90. For the dependance of this process of remembrance on material media, see Régis Debray, *Transmitting Culture* (New York: Columbia University Press, 2000).

[47] Nelson Goodman, *Ways of Worldmaking* (Indianapolis: Hackett Publishing Company, 1978), 1-22. This constructionist perspective does not rule out some version of internal realism, which is granted by God.

[48] For a thorough treatment of this triad, see Thomas Söding, *Die Trias Glaube, Hoffnung, Liebe bei Paulus. Eine exegetische Studie* (Stuttgart: Katholisches Bibelwerk, 1992).

Christ. Human attention is also qualified and reallocated by perceiving to whom Christ paid attention.[49]

The reallocation and qualification of attention by love and hope challenges the economy of attention, because Christians are called to pay attention where it is needed, give attention as a gift, not as a social "currency."[50] Undoubtedly, the church as a social institution attracts and uses human attention. However, the church is also called to break the logic of the market of attention. At least locally and temporarily, it can call into question the logic of this economy as it is so vividly exemplified in the media. According to this logic, the media pay "perceptive attention" to certain events and persons if and only if two conditions are fulfilled. First, there has to be a decent chance that by communicating this perceived event, the media can attract more attention than they invest; and second, a considerable amount of the attention attracted has to be redirected back to, or re-invested in, the media itself. For this reason, good stories raise the ratings of a network, and, in turn, some journalists and filmmakers become celebrities. If the media pay attention, they have to get back more than they pay. For the media, to pay attention has to be a profitable investment.

Again, how can the churches not just mirror this economy of attention but challenge it? The proper practice of faith, love, and hope does not obey this logic. Why? The practice of faith, love, and hope turns attention to the issues and people who do not attract the attention they deserve (seen in Christ's perspective) or who just attract the fleeting attention of "morbid curiosity." Love and hope not only redirect attention but also call for a responsible extravagance in paying attention. Love and hope invest attention in hopeless situations, events, and cases—without the hope of reciprocity in the currency of attention. By doing this, they not only gather but also but act in Christ's name.

---

[49] There is a severe difference in the way most of the time the media turn their attention to the dark and shadow sides of life, on one hand, and Christ's attentiveness on the other. The media's "morbid curiosity" has to be contrasted with Christ's "caring attentiveness." For the former, see Paul Ashdown, James A. Crook, and Jack B. Haskins, eds., *Morbid Curiosity and the Mass Media: Proceedings of a Symposium* (Knoxville: Gannett Foundation, 1984). The media care for the dark sides of life only insofar as the portrayal of these sides attracts attention that can be sold to advertisers. To put it into Kantian terms, suffering people are not an end in themselves but are means to do business.

[50] There are, without doubt, strong links to proponents of humanitarian and justice-oriented politics. "No amount of communication, however stylish and informative, will engage people in politics, unless they pay attention, at least some of the time." This is, rightly, the opening remark in Nick Couldry and Sonia M. Livingstone, eds., *Media Consumption and Public Engagement: Beyond the Presumption of Attention* (Basingstoke: Palgrave Macmillan, 2007), 3.

Finally, academic reflection on religion and theological reasoning needs to focus not only on the life and responsibility of the church, but also on what is needed for the flourishing of communal life. "Seek the welfare of the city where I have sent you" is a demand that also applies to responsible theological reflection. In the face of the current exploitation of human attention, theological reasoning has to work toward an "ecology of attention." Such a project cannot be carried out by theology alone, but needs to be developed in cooperation with other disciplines and in dialogue with other partners in civil society. We still lack a thorough comprehension of the subtle mechanisms through which attention is built into the structures of our society. There is much debate about "dematerialization," "informatization," and "virtualization," but the basic resource for the processing of information in communication is still not thoroughly explored. An ecology of attention as part of theological anthropology and theological ethics takes seriously the finitude of human beings, their call to experience a real polyphony of life, as well as the human responsibility for the consumption of one's own media experiences.[51] Such an ecology of attention would have to consider the unavoidable side-effects of the current distribution of attention. It would help to see that late modernity replaces the forceful control of the human body as an exercise of social power through a more subtle control of persons, that is, by specific ways of attracting attention by the attraction of bodies. Yet, an ecology of attention could not be developed without a vision of the good life that encompasses the human desire for pleasure and joy in the same way as the obligation to deal responsibly with our and other people's time—because life is both: a project and at the same time a gift. The creative tension between both is kept present by theological discourse.

6. Concluding Remarks

The real challenge for theological reflection concerned with our media culture is to understand the dynamics of having, gaining, and losing the property of attention, to understand the subtle processes by which this cultural resource is used, exploited, regenerated, and put to work in social life. Yet the observation of these dynamics should not trigger ecclesiological alarmism and lament about our culture. The current situation can instead challenge the church to discover the strengths and weaknesses of its own life and witness. My argument was that any new and deeper understanding of the culture in which the church lives, and the complex relationship between culture and church, can challenge the church's

---

[51] For the preservation of a "multidimensional and polyphonic" life, see Dietrich Bonhoeffer, *Widerstand und Ergebung. Briefe und Aufzeichnungen aus der Haft* (DBW 8) (Gütersloh: Kaiser, 1998), 453.

self-understanding in a nondeterminate yet creative way. Hence, by taking up this challenge, the church can discover in what way it regenerates, reallocates, and qualifies human attention—in the light of God's own life-sustaining and graceful attentiveness. Over against the general economization of attention, the practice of faith, love, and hope embodies a responsible extravagance in the donation of attention. But, as part of the public responsibility of theological reasoning, theology has to stimulate the development of a constructive public discourse about an ecology of attention that unmasks the power of the economy of attention. The contributions to this discourse will always be colored by God's own style of attentiveness and the Christian vision of the polyphony of life. Yet this might be what Christians owe to the public discussion.

Are Social Networks Media?
The Problematic Financial Classification as Communication Services Companies

Katrin Gülden Le Maire

"Are social networks media?" is a question that entails political, judicial, social, and ethical implications and consequences. This chapter discusses whether social networks are news media as understood in the Western European and, especially, the German context, and whether they are compatible with the division of power as constituted within democratic states. The chapter clarifies and defines the concept of news media, their role, and the relevant actors.

The Media

Since the creation of the printing press, the radio, and television, citizens have consumed and communicated information and news via analogue media in audio-visual and print formats. News dissemination, from the Roman Empire until, approximately, the creation of the *New York Herald* newspaper, in 1835, was primarily characterized by published opinion pieces.[1] Informative, editorial journalism—that is, the professional, continuous, and reliable transmission of news and information—was closely linked to technological advances and developed only with the creation of the telegraph, which allowed for their instant transmission and dissemination.[2] Indeed, the inventors of the telegraph—Samuel Morse in the United States, and William Fothergill Cooke and Charles Wheatstone in Britain—have been declared Victorian internet pioneers.[3] Etymologically, the word "journalism" evolved from the Latin *diurnalis* (belonging to a day) to the French *journal-*

---

[1] Historically, the publisher Johannes Carolus (1575-1634) has been credited with the creation of the first regularly printed newspaper and thus, loosely, with the creation of the occupation of journalist. Yet it was the *New York Herald* newspaper that propagated the idea of the journalist as a stand-alone profession. See Johannes Weber, "Sraßburg 1605: Die Geburt der Zeitung," *Jahrbuch für Kommunikationsgeschichte* 7 (2005): 3-26, at 6-7.
[2] James Carey, *Communication as Culture* (New York: Routledge, 1989).
[3] Tom Standage, *The Victorian Internet* (New York: Berkeley Books, 1999).

isme in the late seventeenth century.[4] Its definition developed from the contents of a prayer book (fifth to fifteenth centuries), to a diary (seventeenth century), to a printed newspaper (as of the eighteenth century). Today, the definition of "media" has been broadened to include digital, social-network content.

Audio and visual broadcasting, print publishing, and the internet are, first of all, each a *medium:* a communication channel that exists in analogue and digital format. They are equally news *media* in the sense that they transmit written and oral code, that is, written and/or spoken language containing information and visual images and created by professional journalists and reporters. Analogue news media remain somewhat limited to particular readerships and viewerships owing to their specific local, regional, or national distribution models. Visual media have transcended these barriers, as have digital broadcasting and publishing media and social networks. Media publishers increasingly use social networks and platforms to disseminate their news, though not without problems. This development addresses the overall changed consumption patterns of news media (in terms of communication channels) and the search for new audiences.[5]

Particular models of the use and distribution of media depend on economic and political factors, such as their ownership and the jurisdictions they operate in and are bound to. Media can be financially and/or politically independent or controlled and restrained by business and/or political institutions. Media ownership models vary from not-for-profit foundations to stand-alone publishing houses, stock market-listed tech companies, and diversified corporations. The *typical* business model of a classic analogue print medium consisted of the generation of revenues through advertising, subscriptions, and kiosk sales. Information shared with advertisers about prospective customer target groups was restricted owing to limited reach, technology, and data availability.

Western European countries have implemented different media structures. In Germany, the public media (several radio and television channels) are financed through a tax-like levy on households. They media statutory corporation (*Körperschaft des öffentlichen Rechts*) is independent from government and tied to the German Interstate Broadcasting Treaty (*Rundfunkstaatsvertrag*). Germany is constitutionally bound to state independence (*Staatsferne*);[6] the country does not pay

---

[4] Muge Demir, "The Importance of Ethics, Credibility and Reliability in Online Journalism," *European Journal of Social Sciences* 24, no. 4 (2011): 537–45.

[5] Kasper Welbers and Michaël Opgenhaffen, "Social Media Gatekeeping: An Analysis of the Gatekeeping of Newspapers' Public Facebook Pages, *New Media & Society* 20, no. 12 (2018), 4728–47.

[6] In reality, this concept has been hotly debated during the COVID-19 crisis in 2020 as the German Bundestag set aside 220 million euros of state aid for the print media sector. See Helmut Hartung, "Pressemedien in der Subventionsfalle," *Medienpolitik.net*, Dec. 10, 2020, https://www.medienpolitik.net/2020/10/pressemedien-in-der-subventionsfalle/.

direct subsidies to its media (in contrast to France, for example).[7] Freedom of speech and press have been constitutionally anchored within the Basic Law since 1949 (Grundgesetz Artikel 5). Indeed, the Western Allied occupying forces considered audiovisual and print media in postwar Germany critical channels to ensure the creation of a democratic, nonexpansionist country. Licenses for German news media were distributed; literary and media reeducation programs were fostered to establish a democratic value order.[8] The postwar German radio broadcasting system was modeled on the British Broadcasting Corporation (BBC), as was the contributary model of the public media. Historically, freedom of speech and of the press dates back to 1789 (Article 11 of the French Declaration of the Rights of Man and of the Citizen). In 1948, the United Nations guaranteed freedom of expression and of the press in Article 19 of the Universal Declaration of Human Rights. All 192 member states have signed the declaration; yet their professed support provides a stark contrast to reality.[9]

German postwar understanding includes the media as the fourth power within the Federal Republic, holding the executive, legislative, and judicative powers accountable not only by the media's critical analysis of general news and information but also by political communication. Publishing houses and media companies, as organizations that are part of the overall societal make-up, are bound by national governing law. They are meant to aid citizens to develop informed views and opinions. The idea of a fourth power goes back to the Austrian philosopher René Marcic, who built on Montesquieu's tripartite system of the division of political powers (1748).[10] Marcic's concept, in turn and in time, also fueled the self-image of twentieth-century German journalists. Marcic, however, was not the first to propose this idea. In 1841, Thomas Carlyle, referring to Ed-

---

[7] The French government has subsidized media since the French Revolution. Subsidies take different forms, from reduced VAT to financial support for journalist institutions or reduced fees for telecommunications services. In contrast, Germany provides an indirect subsidy through a reduced VAT on news media and the TV and radio license fee. Deutscher Bundestag, "Presseförderung in Frankreich und anderen EU-Mitgliedstaaten," Bundestag, https://www.bundestag.de/resource/blob/412162/eade507f04ef9bb0a52e0683fe44ae87/WD-10-021-09-pdf-data.pdf.

[8] Larry Hartenian, "The Role of Media in Democratizing Germany: United States Occupation Policy 1945–1949," *Central European History* 20, no. 2 (1987): 145–90; and Hansjörg Gehring, *Amerikanische Literaturpolitik in Deutschland 1945–1953* (Stuttgart: Deutsche Verlagsanstalt, 1976), 17–21.

[9] "UNESCO Observatory of Killed Journalists," UNESCO, https://en.unesco.org/themes/safety-journalists/observatory.

[10] René Marcic, *Vom Gesetzesstaat zum Richterstaat* (Wien: Springer, 1957), 394–97. Montesquieu, Charles-Louis de Secondat, Baron de, *De l'esprit des lois* [1748] (Paris: Flammarion, 1993).

mund Burke, who equally drew on Montesquieu, articulated idea of the Fourth Estate sitting in the reporters' gallery of the British Parliament.[11]

The first German journalism school opened in 1899 in Berlin; yet the idea of a systematic journalistic education prior to exercising the profession remained disputed.[12] After World War II, German publishing houses, unions, and broadcasting organizations created an association responsible for the future education of German journalists. This was based on the conviction that German journalism (*Publizistik*) should be founded on a democratic, independent ethos and within a European tradition.[13] As in other countries, journalism studies can be pursued today within the general university system. The professional media creator (the journalist), a full- or part-time trained specialist of news creation and transmission, is a relatively recent historical phenomenon. It is tied to the broader access of the middle class to education from the later nineteenth century onward. Scandals, such as the forged Hitler diaries purchased in 1983 by the German magazine *Der Stern*, and the journalistic fraud of the *Der Spiegel* reporter Claas-Hendrik Relotius in 2018, created enormous public criticism and interest and led to the overhaul of journalistic standards in many publishing houses. Remarkably, the question whether journalism is a profession or a vocation has been discussed for many years. Martin Löffelholz and Torsten Quandt provide an extensive overview of the journalism theories that have developed over one hundred years in German-speaking countries.[14] Criticism toward news media and journalists has increased in the past decades (the *Lügenpresse*, or lying press), in particular concerning the selection and/or limitation of newsworthy information.[15]

In contrast, social networks—online communication channels where users interact, share unfiltered content, and collaborate in self-selected communities—are a phenomenon of the early twenty-first century. The idea of citizen news transmission, the public participative communication by ordinary citizens, is not a new concept, but originated with the (physical) public town square in antiquity. As Franklin Foer recounts, the definition of what the public sphere represented developed further over time and came to be embodied by "coffee houses, newspapers, bookstores, theatres, and meeting places, the locales that allowed individ-

---

[11] Thomas Carlyle, *On Heroes and Hero Worship* (London: James Fraser, 1841), 392.
[12] Romy Fröhlich and Christina Holtz-Bacha, "The German Journalism Education Landscape," in *European Journalism Education*, ed. Georgios Terzis (Bristol: Intellect, 2009), 131–48.
[13] "Über uns-Geschichte der Schule," Deutsche Journalistenschule, https://djs-online.de/ueber-uns/geschichte-der-schule/.
[14] Martin Löffelholz and Torsten Quandt, "Journalism Theory," *Ecquid Novi, African Journalism Studies* 26, no. 2 (2005): 228–46, at 230–33.
[15] Astrid Blome, Tobias Eberwein, and Stefanie Averbeck-Lietz, *Medienvertrauen: Historische und aktuelle Perspektiven* (Berlin: de Gruyter, 2020).

uals to come together to form a public."[16] They were places of thinking independent of the monarchic, autocratic state and free from church interference, and they allowed citizens to exchange their views, consume literature and culture, debate politics, and form educated opinions. Jürgen Gerhards and Mike Schäfer provide an overview of how, initially, the internet has been considered a "better" public sphere, providing greater accessibility to a variety of voices and opinions from a range of actors in civil society. In reality, little empirical evidence supports this theory in mature democracies like Germany and the United States.[17]

Jürgen Habermas was initially critical of traditional news mass media and considered them highly regulated; he comprehensively developed the idea of the public sphere and its relevance for democracy.[18] Social critics, such as Noam Chomsky, spoke of a "fifth power," critiquing the perception that the media in democracies are representative of the population and a legitimate mouthpiece of the people's political opinion and will formation. In reality, Chomsky claims, powerful lobbying forces manage and manipulate media content. He thus implies that the idea of the free media is more of an ideal than reality, as in practice most media are for-profit organizations.[19] In line with the tech euphoria of the early 2000 s, William H. Dutton offered a positive definition of the internet and growing related technologies as an emerging Fifth Estate.[20]

In terms of media content, David Manning White in 1950 evaluated the process by which journalists selected, filtered, and subsequently published news. His "gatekeeping" theory concludes that selections are based on highly subjective value judgments.[21] Manning White's idea has been developed further to include social networks and digital media impact.[22] Indeed, media gatekeeping has been well researched, including the systematic bias of information and news selection of overly positive and negative news, news norms, organizational factors, and

---

[16] Franklin Foer, "The Death of the Public Square," *The Atlantic*, Jul. 6, 2018, https://www.theatlantic.com/ideas/archive/2018/07/the-death-of-the-public-square/564506/.

[17] Jürgen Gerhards and Mike Schäfer, "Is the Internet a Better Public Sphere? Comparing Old and New Media in the US and Germany," *New Media & Society* 12, no. 1 (2010): 13.

[18] Jürgen Habermas, *Strukturwandel der Öffentlichkeit, 1962* (Berlin: Suhrkamp Verlag, 1990).

[19] Noam Chomsky, *Manufacturing Consent: The Political Economy of the Mass Media* (New York: Pantheon Books, 1988).

[20] William H. Dutton, "The Fifth Estate Emerging through the Network of Networks," *Prometheus-Critical Studies in Innovation* 27, no. 1 (2009): 1–15.

[21] David Manning White, "The 'Gate Keeper': A Case Study in the Selection of News," *Journalism & Mass Communication Quarterly* 27, no. 4 (1950): 383–90.

[22] Peter Bro and Filip Wallberg, "Gatekeeping in a Digital Era," *Journalism Practice* 9, no. 1 (2014): 92–105.

reality.[23] However, as Stuart N. Soroka argues, this research does not consider *how* a piece of news information is framed in a certain communicative manner.[24] Richard O. Mason evaluated the content of media information based on in his PAPA model (1986). He considered the four ethical issues of privacy, accuracy, property and accessibility (PAPA) as critically important in an information age.[25] Alan Peslak revisited Mason's model twenty years later and validated its ongoing importance.[26] It is noteworthy that IT professionals whom Peslak polled considered ethical concerns as highly important, but thought that the question of media ownership was less important. Facebook had been created only two years prior to Peslak's study and counted merely 12 million members at the time, as compared to almost 2.9 billion users in 2022. The company was privately owned and became listed on the stock exchange only in May 2012.

Social Networks

A medium is, first of all, a channel to communicate content (whether information, newsworthy or interesting facts, opinion, slander, or emotions) from a sender to a receiver.[27] In order to assess the classification of social networks as news media or publishers, one needs to evaluate their ownership structure, business model, market share, aim, accessibility, content, and overall impact on society (including political, societal, cultural and ethical consequences). What kind of description might be appropriate for a tech company that owns a social network, and what (financial market) classification should be envisioned?

Considering the above definition and scope, a social network does *not* qualify as media, even though it is a medium. In fact, a digital medium takes on various forms: there are websites, microblogs, forums, video sharing, and social networking apps. Some of those operate as media. However, Facebook, Instagram (owned by Meta Platforms, Inc.), LinkedIn (a subsidiary of Microsoft Corporation), Goo-

---

[23] Stuart N. Soroka, "The Gatekeeping Function: Distributions of Information in the Media and the Real World," *Journal of Politics* 74, no. 2 (2012): 514-28.

[24] Ibid., 515.

[25] Richard O. Mason, "Four Ethical Issues in the Information Age," *MIS Quarterly* 10, no. 1 (1986): 5-12.

[26] Alan Peslak, "Papa Revisited: A Current Empirical Study of the Mason Framework," *Journal of Computer Information Systems* 46, no. 3 (2006): 117-23.

[27] The Shannon-Weaver model of communication from 1948 still forms the basis of the majority of communication scientific models today. Claude E. Shannon, "A Mathematical Theory of Communication," *The Bell System Technical Journal* 27, nos. 3-4 (1948): 379-423; and Claude E. Shannon and Warren Weaver, *The Mathematical Theory of Communication* (Urbana: University of Illinois Press, 1949).

gle, and Twitter are internationally operating, U.S.-based technology companies. Their equally pervasive Chinese equivalents are Sina Weibo, a microblogging service, and WeChat, a multiservice app that includes messaging, social network, and payment options (both are owned by Tencent Holdings, Inc.). These U.S. and Chinese stock market–listed companies combine a variety of business operations that add to their complexity. Facebook, for example, creates the majority of its earnings through targeted digital advertising sales on their "free" social network and messenger sites. "Free" here means that the network does not charge its members regular user fees. However, Facebook users agree to make their personal data available, although the European Commission increasingly protects citizens through legislation.[28] Yet a European Facebook user generates $15.13 of advertising return for the company (plus $0.36 of other revenue in the first quarter of 2021).[29] Facebook user data is not sold *primarily* as a stand-alone product to advertising clients. Rather, a user's personal data is sold *secondarily*; the data access is *implicitly* acquired in conjunction with targeted advertising slots. Implicit means personal data is sold through the algorithmic selection of a predefined target group corresponding to the purchaser's requirements for advertising purposes. In contrast, "explicit" conveying of data means the sale of direct personal user data. Indeed, tech companies use sophisticated technology that incorporates the latest developments in cognitive scientific and neurological research for their development of products and services. They employ their own scientific research teams (predominantly working on artificial intelligence [AI] developments) and invest larger financial resources in future research and development than some entire countries do.[30]

As for overall digitalization, the scope, speed, reach, and impact of transmitting information and opinion on social networks are unprecedented. Classical analogue media used to communicate news, events, information, the opinions of politicians, and the general public through trained journalists. Social networks, however, permit individual citizens not only to choose their own source of information but also to become a source of information themselves, while simultaneously affecting user opinion through algorithmically preselected and presented

---

[28] General Data Protection Regulation (GDPR) 2018, Digital Markets Act (DMA) 2022, and Digital Services Act (DSA).

[29] "Facebook Earnings Presentation Q1 2021," Facebook, https://s21.q4cdn.com/399680738/files/doc_financials/2021/FB-Earnings-Presentation-Q1-2021.pdf.

[30] Sam Shead, "Facebook Plans to Double Size of AI Research Unit by 2020," *Forbes*, Oct. 1, 2018, https://www.forbes.com/sites/samshead/2018/10/01/facebook-plans-to-double-size-of-ai-research-unit-by-2020/?sh=3d9441184c4f.

content.[31] Moreover, social networks are easily accessible and have low entry barriers. Indeed, the communicative power that a single citizen potentially holds within an internet-enabled network over a person or a political, social, or economic institution can be enormous.[32] The selection, evaluation, interaction, and reaction of personal users and, thus, their communication are different from those of trained journalists, who are liable to professional publishing guidelines and ethical, institutional, and industry standards.

The classification (categorization on the financial markets) of a tech and social network company is extremely sensitive. In 2018, Facebook CEO Mark Zuckerberg defended his company as a tech platform rather than a publisher.[33] Yet in February 2020, he called upon regulators to consider Facebook a cross between a media publisher and a telecommunications company.[34] His argument is likely based both on financial and judicial aspects. First, Facebook was reclassified on the financial markets in September 2018. The technology sector of the S&P500 and the Global Industry Classification Standard (GICS) were "de-FAANGing,"[35] effectively shifting companies from the telecommunications and information technology sector into the communications services sector because of the increased similarity of these companies to communications services.[36] Second, Zuckerberg's differentiation is legally important: a publisher (an originator of news) is subjected to different regulatory and ethical responsibilities than a platform provider (a transmitter of news and posted content). In the United States, freedom of speech is secured by the First Amendment; moreover, tech companies are safeguarded by Section 230 of the Communications Decency Act (1996), which immunizes web platforms from liability for third-party content. The defi-

---

[31] In general, (German) journalists who engage and communicate via social networks highlight their accounts as *private*, and refer to the fact that their personal opinions do not necessarily represent the stance of the organization they work for.

[32] Kevin Werbach, "The Impact of Social Media: Is It Irreplacable?," *Knowledge at Wharton*, Jul. 26, 2019, https://knowledge.wharton.upenn.edu/article/impact-of-social-media/.

[33] Heather Whitney, "Search Engines, Social Media and the Editorial Analogy," Knight First Amendment Institute at Columbia University, Feb. 27, 2018, https://knightcolumbia.org/content/search-engines-social-media-and-editorial-analogy.

[34] Reuters Staff, "Treat Us Like Something between a Telco and a Newspaper, says Facebook's Zuckerberg," Reuters, Feb. 15, 2020, https://www.reuters.com/article/us-germany-security-facebook/treat-us-like-something-between-a-telco-and-a-newspaper-says-facebooks-zuckerberg-idUSKBN2090MA.

[35] The acronym FAANG represents the stock-market-listed tech companies Facebook, Amazon, Apple, Netflix and Google.

[36] Noel Randewich, "Facebook, Alphabet Shifted in Sector Classification System," Reuters, Jan. 11, 2018, https://www.reuters.com/article/us-s-p-sectors-idUSKBN1F037G. The reclassification increased the S&P trading volume substantially.

nition of what constitutes hate speech and slander is broader in the United States than in Germany. It is also subject to intense recurring political and judicial debate. In contrast, the German criminal code addresses the issues of incitement of the masses (*Volksverhetzung/Strafgesetzbuch* § 130), the disruption of public peace (*Störung des öffentlichen Friedens/Strafgesetzbuch* § 126), and, separately, the protection of minors (*Jugendschutzgesetz*). Several challenges have arisen and are highlighted in the view of social networks as news media and publishers: among them are the selective presentation of news through algorithmic intervention, the high volume of advertising, and the volume of disinformation spread by users. Increasingly, empirical evidence of the negative cognitive impact of social networks becomes available.[37] Moreover, the subjects of freedom and integrity in relation to personal data sovereignty are scrutinized critically as tech companies effectively have become global data-harvesting sites.[38]

Around 35.6 percent of the world's population use Facebook. Social networks are transnational phenomena; their consumption has increased sharply again since the beginning of the COVID-19 crisis in 2019.[39] Citizens increasingly consume media news via social network channels rather than classic media outlets.[40] Overall, the use of Facebook has increased among the four generational cohorts, with baby boomers being their strongest growth group. The youngest generational cohort, Generation Z, which is just now approaching adulthood, has been characterized as hypercognitive.[41] Michael Dimock explains:

---

[37] Ronald Deibert, "The Road to Digital Unfreedom: Three Painful Truths about Social Media," *Journal of Democracy* 30, no. 1 (2019): 25–39; and Wu Youyou, Michal Kosinski, and David Stillwell, "Computer-Based Personality Judgments Are More Accurate Than Those Made by Humans, PNAS 112, no. 4 (2015): 1036–40.

[38] Nathan Bronson and Janet Wiener, "Facebook's Top Open Data Problems," Meta, https://research.fb.com/blog/2014/10/facebook-s-top-open-data-problems/.

[39] "Meta Reports Fourth Quarter and Full Year 2021 Results," Meta, https://s21.q4cdn.com/399680738/files/doc_financials/2021/q4/FB-12.31.2021-Exhibit-99.1-Final.pdf; and "Media Consumption in the Age of COVID-19, FrankWBaker.com, https://frankwbaker.com/mlc/wp-content/uploads/2020/04/1-main-graphic_covid-media-2-scaled.jpg.

[40] Nic Newman et al., *Reuters Institute Digital News Report 2020* (Oxford: Reuters Institute for the Study of Journalism, 2021), 71,88; and Mason Walker and Katerina Eva Matsa, "News Consumption across Social Media in 2021," Pew Research Center, Sep. 20, 2021, https://www.pewresearch.org/journalism/2021/09/20/news-consumption-across-social-media-in-2021/.

[41] Tracy Francis and Fernanda Hoefel, "The Influence of Gen Z, the First Generation of True Digital Natives, Is Expanding," McKinsey, Nov. 12, 2028, https://www.mckinsey.com/industries/consumer-packaged-goods/our-insights/true-gen-generation-z-and-its-implications-for-companies.

The implications of growing up in an "always on" technological environment are only now coming into focus. Recent research has shown dramatic shifts in youth behaviours, attitudes and lifestyles—both positive and concerning—for those who came of age in this era. What we don't know is whether these are lasting generational imprints or characteristics of adolescence that will become more muted over the course of their adulthood. [42]

Interestingly, for these digital natives, the concept of news *media* includes social networks. By default, as this generation has not known a nondigital age, their comprehension of who and what constitutes news and media involves mobile systems and the internet. Effectively, social networks such as Facebook have become systemic communication channels, in that a large part of nations' populations prefer to communicate and inform themselves via social networks.

Tech companies that own social networks can potentially act as hybrid corporate-political organizations because of their size, their monopolistic dominance, their vast data collection, and their gatekeeping function in the digital economy. Their enormous economic power has been recognized and recently been regulated by the European Union.[43] Interestingly, Zuckerberg's initial vision was: "Many of us got into technology because we believe it can be a democratizing force for putting power in people's hands. I believe the world is better when more people have a voice to share their experiences, and when traditional gatekeepers like governments and media companies don't control what ideas can be expressed."[44] Zuckerberg was nineteen years old when he created Facebook. This utopian vision of democracy and the human person seems prevalent among U.S. college students and based on a bias called WEIRD (white, educated, industrialized, rich, democratic) impacting their worldview and political assumptions.[45]

---

[42] The Pew Research Center categorizes the revised classification of generational cohorts; this chapter adheres to their definition, which is as follows: the Silent Generation (1928–45), Baby Boomers (1946–64), Generation X (1965–80); Millennials (1981–97), Generation Z (1997–2012). See Michael Dimock, "Defining Generations: Where Millennials End and Generation Z Begins," The Pew Research Center, Jan. 17, 2019, https://www.pewresearch.org/fact-tank/2019/01/17/where-millennials-end-and-generation-z-begins/.

[43] See footnote 28.

[44] Mark Zuckerberg, "A Blueprint for Content Governance and Enforcement," Facebook, https://m.facebook.com/nt/screen/?params=%7B"note_id"%3A751449002072082%7D&path=%2Fnotes%2Fnote%2F&refsrc=http%3A%2F%2Fwww.google.de%2F&_rdr.

[45] Joseph Henrich, Steven J. Heine, and Ara Norenzayan, "The Weirdest People in the World?," *Behavioral and Brain Sciences* 33, nos. 2–3 (2010): 61–83; and Marshall H. Segal, Donald T. Campbell, and Melville J. Kerskovits, *The Influence of Culture on Visual Perception* (Indianapolis: Bobbs-Merrill, 1966).

Evaluation of the underlying political and economic philosophy of Silicon Valley technology investors and CEOs provides further insight into the compatibility of social networks as news media with democratic values. The German-American billionaire investor Peter Thiel is a vocal example:

> Most importantly, I no longer believe that freedom and democracy are compatible. ... In the 2000 s, companies like Facebook created the space for new modes of dissent and new ways to form communities not bounded by historical nation-states. . . . The hope of the internet is that these new worlds will impact and force change on the existing social and political order.[46]

Thiel is a proponent of conservative libertarianism. Implicit to his view is the economic theory of laissez-faire capitalism that proposes a radically free market without any government intervention. Jon Askonas points out the naïve view of human nature coupled with tech utopianism fueled by what he considers "smart paternalism" prevalent among Silicon Valley executives and investors.[47] Yet Thiel's vision goes further, as it includes autocratic features: "Unlike the world of politics, in the world of technology the choices of individuals may still be paramount. The fate of our world may depend on the effort of a single person who builds or propagates the machinery of freedom that makes the world safe for capitalism. ... We are in a deadly race between politics and technology."[48]

Gatekeeping

In fact, one can observe a kind of nondemocratic behavior being exercised *through* tech companies by users but also *by* tech company executives. Select anarchic and violent effects were witnessed with the storm on Capitol Hill in Washington in 2021. There is empirical evidence that the storm was organized *via* social networks, such as Facebook, Parler, and Twitter. It had built up over several months through targeted misinformation of the larger public from both political represen-

---

[46] Peter Thiel, "The Education of a Libertarian," *Cato Unbound*, Apr. 13, 2009, https://www.cato-unbound.org/2009/04/13/peter-thiel/education-libertarian; and Benjamin Wallace-Wells, "The Rise of the Thielists: Has the Republican Party Found Its Post-Trump Ideology?," *The New Yorker*, May 13, 2021, https://www.newyorker.com/news/annals-of-populism/the-rise-of-the-thielists.

[47] Jon Askonas, "How Tech Utopia Fostered Tyranny: Authoritarians' Love for Digital Technology Is No Fluke—It's a Product of Silicon Valley's 'Smart' Paternalism," *The New Atlantis* 57 (2019): 3–11.

[48] Thiel, "Education of a Libertarian."

tatives and citizens alike.[49] Moreover, tech executives exercise political power and actively interfere in political communication and judicial affairs. Twitter permanently suspended then U.S. President Trump's account (which he used as his main channel of communication during his term in office) on January 8, 2021, after "assessing" his tweets against the company's "Glorification of Violence Policy."[50] The ban swiftly drew worldwide criticism from democratic political leaders, who questioned both the judicial and ethical basis of the censorship (especially in light of other disputed political leaders keeping their accounts). Depending on one's perspective, the exercise of governance, censorship, and control was based not on existing law but on autoscripted corporate guidelines. At the same time, tech companies create organizational structures and bodies to implement their own rules. Following the Cambridge Analytica scandal in 2018, Facebook set up a highly remunerated forty-member oversight board made up of scientists and former politicians. The board operates similarly to a court panel. Users can appeal to it, and the oversight board can overrule Facebook decisions concerning problematic published content. Moreover, moderation of commercial content has become an indispensable feature of social networks. Tech companies employ thousands of content moderators who, together with machine learning technology, are responsible to find, evaluate, and remove problematic social network content. Moderators are often badly paid, badly trained professionals, employed through third party companies.[51] The chaotic work environment, the mental and emotional impact of content moderation, guideline creation, and

---

[49] Atlantic Council DFRLab, "#Stopthesteal: Timeline of Social Media and Extremist Activities Leading to 1/6 Insurrection," *Just Security*, https://www.justsecurity.org/74622/stopthesteal-timeline-of-social-media-and-extremist-activities-leading-to-1-6-insurrection/; and Luke Munn, "More Than a Mob: Parler as Preparatory Media for the U.S. Capitol Storming," *First Monday* 26 (2021), https://firstmonday.org/ojs/index.php/fm/article/view/11574/10077.

[50] Former president Trump was initially banned from Facebook for two years. See "Permanent Suspension of @realDonaldTrump," Twitter, Jan. 8, 2021, https://blog.twitter.com/en_us/topics/company/2020/suspension.html; and Nick Clegg, "In Response to Oversight Board: Trump Suspended for Two Years; Will only be Reinstated if Conditions Permit," Facebook web site URL: https://about.fb.com/news/2021/06/facebook-response-to-oversight-board-recommendations-trump/.

[51] Paul M. Barrett, "Who Moderates the Social Media Giants? A Call to End Outsourcing," NYU Stern Center for Business and Human Rights, Jun. 8, 2020, https://www.stern.nyu.edu/experience-stern/faculty-research/who-moderates-social-media-giants-call-end-outsourcing.

transparency standards remain highly problematic despite Facebook's "Community Standards" (2018) and Transparency Center (2021).[52]

Finally, tech companies have the potential power to restrict professional news media distribution and overall public communication and thus impact citizens' general education, not just through algorithmic preselection of content but also through actual interference in governmental affairs, as in Australia.[53] The Australian government proposed legislation for tech giants like Facebook and Google to remunerate professional news creators and media for republished content on social networks.[54] In response, Facebook blocked third-party news for Australians on their accounts. The company effectively forced the government to review and amend its proposed law, which it did.

Summary

News media are recognized as gatekeepers and are regulated accordingly. Tech companies providing social-network services have equally been recognized as gatekeepers by the European Union. However, this recognition pertains to their economic force, their market accessibility, and competition. As outlined, social networks do not qualify as news media, even though they are a medium and a communication channel. News control and channel manipulation are not new phenomena. In fact, over a hundred years ago, telegraphic communication was manipulated in order to falsify political messages and to tamper with the prices of goods.[55] Similarly, journalists are human beings, not free of error, bias, and worldviews. Yet they form a vital institution of democracy, evaluating and criticiz-

---

[52] San Mateo County, Civil Action No. 18CIV05, Selena Scola, Erin Elder, Gabriel, Ramos, April Hutchins, Konica Ritchie, Allison Tebracz, Jessica Swarner, and Gregory Shulman, individually and on behalf of all others similarly situated, Plaintiffs, v. FACEBOOK, INC, Defendant: see Scola v. Facebook Settlement, https://contentmoderatorsettlement.com/.

[53] Stephan Lewandowsky et al., *Technology and Democracy, Understanding the Influence of Online Technologies on Political Behaviour and Decision-Making* (Brussels: Publications Office of the European Union, 2020).

[54] Australian Communications and Media Authority, News Media Bargaining Code, https://www.acma.gov.au/news-media-bargaining-code#:~:text=The%20News%20Media%20and%20Digital,platforms%20and%20Australian%20news%20businesses.

[55] David Hochfelder, *The Telegraph in America, 1832–1920* (Baltimore: Johns Hopkins University Press, 2012), 9, 15. In France, the fraud of the brothers Louis and François Blanc, between 1834 and 1836, called the "piratage du télégraphe Chappe," was widely publicized and also picked up by Alexandre Dumas in his work *Le Comte du Monte Christo*. See *Gazette des Tribunaux*, No 3506, Dec. 10, 1836, data.decalog.net/enap1/Liens/Gazette/ENAP_GAZETTE_TRIBUNAUX_18361210.pdf.

ing political and economic communication and contributing to the creation of rational political opinion of citizens. The majority are trained professionals bound to publishing and industry standards, in contrast to ordinary citizens expressing themselves on social networks.

The above examples concerning both the use of social networks by citizens to impact the public sphere and the limitation of its services by tech companies (in these cases the algorithmic and actual account restrictions) to influence political decision-making about the public sphere are highly problematic. In Habermas's critique, the democratic system in its totality is damaged if the public sphere no longer directs the attention of citizens to relevant and necessary topics. In contrast to his theory fifty years ago, he affirms the importance of qualitatively filtered new media information for citizens; indeed, he has reviewed his initial theory in light of a digitalized society.[56]

Overall, it appears easier to define what social networks are *not* than to say what they are or might be. It is increasingly argued that tech companies like Google or Facebook have become essential communications infrastructure goods, indispensable to daily life.[57] Considering Zuckerberg's own words that his company may be a hybrid telecommunications company, it might be worthwhile to take note of the ongoing U.S. discussion whether social networks are systemic, indispensable common carriers. Historically, the telegraph and the telephone were at one point considered systemic, indispensable common carriers and highly regulated in order to limit their gatekeeping function. This was done to regulate competition within the market. The argument concerning social networks surpasses competition: it has been extended to focus on the definition of the overall public sphere, the social network's potential qualification as a natural monopoly and, especially in the United States, the question concerning freedom of speech. Any financial classification of a company has social, political, and judicial implications. It potentially even touches on the social capital of a society.[58] In the case of tech companies providing social-network services, the classification remains difficult.

---

[56] Jürgen Habermas, "Überlegungen und Hypothesen zu einem erneuten Strukturwandel der politischen Öffentlichkeit," *Sonderband Leviathan* 37 (2021): 470–500, at 497.

[57] Matthew Feeney, "Are Social Media Companies Common Carriers?," *Cato Institute*, May 24, 2021, https://www.cato.org/blog/are-social-media-companies-common-carriers. Eugene Volokh, "Treating Social Media Platforms Like Common Carriers?," *Journal of Free Speech Law* 1, no. 1 (2021): 377–462.

[58] Ernst Wolfgang Böckenförd, *Staat, Gesellschaft, Freiheit* (Frankfurt: Suhrkamp Verlag, 1976).

Part Three:
Media, Values, and Crises

Datafied Media and the Silent Derangement of Ethics

Nick Couldry

> In conditions of late modernity we live "in the world" in a different sense from previous eras of history.
> —Anthony Giddens, *Modernity and Self-Identity*[1]

> A silent catastrophe that occurs almost unperceived.
> —W. G. Sebald, *After Nature*[2]

Our language of character, values, and ethical education is something we inherit: we cannot form it, and rarely even reform it, individually. But this does not mean that what we inherit is immune to historical change: quite the contrary, the history of earlier eras confronts us with many examples of ethical languages strikingly different from our own. One of the most developed philosophical frameworks, and certainly the oldest, for understanding character, Aristotle's account of virtue, is notorious for its apparent disinterest in historical change. But in the past two centuries, starting with Hegel, a related account of ethics has developed which *is* socially embedded and so *does* recognize the role that historical change plays in forming the language in which our ethical understandings are possible. This historical rethinking of ethics and character acknowledges a disturbing possibility: that forms of ethical life can, at particular points in history, become contradictory, generating tensions between the various commitments which they require. If this happens, there is a risk that, as one commentator on Hegel put it, "the lives in a form of life become uninhabitable."[3] It is exactly this sort of deep, one might say foundational, conflict in our ethical life to which, I will argue, contemporary media give rise.

---

[1] Anthony Giddens, *Modernity and Self-Identity* (Cambridge: Polity, 1994).
[2] W. G. Sebald, *After Nature* (Harmondsworth: Penguin, 2003).
[3] Terry Pinkard, *Hegel's Naturalism* (Oxford: Oxford University Press, 2012), 118. Compare ibid., 8, 115, 117, and Robert B. Pippin, *Hegel's Practical Philosophy* (Cambridge: Cambridge University Press, 2008), 5.

The problem derives not from particular stories that media tell, or from particular forms of media production or media habit. The problem derives from the broader phenomenon of what I call "*datafied* media," a term that needs a little unpacking. Everything depends on how we interpret "the internet." While the space of the internet has been widely celebrated since it became a part of everyday life in the early 1990s, the past decade has seen more critical perspectives emerge on the costs of how the internet has developed. I mean three developments in particular: the commercialization of internet space and its underlying infrastructure, from browsers and search engines to undersea cables and satellites;[4] the massive growth of the commercial intranet as the basis for economic production;[5] and, since the early to middle years of this century's first decades, the emergence of privately owned digital platforms for the conduct of much of economic and social life.[6] Much of life and, through new forms of media production and new ways of recirculating media, much of media themselves now exist for us principally online. But why "*datafied*" media? Because widely, though not inevitably, most of our online activities occur in spaces, whether platforms or not, that bear a striking feature: they require those activities, as a very condition of their possibility, to be registered and tracked in ways that *through the resulting data* create economic value for corporations, very often without the actors' full knowledge or consent. This "datafication" of media[7] has consequences, not just in itself, but because of the types of space and movement online that it fuels. To consider the consequences of datafied media (even in this highly compressed way) is therefore to consider the consequences of how, in general, we are today living our lives *with* media. The implications for ethics are striking and, so far, insufficiently understood.

To approach these issues, we need to identify the level at which datafied media can be seen to shape something as broad as ethics. Very often, popular debate about the media's moral impacts focuses on individual characters (particular bad people corrupted by media) or moral panics that supposedly "reveal" a general truth about society. But this is to miss underlying patterns that matter more. We need to consider how datafied media are changing *the general conditions of character formation* in contemporary societies. Fortunately, there is for this an inherited concept, at least in German culture and philosophy: the concept of *Bildung*. Although this term has often been criticized for its association with particular forms of elitist education, I will use it more generally to point to a persistent and

---

[4] Andrew Keen, *The Internet Is Not the Answer* (London: Atlantic Books, 2015).
[5] Dan Schiller, *Digital Depression* (Urbana: University of Illinois Press, 2014).
[6] Tarleton Gillespie, "The Politics of 'Platforms,'" *New Media & Society* 12, no. 3 (2010): 347-64.
[7] Jose Van Dijck, "Datafication, Dataism and Dataveillance: Big Data Between Scientific Paradigm and Ideology," *Surveillance and Society* 12, no. 2 (2014): 197-208.

discernible level at which societies are configured so as to form characters in particular ways and not others. This broader usage of the term *Bildung* links to contemporary ethical debates in the neo-Aristotelian tradition.

My argument in this chapter has two main sections, both oriented to the question whether datafied media—or, more precisely, the particular configuration of media resources and media-related practices associated with datafied media—affect the conditions of character formation in contemporary societies. The first section discusses the philosophical antecedents to this question, and the second reviews some features of datafied media that are of particular concern. In conclusion, I discuss our response, if this analysis is even partially correct: is the answer a revived and extended media ethics, or is something bolder and broader required?

Philosophical Anticipations

In recent years, there has been a revival of philosophical interest in *Bildung* prompted by the work of John McDowell. In his attempt to reconcile Aristotelian, Hegelian, and Kantian perspectives on rationality and ethics, McDowell argues that we must go beyond the notion of a fixed human "nature" of which crude understandings accuse Aristotle: "if we generalize the way Aristotle conceives the moulding of ethical character, we arrive at the notion of having one's eyes opened to reasons at large by acquiring a second nature. I cannot think of a good short English expression for this, but it is what figures in German philosophy as Bildung."[8] McDowell, boldly, is arguing that, if we read Aristotle correctly, his ethics already contains the seeds of the notion of *Bildung,* a broad social process through which character is molded. McDowell's argument operates at a high level of abstraction, and it is clear that he is not referring to any specific form of educational provision or curriculum design (which is how *Bildung* is often interpreted). His key points are the following. First, human beings' rationality—their possibility of "being at home in the space of reasons"[9]—depends on their being initiated, as embodied beings, into language. Second, language—and the possibility of rationality generally—is not outside, or prior to, the trajectory of human interactions, but is intrinsically a social phenomenon. As McDowell puts it, "rationality is a normative status [so] understanding it requires a social context."[10] *Bildung,* on this view, is the process of formation—the process of being initiated into an inherited

---

[8] John McDowell, *Mind and World* (Cambridge, MA: Harvard University Press, 1994), 84.
[9] Ibid., 125.
[10] John McDowell, *Having the World in View* (Cambridge, MA.: Harvard University Press, 2009), 166.

historical trajectory of reasoning and thinking ethically about the world–that enables humans to become ethical subjects.

This is indeed abstract, and McDowell himself insists that his intention is not to comment on how particular ethical traditions or versions of *Bildung* have evolved.[11] That, however, has not stopped commentators on McDowell's work from opening up an interesting line of debate. First, J. M. Bernstein argues that McDowell pays too little attention to the possibility that, under particular historical conditions, our space of reasons gets perverted or corrupted into forms of "rationalized reason," as, for example, Adorno argued:[12] it is this comment that provoked McDowell's denial just mentioned. Second, the late Rüdiger Bubner interprets McDowell's understanding of *Bildung* in ways that open up important possibilities of historical contradiction and conflict.

Bubner's argument is worth exploring in more detail. McDowell's key move, from which Bubner builds, is to insist that Aristotle's idea of a basic or "first" nature of animal life implies, for humans, a *"second" nature*, which captures how humans are initiated, via language, into a space of evolving reasons, where practices such as ethics emerge. This space of reasons can emerge only *in* history, even though the *fact* that it is a necessary feature of human life does not itself depend on, and is not caused by, any particular history.[13] Bubner goes further in bringing out the implications of McDowell's concept of second nature. According to Bubner, "Bildung means the discovery of possibilities and capacities whereby character is shaped, not only in the direction of a socially fixed and pre-given ideal of virtue, but in the acquisition of a personality. Everyone has the means of realizing this end, but it takes a lot to bring it into concrete existence."[14] *Bildung*, on this reading, therefore involves the inherent possibility of each person acquiring a distinctive personality, but under conditions that are both historical and experienced individually, transforming Aristotle's concept of virtue into something less generic and more contextual.

As a result, according to Bubner, *Bildung* (the particular form that initiation into the space of reasons takes in particular lives) is not the same as second nature (the general concept), but in dialectic with it: "our own second nature [is] something we must endeavour to realize though *our very concern* with Bildung."[15] This creates a possibility of instability when "second nature loses its fundamental ability to endure through time, as well as its stability in the face of conflicts, when and

---

[11] John McDowell, "Responses," in *Reading McDowell: On Mind and World*, ed. Nicholas H. Smith (New York: Routledge, 2002), 269–305, at 300.

[12] J. M. Bernstein, "Re-enchanting nature," in Smith, *Reading McDowell*, 217–45, at 239.

[13] McDowell, *Having the World in View*, 169.

[14] Rüdiger Bubner, "*Bildung* and Second Nature," in Smith, *Reading McDowell*, 209–16, at 211.

[15] Ibid., 214–15.

in so far as we do not all affirm it together time and again in daily action."[16] So, in particular historical circumstances, *Bildung* may not always evolve in ways that confirm our second nature—that is, our shared and inherent possibility of being rational beings. This happens when *Bildung* fails to be socially reproduced. In making this connection, Bubner aligns McDowell's insights with broader sociological notions of social reproduction and structuration.[17]

How, more concretely, can we imagine *Bildung* not being reproduced, and our second nature as rational animals thereby being destabilized? To make sense of this, we must make explicit a premise assumed in all the philosophical positions so far discussed; that *Bildung*, and the enactment of our second nature, is something human beings achieve through their dealings *with each other as human beings*. What if human life today were starting to incorporate not just human beings' use of external tools (as has happened throughout recorded history), but also external processes and systems that are *not* responsive to humans' ethical reasoning and so are not part of the "space of reasons"? This is the possibility that, with Andreas Hepp, I explored in the book *The Mediated Construction of Reality*.[18]

What if human history—through the proliferation of datafied media and, underlying them, the huge and rapid growth of partly autonomous artificial intelligence and machine learning systems—is evolving in a direction where human life and reasoning is structured not only by encounters with other human beings in the space of reasons, but also by interfaces with impersonal computing systems, programmed by individuals, no doubt, but operating in nonlinear pathways that go far beyond the initial designs of their programmers?[19] Then we would have to acknowledge an uncomfortable possibility: that, far from the social world being (as Peter Berger and Thomas Luckmann once conceived it[20]) constructed out of human beings' encounters with, and mutual knowledge of, each other, the social world is now, itself, in part *datafied*—datafied through the continuous embedding within it of contemporary media with their capacities of autonomously tracking and nudging human decision-making and experience.[21] If so, then human life and its space of reasons—and therefore the very possibility of a rational ethical life—would have become shaped by a *third* nature "driven by the economic imperatives

---

[16] Ibid., 215.
[17] Anthony Giddens, *The Constitution of Society* (Cambridge: Polity, 1984).
[18] Nick Couldry and Andreas Hepp, *The Mediated Construction of Reality* (Cambridge: Polity, 2017).
[19] Stuart J. Russell, *Human Compatible: AI and the Problem of Control* (London: Allen Lane, 2019).
[20] Peter Berger and Thomas Luckmann, *The Social Construction of Reality* (Harmondsworth: Penguin, 1966).
[21] Karen Yeung, "'Hypernudge': Big Data as a Mode of Regulation by Design," *Information Communication and Society* 20, no. 1 (2017)): 118-36.

of the data industries and all the wider goals of capitalist expansion that, in turn, drive those industries."[22]

This, I believe, is the possibility that political and theological philosopher Giorgio Agamben envisaged when, in the important essay "What is an Apparatus?," he argued that technology generates a problem of "subjectification" through the new relations between human beings and their devices. The ways in which we are made subjects through our data-extracting devices involves what Agamben calls "a pure activity of governance devoid of any foundation in being"[23] –that is, in McDowell's terms, a mode of governing subjects, the logic of which does not pass through our human space of reasons. A similar problem is raised by legal philosopher Mireille Hildebrandt in her discussion of how AI-driven automated judgments quietly undermine our embodied and humanistic conceptions of legal rationality.[24]

From multiple directions, then, by building on the suggestions of interpreters of both Hegel and McDowell as they have updated Aristotle's fixed view of human nature, we arrive at the possibility that the social world today may be reproducing itself in ways that are in tension with our possibilities, as human beings, for being ethical, that is, to become beings motivated by reasons. Or, to return to the language of the quotation from sociologist Anthony Giddens at the start of this essay, we must acknowledge that datafied media are changing how we are "in" the world and so reconfiguring our possibilities of being formed *as* ethical subjects fitted to live and act in that world, reshaping, that is, our very possibilities for *Bildung*. If so, we are back with the historical paradoxes of problematic human interdependence that Hegel anticipated two centuries ago. To quote Pinkard once more: "[O]ur very metaphysical status as the agents we are is realizable only from within these complex social dependencies within the fabric of recognition."[25] But what if those dependences created contradictions with our attempts to be ethical?

In the next section, I provide evidence that this alarming potential of contemporary mediascapes is more than speculation.

Bildung in a Datafied World: Some Problems

I turn here from abstract philosophical debate about the preconditions for ethics and character formation to more concrete discussion about the dynamics of to-

---

[22] Couldry and Hepp, *The Mediated Construction of Reality*, 142.
[23] Giorgio Agamben, *What Is an Apparatus? And Other Essays* (Palo Alto, CA: Stanford University Press, 2009), 11.
[24] Mireille Hildebrandt, *Smart Technology and the End(s) of Law* (London: Edward Elgar, 2015).
[25] Pinkard, *Hegel's Naturalism*, 193.

day's media and social landscapes. I noted above that earlier philosophical theories assumed that the preconditions of ethics derive from the historically specific and accumulating resources of *human* interaction, in other words from "tradition." To abandon the idea of tradition as a shaper of ethics would be not only to abandon the neo-Aristotelian legacy, but also to abandon the idea of history itself, since history's continuity in part comprises the passing between generations of resources and frameworks of understanding that we call tradition. But, until recently, there has been a latent assumption in the notion of history mobilized via *Bildung* and related understandings of ethics: the assumption that history is a matter of humans' interactions with each other, albeit supplemented by their use of tools and the material resources and infrastructures that humans build together. Social phenomenology (from Schütz to Berger and Luckmann) made similar assumptions about the centrality of human interaction and knowledge construction, building a cognate understanding of social institutions. In today's world, where media companies and digital online platforms have such prominence, it would be negligent not to include such companies and platforms as part of the institutional setting for social life. But what are the implications of this?

By media here, I mean "technologically based media of communication that institutionalize communication" and stabilize its practices on various levels.[26] There is not enough space here to elaborate on this definition, but at the very least "media" for this purpose include not only traditional (often called, "legacy") media—television, film, radio, the press—but also online platforms and websites, and the vast infrastructure of the internet and the many levels of data processing that underlie particular platforms and websites.

An important feature of media in this expanded sense is their deep embedding in everyday life. Before the age of the internet, traditional media mattered because of the large-scale narratives they supplied and the everyday habits of attention and entertainment they supported, yet, as media, they remained detachable from many of the basic resources on the basis of which we construct our daily lives. This began to change in the 1980s, when credit and bank cards became common means of payment, supported by large-scale infrastructures of data collection and monitoring in what Craig Calhoun called "quaternary" social relations.[27] Change accelerated massively in the 1990s, as internet use, such as email, became an ever more persistent feature of daily transactions, and the World Wide Web became the predominant source of much information for daily use. Another massive transformation occurred from around 2005, when social platforms such as Myspace and Facebook became standard means for presenting

---

[26] Couldry and Hepp, *The Mediated Construction of Reality*, 32.
[27] Craig Calhoun, "The Infrastructure of Modernity," in *Social Change and Modernity*, ed. Hans Haferkamp and Neil J. Smelser (Berkeley: University of California Press, 1992), 205–36.

one's self to others and interacting with them regularly. Meanwhile, mobile phones had come to be used for much more than spoken conversations, including continuous text interaction, and by the 2010 s, all these communication functions became integrated in single devices, such as the smartphone and tablet.

This history is all too familiar; it is the banal backdrop to life during the past two or three decades. But it has underlying features of critical importance that are less often noted. A key commentator here has been U.S. legal theorist Julie Cohen. In the book *Configuring the Networked Self*, Cohen argues that underlying the massive expansion of activities and services available online is something less noted by celebrants of media: human beings' increasing dependence on impersonal computer systems for the conduct of basic transactions, for access to those they care about, and for the management of daily life. The result, as Cohen strikingly puts it, is "a gap between the rhetoric of liberty and the reality of diminished individual control."[28] Rather than this political implication, I want to focus on the ethical import of the processes that underlie this gap.

For Cohen, the key transformation is spatial: "the information society is not simply an abstract collection of categories and privileges; its inhabitants exist within real spaces and experience artifacts and architectures as having material properties" (26). We inhabit "a new kind of social space . . . networked space," whereby information technologies "reshape our embodied perceptions and experiences" (33, 41). Cohen is not talking about a crude and direct molding of character by media, but a more open shaping of the *conditions* of social existence. Her argument emerges in counterpoint to how, until the age of datafied media, we understood freedom: "human flourishing requires both boundedness and some ability to manage boundaries" (152), that is, something different from the unboundedness of networks. The more time we spend on online platforms, governed not by us as users but by the protocols of the companies who own the platforms, the less control we have over the basic conditions of our social interaction. Cohen captures this problem through the notion of platforms' "architectures of control." These architectures "reflect a fundamental shift in our political economy toward a system of governance on precisely defined, continually updated authorization of access by, and to, actors, resources and devices" (188).

We are, in other words, increasingly, in richer nations at least, spending ever higher proportions of our time in spaces governed by systems that human beings do not control (even if those systems were initially programmed by certain human beings), systems whose terms are imposed on platform users without any meaningful consent. Both platforms and systems are oriented to commercial ends, rather than any desire to enhance social interaction, and, as Cohen notes, they generally operate opaquely, far beyond the detailed understanding of their users.

---

[28] Julie E. Cohen, *Configuring the Networked Self* (New Haven: Yale University Press, 2012), 4. Further citations to this work are in parentheses in the text.

What might be the specific implications of this for the idea of *Bildung* as a process whereby ethical subjects are formed?

Who/What Do We Interact with Online?

It has been an unspoken assumption of ethics until the twenty-first century that the interactions from which a process of *Bildung* or ethical formation[29] emerges are interactions between human beings, or between human beings and the institutions they build. In their dealings with the world, human beings of course use tools and, more generally, take advantage of the resources which, individually or collectively, humans manage, including at the broadest level the infrastructures on which everyday life is built. Within this understanding of action, there are plenty sources of friction with individual goals and plans, but at no point does human life confront something external to human life—until, that is, it confronts the natural conditions of its existence (which can be interpreted purposively or not, depending on one's theological or secular position). Put crudely, ethics is the measure of how well human beings confront the external conditions of their existence and, on that basis, interact with each other and with the resources that, as human beings, they have built. *Bildung*—the process of forming ethical subjects, even if actualized via institutions—is always, therefore, in the end, a residue of prior human actions.

But what if the process whereby ethical subjects are today formed is different? Consider platforms such as Facebook and Twitter, chosen only because they are so well known. It would be hard to deny that interactions on those platforms, and countless similar platforms, play a key role in how all but the youngest people today are formed as ethical subjects across both public and private matters. For these platforms are where most of us encounter many of the people we encounter. Are Facebook and Twitter populated only by human beings and the content traces left by human beings? Clearly not: a significant proportion of the "inhabitants" and the content found on these platforms are respectively automated agents (such as "bots") and content generated by automated systems.[30]

This would not necessarily be a problem if it were generally clear *whether* the entity you are interacting with is a bot or not, and, independently, whether a particular piece of content has been posted by a human being or by an automated system. But the whole *point* of bots and systems for automated content generation is to ensure that it is not easy to tell the difference between them and real human

---

[29] Sabina Lovibond, *Ethical Formations* (Cambridge, MA: Harvard University Press, 2002).
[30] Philip N. Howard, *Lie Machines* (New Haven: Yale University Press, 2020); and Damian Tambini, "In the New Robopolitics, Docial Media Has Left Newspapers for Dead," *The Guardian*, Nov. 18, 2016.

beings and the content they generate. The result is to regularly trick people on such platforms into interactions, perceptions, and long-term judgments that rely, falsely, on the assumption that they have been responsive to interactions with real human beings. This is a problem. When much of the content that contributes to ethical formation in digital spaces is not only not generated by other human beings but, perhaps, generated with the explicit goal of tricking human judgment quietly and invisibly, then we start to doubt whether it is part of *Bildung* at all. Societies where human beings emerge with regular characteristics that are *not* shaped by the space of human reasons but perhaps, at worst, shaped by a space of automated *un*reason are spaces where the very possibility of ethical formation is challenged.

We begin to glimpse here a deep conflict between human goals and system goals[31] that dismantles the boundary on which our inherited notions of ethics depend: the boundary between the accumulated histories of human interaction and the external (nonhuman) conditions of human life. It is as if, in automated programmed form, we were starting to delegate to external machines part of the task of sustaining ourselves as ethical beings. But that is exactly what human beings cannot do if they are to remain ethical and human.

What Shapes the Environments We Encounter Online?

The question of bots and other automated agents is a problem to which, no doubt, platform operators are giving some attention, if only because of the reputational damage they risk from not being seen to care about the problem. But it is only one aspect of a larger issue that platforms cannot avoid or regulate, since it derives directly from the business model that drives their operations.

Another key assumption of theories of ethical formation and *Bildung*, until the era of datafied media, has been that the interactional environments in which human subjects are formed are themselves shaped by what we might call the dynamics of human interaction. Whatever theory of psychology or historical understanding one relies upon, it is clear that those dynamics are very often oriented to goals other than ethics, and that the outcomes are very often far from ethical. Since, however, such dynamics are, we assume, characterized by whatever forces have distinctively driven humans as particular types of natural beings, we have taken those dynamics and the human environments, good or bad, to which they give rise as material on which ethics must reflect. But what if today's interactional environments are governed, in large part, not by the dynamics of human interaction but rather by *algorithmically sorted* human traces—that is, not by patterns in the goals and passions that historically have shaped human behavior, but pat-

---

[31] Robin Mansell, *Imagining the Internet* (Oxford: Oxford University Press, 2012).

terns in the goals of those particular humans who profit from "curating" the traces of human interactions online in particular ways?

Since *Bildung* today takes place in large part in such platform environments, we would seem to be allowing *Bildung* to be shaped, perhaps decisively, by forces that have not until now shaped how human beings interact with each other.

Note that platform operators must *deny* that what goes on between humans on their platforms is anything other than "natural." This indeed is the ideology of a digital platform like Facebook: to claim that Facebook's mechanisms of, for example, heightening the visibility of this or that content simply highlights what was already there in human interaction naturally. Consider the language of an email directed to me as a supposed member of the "Facebook Community" on December 1, 2020 (I almost never use Facebook, but a bonus of my retained membership is to receive such material): "Facebook groups are more than just online meeting places—they are also an extremely valuable tool for community organizing, in real life. Bringing the relationship-forging power of groups to your real-life community can help strengthen your community's bonds and connect you with a much wider pool of potential members." Or take this statement by Facebook founder Mark Zuckerberg in a long memorandum addressed to "our community" on February 16, 2017, less than a month after the inauguration of President Trump:

> History is the story of how we've learned to come together in ever greater numbers—from tribes to cities to nations. At each step, we built social infrastructure like communities, media and governments to empower us to achieve things we couldn't on our own. Today we are close to taking our next step. ... Progress now requires humanity coming together not just as cities or nations, but also as a global community. ... For the past decade, Facebook has focused on connecting friends and families. With that foundation, our next focus will be developing the social infrastructure for community.[32]

Such language ignores completely the shaping role that Facebook's own algorithms play in selecting and prioritizing what appears to us as "news" or as relevant content and interactions on the platform. Four years later, after a series of furors about Facebook's role in, at the very least, not preventing the spread of damaging potential misinformation in elections in various countries, it is impossible to look back on Zuckerberg's words other than ironically. But the statement is sign of more than naivete: it represents a form of necessary bad faith on the part of digital platform operators whose business is to engineer the social in ways that are profitable.

---

[32] Mark Zuckerberg, "Building Global community," https://m.facebook.com/nt/screen/?params=%7B%22note_id%22%3A3707971095882612%7D&path=%2Fnotes%2Fnote%2F&_rdr, Feb. 16, 2017.

That bad faith becomes clear when we consider the actual dynamics of platforms such as Facebook: that is, their business model. As Dipayan Ghosh and I recently argued, the features of that business model are clear: "first, the *collection* of data on the user so as to generate behavioral profiles; second, the refinement of sophisticated *algorithms* that curate the content in her social feeds and target ads; and third the sustaining of engaging—and perhaps addictive—*content* on platforms that keep her hooked, to the exclusion of rivals."[33]

This business model is what underlies Facebook's engagement today in the "direct management of key domains of social life so as to maximize profit—*whatever the cost to social, political and market functioning.*"[34] The resulting contradiction between Facebook's business model and its self-description as a sustainer of social life is more than self-misrecognition. It disguises a key feature of today's datafied media that undermines their contribution to *Bildung*. Facebook presents itself as our tool to engineer a better social world on a large, indeed global, scale. But—as popular debate has grasped for some time in the phrase "if the service is free, then you are the product"—Facebook is not the tool of its users, or indeed of humanity in general; rather, Facebook's users are the tool—or, better, the raw material—that fuels Facebook's business model. This is an example of the "tool reversibility" that Andreas Hepp and I argue characterizes all datafied media and the social systems that incorporate them: that, though they appear to be our tools, datafied media must, by the very fact that we are using them, have already been using us as a source of data.[35]

Underway today is a fundamental change in the nature of human tools: think of the Internet of Things and its suite of domestic devices that operate to extend the domain of routine data extraction across everyday life. This might seem remote from questions of ethical formation, until we note that this is just one example of how deeply datafied media have come to reshape the space of everyday action. This matters for *Bildung*, because our understanding of the processes through which human ethical subjects are formed did not, until recently, include such asymmetries, let alone the commercially driven distortions of social interaction we have just noted. Before concluding, let me make one more point about asymmetries and datafied media.

---

[33] Dipayan Ghosh and Nick Couldry, "Digital Realignment: Rebalancing Platform Economies from Corporation to Consumer," Harvard Kennedy School, Oct. 2020, https://www.hks.harvard.edu/centers/mrcbg/publications/awp/awp155, p. 16 (emphasis in original).

[34] Ibid., 22 (emphasis in original).

[35] Couldry and Hepp, *The Mediated Construction of Reality*, 132-32.

The Death of Communicative Symmetry?

Datafied media, such as the social media platforms where we appear to each other, not only are based on data extraction but are, basically, databases, and this affects fundamentally how they contribute to our ethical life. All databases operate on an "exclusionary principle" that determines what can and cannot be stored in a particular form:[36] in other words, "what is not classified [as data, NC] gets rendered invisible."[37] The exclusions on which databases operate fix the starting point from which data operations (counting, aggregating, sorting, evaluation) begin. The knowledge that results (including our knowledge as platform users) cannot easily be separated out from the selections that formed the database.

Consider our interactions with each other on a platform such as Facebook, which, once again, we must assume contributes potentially to how characters today are formed. What appears as having just happened to, and for, us on a social media platform can appear *as such* only by virtue of its place in archives ordered according to principles quite different from those that regulate everyday face-to-face social interaction: principles that optimize traffic on the platform.[38] Social media "appearances" are always the result of prior processing. There must always, therefore, be a gap between the categorizations that generate those appearances and our experience of those appearances as platform users. This gap is not accidental but inherent to the "platformed sociality"[39] that Facebook or similar social platforms provide.

This phenomenon has a radical impact on the very forms of online social interaction, for the basic level of symmetry we take for granted in face-to-face social interaction cannot be assumed online. Let me explain. When two native speakers of a language speak together, one speaks in the language in which she expects her interlocutor to respond, and so does the interlocutor, and from this follow many other more detailed symmetries. The flow of everyday conversation between those who share a language is based on two key assumptions that Alfred Schütz called "interchangeability of standpoints" and "congruence of relevance systems."[40] Put differently, the elements in any stream of social interaction are

---

[36] Geoffrey C. Bowker, *Memory Practices in the Sciences* (Cambridge, MA: MIT Press, 2008), 12.
[37] Ibid., 153.
[38] Cristina Alaimo and Jannis Kallinikos, "Encoding the Everyday: The Infrastructural Apparatus of Social Data," in *Big Data Is Not a Monolith: Policies, Practices, and Problems*, ed. Cassidy R. Sugimoto, H. R. Ekbia, and Michael Mattioli (Cambridge MA: MIT Press, 2016), 77–90.
[39] Jose van Dijck, *The Culture of Connectivity* (Oxford: Oxford University Press, 2013), 5.
[40] Alfred Schütz and Thomas Luckmann, *The Structures of the Life World: Volume II* (Evanston, IL: Northwestern University Press, 1973), 60.

treated by participants as continuous with each other. But the symmetry of such exchanges cannot be so easily assumed on social media platforms, where whatever appears "back" to us does so only because it has already complied with the categorization criteria of the platform, not those of the interlocutors. Even more important, what appears back to me is determined by algorithms that work from the personal data stored about my interactions with the platform, and that of persons linked to me; the same is true with what appears back to you, but with no necessary coincidence between the dynamics that share what appears to you or to me. In short-term exchanges, we might not notice any consequences from this underlying difference: our stream of interaction might seem to be frictionless and unimpeded; on a larger scale, however, the results may well be more misleading, since each of us is reacting to differently structured sets of appearances. As a result, there is a deeper asymmetry hidden within claims that data from social media platforms yield knowledge about the social. As Jose van Dijck puts it, "it is easier to encode sociality into algorithms than to decode algorithms back into social action."[41] Yet this is exactly what we try to do, and Facebook purports to do, when we read social media data streams as if they were simply an extension of our natural forms of sociality.[42]

Conclusion

I have argued that some key features of today's datafied media environment alter the conditions under which we interact socially with each other, and that those alterations are of significance not only in themselves, but because of their implications for how we conceive ethical subjects to be formed today. I have formulated these issues by reference to the concept of *Bildung*, as the only widely available concept that registers the knowledge and social structures underlying the possibility of ethics. Yet our exposure to automated agents online, the general shaping of online interactions by platforms' commercial objectives, and the ways in which algorithms interfere even with something as basic as how we appear to each other online all illustrate how we are not formed ethically in datafied environments in the ways we once assumed as intrinsic to the formation of ethical subjects.

I have not argued that character as such is transformed, let alone corroded, by datafied media. That would be too moralistic a tale: the consequences of media for social life rarely take such a linear form. As a result, the appropriate response to the diagnosis offered in this chapter is not simply renewed effort to behave more

---

[41] Van Dijck, *The Culture of Connectivity*, 172.
[42] For more detailed discussion of this point, see Nick Couldry and Jannis Kallinikos, "Ontology," in *The Sage Handbook of Social Media*, ed. Jean Burgess, Alice Emily Marwick, and Thomas Poell (Los Angeles: Sage, 2018), 146–59, at 149–52.

ethically in mediated settings; for that ignores the deeper ways in which the *conditions of possibility* for being ethical today are being reshaped in a largely online world.

Rather, it is more important to turn our gaze away from individuals and toward the wider social domain, shaped as it is by deep economic forces that have been characterized variously as surveillance capitalism and data colonialism.[43] Are we registering in the unsettling of our inherited assumptions about *Bildung* the reverberations of a wider disruption of social life? Are our very possibilities for an ethical life being deranged by the eruption within our spaces of everyday interaction of external dynamics driven by corporate, not individual human, interests? Is the very space of the free self, by which we make sense of ethical reflexivity, prised apart by the continuous tracking of individuals not by external infrastructures responsive to us as ethical beings, but by business models for which platforms are responsible to their shareholders?[44]

If so, something profound is amiss in our ethical life in the age of datafied media. We will need to work hard to avoid ethics facing the "catastrophe that occurs almost unperceived," which W. G. Sebald once named with his special acuity.

---

[43] Shoshana Zuboff, *The Age of Surveillance Capitalism* (London: Profile Books, 2019); and Nick Couldry and Ulises A. Mejias, *The Costs of Connection* (Palo Alto, CA: Stanford University Press, 2019).

[44] See Couldry and Mejias, *The Costs of Connection*, chap. 5, for more discussion.

Seeing a Crisis Through Media: Narrating the Coronavirus Pandemic in the Early Twenty-First Century

Julia Sonnevend and Olivia Steiert

As we are writing this chapter in early 2021, a deadly pandemic is altering everyday life around the globe. A novel coronavirus emerged in late 2019 that wreaks havoc on societies, communities, and individuals, separating grandparents from grandchildren, causing economic recession, and altering even our ability to interact with each other. The coronavirus crisis is an event that we mostly see only *through* the media. It is a mediated crisis in which both the representations of events and our basic ability to communicate are subject to contemporary media technologies. Unlike in the case of an earthquake or a tsunami, we do not see the epicenter and the remnants of the crisis. There are no ruins to clean up, houses to rebuild. What we need to maintain and rebuild daily are human relationships in a time of extreme social distancing. This crisis thus offers a unique lens to look at the role of media in contemporary social life. In this chapter we focus on what we *see* and do *not* see with the help of the media during this pandemic. By looking at this highly mediated crisis, we hope to give a glimpse into the more general roles the media play in contemporary societies worldwide.

Eventfulness and the Media

An event's construction tends to involve a process of naming, narrating, and visualizing.[1] Narrators locate an event by addressing it with a name, developing its core social meaning, and attaching, if possible, visual representations to it. The media, along with other storytellers, work on "taming" the event, marking its beginning, middle, and potential end.

---

[1] Julia Sonnevend, *Stories without Borders: The Berlin Wall and the Making of a Global Iconic Event* (Oxford: Oxford University Press, 2016).

This process involves dealing with the inherent "restlessness" of events, their constant flux.² It is never easy to pinpoint events, but an ongoing pandemic poses unique challenges in this respect. At the moment of writing this chapter, there are still intense discussions about the origins of the current pandemic, as some suggest animal-to-human transmission, while others argue for the escape of a virus from a laboratory in Wuhan, China. The exact timing of the beginning is still disputed. Moreover, this event comes in waves that hit distinct countries and regions at different times, creating multiple temporalities. Finally, at this point no end to the event is in sight; it is even possible that this pandemic will become an ongoing process that poses a recurring yet relatively manageable threat. In cases of "restless" events, such as the current pandemic, even situating ourselves in relation to the event is challenging, as it is often unclear whether we are "inside" or "outside" of the event.³

A pandemic is also part of the "difficult past" category of events. A difficult past "is constituted as a result of an inherent moral trauma, disputes, tensions, conflict."⁴ In some sense this pandemic is already constructed as a traumatic event reflected, for instance, in commemorative COVID memorials erected worldwide. But over time, as the pandemic's toll becomes clear, and the focus of governments might shift from crisis management to trauma processing, it will likely be further constructed as a cultural trauma regionally, nationally, and even internationally.⁵ Given the differing political views on the pandemic's adequate handling, it will likely be highly disputed for a while. But over time, some consensus might emerge, at least over the pandemic's undeniably high human toll. During this narrative process, journalists will play a major role in naming, narrating, and visualizing the event, both enabling consensus and further entrenching division.

Journalists as Storytellers and Builders of Mythological Narratives and Sites

In Western tradition, there is a long-held understanding that the central role of journalism is to share information as adequately and objectively as possible. No-

---

[2] Robin Wagner-Pacifici, "Theorizing the Restlessness of Events," *American Journal of Sociology* 115, no. 5 (2010): 1351–86; and Robin Wagner-Pacifici, *What Is an Event?* (Chicago: University of Chicago Press, 2017).

[3] Wagner-Pacifici, *What Is an Event?*

[4] Vered Vinitzky-Seroussi, *Yitzhak Rabin's Assassination and the Dilemmas of Memory* (Albany: State University of New York Press, 2009), 3.

[5] Jeffrey C. Alexander et al., *Cultural Trauma and Collective Identity* (Berkeley: University of California Press, 2004).

body questions that this is one of journalism's central roles, but it is increasingly disputed whether it is indeed its primary role. Focusing on the role of journalism in shaping democracies, Michael Schudson argued that there are six, or even seven, things journalists can do for democracy: they inform, investigate, analyze.[6] News can also serve as a public forum to share diverse perspectives, it can be a tool for social empathy, and journalists can even mobilize people to take action. Ideally, journalism also supports representative democracy by promoting minority rights. Recently, building on Schudson's work, Ethan Zuckerman offered six or seven things that social media can do for democracy: social media can inform us, amplify important voices and issues, enhance solidarity by connection, and be a space for mobilization and deliberation.[7] Social media, in Zuckerman's view, can show a diversity of views and thus be a model for democratically governed spaces. Zuckerman is, of course, keenly aware that social media often do not live up to these expectations, and that they likely serve more functions than these. But both authors list more roles for the media than just information sharing, even in the narrow context of democratic capacity building.

Media analysts often adopt a narrow focus on the media's information-sharing role, and this leads to assumptions that unwelcomed social and political developments are the outcomes of "information deserts" or "rampant misinformation." But once we move beyond a restrictive focus on information, it becomes clear that societies and individuals also look to the media to adopt frameworks of thought[8] and to confirm their already existing identities.[9] If we shift our focus from what journalists can do for democracy to how the media can shape societies in general, there are even more roles journalists can play. First and foremost, the media can tell eternal stories that move us, shake us, and shape our worldview in a lasting way. In other words, journalists build up mythologies that guide us through challenging and uplifting times. Considering the mythological role of journalism, Jack Lule argued that journalists present heroes, villains, and other stereotypes and tropes that can help us navigate complex information environments.[10] In the context of the pandemic, the mythological role of the media is particularly prevalent. The lead actor of the crisis, the coronavirus, is not

---

[6] Michael Schudson, *Why Democracies Need an Unlovable Press* (New York: Polity, 2008).

[7] Ethan. Zuckerman, "Six or Seven Things Social Media Can Do for Democracy" (blog), May 30, 2018, https://ethanzuckerman.com/2018/05/30/six-or-seven-things-social-media-can-do-for-democracy/.

[8] Julia Sonnevend, "Facts (Almost) Never Win Over Myths," in *Trump and the Media*, ed. Pablo J. Boczkowski and Zizi Papacharissi (Cambridge, MA: MIT Press, 2018).

[9] Daniel Kreiss, "The Media Are about Identity, Not Information," in Boczkowski and Papacharissi, *Trump and the Media*.

[10] Jack Lule, *Daily News, Eternal Stories: The Mythological Role of Journalism* (New York: The Guilford Press, 2001).

available to the human eye.[11] In order to make audiences relate to this crisis, journalists construct heroes and villains as the event's substitute protagonists. Journalists are active in offering these mythological figures. Who is considered a villain, and who is presented as a hero is largely influenced by our "tribal" political identities? For instance, in the United States, for Republicans villains range from COVID-conscious, lockdown-favoring governors to mask-wearers to President Biden. For Democrats, villains are mostly those who flout COVID regulations, who question the seriousness of the crisis, and who are aligned with former President Trump. Journalists cater mythological narratives to both sides.

As the pandemic continues, the central figures of the drama often shift. Early heroes were essential workers, who continued to work in person in hospitals and grocery stores. Later heroes include, for instance, inventors of coronavirus vaccines (unless you are an antivaxxer), politicians, and public-health experts who successfully manage the crisis according to your distinct expectations. We might also admire celebrities and align our behavior with theirs, as they communicate the crisis in a relatable way. Consider, for instance, American actor Tom Hanks's role in the early narration of the crisis.[12] At the very beginning of the pandemic, in March 2020, the announcement of Hanks's and his wife's infection and the online sharing of their experiences made the crisis relatable to a broad American and international audience. We might also have our own personal heroes as well, among family and friends—people who succumbed to or survived the illness, who dedicatedly cared for family members, who taught children during these challenging times, or who did groundbreaking research about the virus.

The infected person occupies a strange in-betweenness. There is generally solidarity toward her suffering, unless somehow her own behavior is to blame. The "superspreader" is equally ambiguous, as she is mostly unaware of her ability to infect others at the time of the "superspreader" event, but is often identified and blamed retrospectively. As vaccinations ramp up, albeit in an unequal way internationally, the divide between vaccinated and unvaccinated is also becoming increasingly prevalent, providing yet another ambiguous category. We do not know who is vaccinated, unless we ask for or show documentation. This means, in everyday interaction, that we have mostly no way of knowing, and thus we look for

---

[11] Julia Sonnevend, "A Virus as an Icon: The 2020 Pandemic in Images," *American Journal of Cultural Sociology* 8 (2020): 451–61; and Julia Sonnevend, "'The Big Clean Up': The 2020 Pandemic as a Representational Crisis," *SSRC Items*, Sep. 17, 2020, https://items.ssrc.org/covid-19-and-the-social-sciences/mediated-crisis/the-big-clean-up-the-2020-pandemic-as-a-representational-crisis/.

[12] Jessica Gall Myrick and Jessica Fitts Willoughby, "A Mixed Methods Inquiry into the Role of Tom Hanks' COVID-19 Social Media Disclosure in Shaping Willingness to Engage in Prevention Behaviors," *Health Communication*, Jan. 14, 2021, https://www.tandfonline.com/doi/citedby/10.1080/10410236.2020.1871169?scroll=top&needAccess=true.

clues or simply assume vaccination status. In many countries, holders of "vaccine passports" are the only ones who can enjoy pools, restaurants, and public events. In some places, coronavirus vaccines are even required for work and school, as has been the case with many other diseases in recent history. The uncertainties around vaccination status and the ways to clarify this status all offer unique "interaction rituals"[13] for people. The vaccinated/unvaccinated divide also presents journalists with a new pool of hero/villain candidates and ambiguous in-between categories.

During a crisis, journalists also show key sites of the event, offering spaces that we can relate to. Just as in theatrical performances, the stages of social performances mostly involve people. As such, they are marked by presence. Usually the stage, the mise-en-scène of the event, is filled with actors. Strangely, in the case of the coronavirus pandemic, we have experienced the opposite. We see the power of absence in previously populated places like the Eiffel Tower, and the power of presence in previously abandoned places, like our emerging home offices. By showing the key sites of the event, the media also draw the event's spatial boundaries. The pandemic has reinforced national borders and boundaries as new travel bans and travel restrictions have emerged. Journalists communicate this divide, reminding readers and viewers of the recurring power of nation-states. Through the presented spatial boundaries, journalists also tacitly communicate who belongs to "us" and who constitutes the vague category of "them."

Engagement with Media as Ritual

These categories of "us" and "them" are not only a basic ingredient to mythologies but also an inherent aspect of society, community, and solidarity. In one of the most enduring classics of sociology, *The Elementary Forms of Religious Life*,[14] Émile Durkheim, in his analysis of aboriginal clan societies, observed how community and exclusion are two sides of one coin. He also introduced a theoretical mechanism behind this claim: rituals. In premodern tribal communities, recurring periods of intense rituals shaped and maintained collective life, solidarity, and identity and produced the symbolic "totems" around which it all revolved. In modern societies, we regularly find the equivalents for such rituals in sports, community celebrations, or media events—and, of course, religious ceremonies.[15] James Carey, in his classic book *Communication as Culture* (1989), put the ritual-

---

[13] Erving Goffman, *Interaction Ritual: Essays on Face-to-Face Behavior* (New York: Doubleday, 1967).

[14] Émile Durkheim, *The Elementary Forms of Religious Life* [1912] (Oxford: Oxford University Press, 2001).

[15] Alexander et al., *Cultural Trauma and Collective Identity*.

istic side of media and communication onto the agenda of media studies. In his view, the simple act of reading a newspaper not only transmitted information from the journalists to the readers but also evoked the moral universe of contending forces that both author and reader live in. The news activated the reader's roles in the social world as supporter, opponent, or citizen. Regarding the centrality of news to society and individual lives, he states that "as with religious rituals, … news changes little and yet is intrinsically satisfying; it performs few functions yet is habitually consumed."[16] What is certain, then, is that news profoundly shapes society, not only in the form of exceptional rituals, but even on the level of habitual practice.

During the coronavirus crisis, the media were in many ways "our window" to the world. Our often "ritualized" consumption of journalism (daily news reads, checking of daily numbers) offered sanctuaries and the calmness of repetition in a world of constant flux. Overall, these functions seemed essential to navigate this crisis. For instance, meticulously staged daily press conferences obtained a ritual character. As Celso Villegas analyzed for the case of Ohio's Governor Mike DeWine, his media performances during the early weeks of lockdown in spring 2020 rose far beyond the role of merely conveying information to the status of a "mediatized sanctuary" for isolated Ohioans.[17] Shannon Mattern made a similar argument about New York's governor, Andrew Cuomo, who guided his state's citizens through the troubling waters of an unsettling political situation with daily press conferences featuring PowerPoint slides and an elaborate mise-en-scène.[18] These culturally versed analyses are just the latest examples of how the notion of press conferences as "pseudo-events"[19] has been superseded to allow for a more comprehensive understanding of media's role in people's everyday lives and social imagination today.

---

[16] James Carey, *Communication as Culture: Essays on Media and Society* (New York: Routledge, 1989), 17.

[17] Celso M. Villegas, "Performing rituals of Affliction: How a Governor's Press Conferences Provided Mediatized Sanctuary in Ohio," *American Journal of Cultural Sociology* 8 (2020): 352–83.

[18] Shannon Mattern, "Andrew Cuomo's COVID-19 Briefing Draw on the Persuasive Authority of PowerPoint," *Art in America*, Apr. 13, 2020, https://www.artnews.com/art-in-america/features/andrew-cuomo-covid-briefings-powerpoint-slideshow-authority-1202683735/.

[19] Daniel J. Boorstin, *The Image: A Guide to Pseudo-Events in America* [1962] (New York: Vintage Books, 1992).

Boundaries, Othering, and Surveillance

While so far we have mostly focused on the narrative abilities of the media, there are other lenses to use as well. Taking one step back, it is also worth noting the flipside that comes with technologies for visualizing and narrating a pandemic: practices of tracking, accumulation of data, and the possibility of "preemptive" surveillance of individuals. As Yougrim Kim shows for the case of South Korea after the 2015 MERS epidemic, fears of contagion and the perceived need for national management rapidly led to the emergence of a "global health security" paradigm.[20] By the time the 2019 coronavirus hit South Korea in 2020, global tracking practices by a South Korean telecommunications company had long been justified as a preemptive measure for the sake of identifying potentially contagious individuals at the national borders. Arguably, this regime proved effective in limiting the impact of COVID-19 on South Korea, but it has also normalized potentially discriminatory practices.

Tracking, of course, has its own mythical base in the familiar idea that a deviant, contagious "other" threatens a cohesive, pure, and homogeneous "us." Like mapping, it serves the functions of information and identification alike. Both technologies are part and parcel of so-called outbreak narratives, which emerged in times of epidemics from bubonic plague to HIV and SARS.[21] The fact that a South Korean company starts its tracking strategies in central Africa is in line with the stock characters inhabiting myths. A similar dynamic played out in an increase in hate speech and incidents of severe violence against Asians and Asian-Americans in the United States, racialized and mythically understood as threatening intruders into a "pure" idea of American society. The pandemic again made these dynamics pitting variably constituted in-groups against out-groups very salient.

(Mis)understanding Misinformation

This perspective can also decisively inform and reorient our understanding of the highly debated, so-called infodemic, which threatens the efficacy of governmental efforts to convince people to comply with social-distancing rules, mask wearing, and vaccinations. The dominant explanation of the phenomenon has been that people are being duped into believing false information by manipulative instiga-

---

[20] Yougrim Kim, "Tracking Bodies in Question: Telecom Companies, Mobile Data, and Surveillance Platforms in South Korea's Epidemic Governance," *Information, Communication & Society* (2021), https://www.tandfonline.com/doi/full/10.1080/1369118X.2021.1883704.

[21] Priscilla Wald, *Contagious—Cultures, Carriers, and the Outbreak Narrative* (Durham, NC: Duke University Press, 2008).

tors. But the more obviously rigged the misinformation, the less understandable the ready acceptance of it. For those observing the infodemic from a distance, people seem to be acting against their own interests, and thus deserve to be scorned by an enlightened, democratic public. Often, the last resort is to frame communities or individuals verging toward conspiracy theories as irrational, deviant, and somehow cognitively deficient.

Fact-checking is a widely chosen tool to counter the issue, assuming that the infodemic marks a lack of true, fact-based contents. While this might technically balance the available information, there is evidence that the approach is less effective in correcting what people actually believe to be true.[22] The crucial point is whether and by whom information is taken up as truth—accepted and shared. Assuming that people must have been successfully duped thus misses a crucial point. As Daniel Kreiss put it, for highly politicized matters "identity comes prior to information. Identity shapes epistemology."[23] In other words, information is not taken up to assess reality objectively. On top of such concerns regarding uptake, fact-checking also reinforces the idea that there can always be a clear line drawn between "knowledge" and "nonknowledge," ignoring the debates in social sciences, and especially in science and technology studies, that have complicated such dichotomies for decades.[24] While in many cases "facts" are relatively clear, in others the boundaries are at least blurred. In any case, authority over truth rests on the rather shaky ideal of objectivity.[25]

Misinformation and the Power of Belonging

As one example, it has been shown that a lot of the skepticism around vaccination originates in what is perceived as "gut beliefs" rather than explicit misinformation.[26] We not only make our decisions based on one or another argument we come across in the media, but also perceive and process what resonates with our own experiences. And we do not form and articulate our own opinions in an isolated, contemplative manner either. Zeynep Tufekci describes our encounter with

---

[22] Brendan Nyhan and Jason Reifler, "When Corrections Fail: The Persistence of Political Misperceptions," *Political Behavior* 32 (2010): 303–30.

[23] Kreiss, "The Media Are About Identity, Not Information," 98.

[24] Noortje Marres, "Why We Can't Have Our Facts Back," *Engaging Science, Technology, and Society* 4 (2018): 423–43.

[25] Lucas Graves, *Deciding What's True: The Rise of Political Fact-Checking in American Journalism* (New York: Columbia University Press, 2016).

[26] Sabrina Tavernise, "Vaccine Skepticism Was Viewed as a Knowledge Problem. It's Actually about Gut Beliefs," *The New York Times*, Apr. 29, 2021, https://www.nytimes.com/2021/04/29/us/vaccine-skepticism-beliefs.html?smid=tw-share.

information on social media as primarily shaped by the social. In contrast to reading a newspaper in the privacy of the living room, Twitter feels more like the context of a football stadium, in which we sit amidst fellow fans and experience effervescence and in-group bonding by screaming across the stadium at the opposite team supporters. This context, she concludes, facilitates that when reading a piece of news on social media, perception will be shaped by belonging rather than facts.[27] Indeed, an experimental survey study from 2013 shows how far the analogy of team sports in understanding political polarization carries: it finds clear evidence that for polarized matters, respondents will answer questions about policy preferences in line with their party affiliation, no matter what other arguments are being provided or whether personal interests are at stake.[28]

An exemplary case of a fake post spread by individual Twitter accounts and tabloid media in the United Kingdom and Australia in early 2020 included an image of a world map thickly covered in slightly curved red lines. While it was originally created to illustrate the total of global air traffic in 2011, in 2020 the same image reemerged as alleged evidence for the routes that fleeing Wuhan residents used before Wuhan went into lockdown in January 2020. Thus, the image in this recontextualization went from depicting a morally neutral fact to showcasing the threatening irresponsibility of potentially infected individuals. It was acknowledged that the use of the color red in the original design proved problematic, with its alarming connotations, arguably lending itself to the reinterpretation in an evolving global state of emergency.[29] Fact-checking services quickly jumped to correct the misrepresentation, but—as so often in these cases—the use of such corrections remains limited vis-à-vis a fast and wide-spreading piece of scandalous drama building on familiar characters of pure and threatened members of "us" versus contagious and threatening "others."

This example is also one of *visual* misinformation, which has garnered some attention as especially effective, due to its likelihood of being shared, watched, and remembered and thus more accessible to our cognitive processes.[30] Visuals more directly speak to the emotions that trigger or prevent skepticism. Anger has

---

[27] Zeynep Tufekci, "How Social Media Took Us from Tahrir Square to Donald Trump," *MIT Technology Review*, Aug. 14, 2018, https://www.technologyreview.com/2018/08/14/240325/how-social-media-took-us-from-tahrir-square-to-donald-trump/.

[28] James N. Druckman, Erik Peterson, and Rune Slothuus, "How Elite Partisan Polarization Affects Public Opinion," *American Political Science Review* 107, no. 1 (2013): 57–79.

[29] AFP Australia, "This Map Shows Flight Paths Worldwide—It Does Not Show the Movement of Wuhan Residents," AFP Fact Check, Feb. 18, 2020, https://factcheck.afp.com/map-shows-flight-paths-worldwide-it-does-not-show-movement-wuhan-residents.

[30] Margaret Anne Defeyter et al., "The Picture Superiority Effect in Recognition Memory: A Developmental Study Using the Response Signal Procedure," *Cognitive Development* 24 (2009): 265–73.

been found to raise people's readiness to believe, while anxiety lowers trust in unsettling information.[31] Such sentiments, fraught with consequences, however, are not spontaneously triggered if there is not already a fertile ground for them. Widespread readiness to indulge in fears and go with the enticing drama often offered in misinformation preexists the infodemic. An unjust or difficult political situation that stokes anger at a government among a disfranchised population will consequently help the acceptance of misinformation, as it serves to deride the perceived opponents.[32]

With social media, assigning the public not only the role of audience but also that of replicator, the question is not only why people accept a piece of information that is likely untrue, but also why they would share and reproduce it? Conceptualizing a click of the sharing button as a social act helps understand this better. The act of telling stories in personal settings or to social media followers is a social activity and, as such, "governed by norms of performance."[33] This emphasizes the potential pleasure in sharing scandalous stories about the imagined opposite team, with which "people may have been seeking less to persuade recipients (by way of the plausibility of the story) than to strengthen their membership in the group (by way of their disinclination to question the plausibility of the story)."[34] Not questioning what seems more than questionable on the surface, then, can be understood as a conscious performance of partisan allegiance. The value of stories is less in truth than in reminding people what side they are on.

The Drama of (Mis)information

Misinformation, then, serves the same purpose for those who believe in it as does any mediated form of information. It reassures and offers belonging; it appears to tame and frame an otherwise ungraspable event. Simultaneously, misinformation is also prone to produce less-positive emotions toward perceived out-groups. On the state level, it often eats away at a society's generalized trust in institutions, the crucial "resting places"[35] that societies need in order to function every day

---

[31] Christian Vaccari, "Online Content and Political Polarization," in *Social Media, Political Polarization, and Political Disinformation: A Review of the Scientific Literature*, ed. Joshua A. Tucker et al., Mar. 2018, https://eprints.lse.ac.uk/87402/1/Social-Media-Political-Polarization-and-Political-Disinformation-Literature-Review.pdf.

[32] See Tufekci, "How Social Media Took us from Tahrir Square to Donald Trump."

[33] Francesca Polletta and Jessica Callahan, "Deep Stories, Nostalgia Narratives, and Fake News: Storytelling in the Trump Era," *American Journal of Cultural Sociology* 5 (2017): 392–408.

[34] Ibid., 402.

[35] Wagner-Pacifici, "Theorizing the Restlessness of Events."

and protect themselves from falling into an infinite regress of doubting common grounds. The application of a specifically cultural sociological perspective in which the public sphere is conceptualized as a site of social drama and performance seems fruitful here.[36] In this framework, "fusion" describes an ideal state in which audiences (the public) go along with the performances of public figures (for example, politicians) as if they were actors on stage in a Shakespeare play. In that state, legitimacy is secured through authentic performances. The rejection of established authorities, however, marks a dissolution of fusion, which will alienate people from politicians, institutions, and elites. This dissolution will make their appearances and public statements appear phony, call their intentions into question, and thus discredit their legitimacy. In the case of fact-checking during the pandemic, Maria Luengo and David Garcia-Marin have argued that fact-checking sites either promote fusion when they find "truth" in claims of public figures and institutions—therefore reestablishing trust—or inhibit fusion when they judge a claim as fake—asking people to mistrust an individual or other sources.[37] Such analyses certainly offer a highly valuable perspective on the phenomenon of misinformation and account for the cultural importance truth claims hold, especially in moments of crisis, whether crises of health or democracy. These analyses can give us a sense of the advantages openly partisan political commentators hold when communicating to audiences as if in personal conversation around the dinner table—a perfectly authentic mise-en-scène,[38] which will determine how audiences perceive the contents presented.

Institutionalized social inequalities are not irrelevant to this struggle over interpretive power, belonging, othering, and deviance. Vulnerable populations and marginalized groups are consistently more at risk of being "othered" through the means of misinformation as well as "neutral" representations, such as pandemic tracking practices and maps. If we think back to the example of the world map showing flight routes, people from Wuhan—the place that came to stand for contamination in 2020—were framed as a threat to the rest of the ("Western") world by tabloid media in the UK and Australia, and thus went from victims to villains in the false claims about their mobility. More than individual users on social media, mass media equipped with interpretive power and resources of dissemination

---

[36] Jeffrey C. Alexander, "Cultural Pragmatics: Social Performance Between Ritual and Strategy," in *Social Performance. Symbolic Action, Cultural Pragmatics, and Ritual*, ed. Jeffrey C. Alexander, Bernhard Giesen, and Jason L. Mast (Cambridge: Cambridge University Press, 2006).

[37] Maria Luengo and David Garcia-Marin, "The Performance of Truth: Journalism, Fact Checking Journalism, and the Struggle to Tackle COVID-19 Misinformation," *American Journal of Cultural Sociology* 8 (2020): 405-27.

[38] See Polletta and Callahan, "Deep Stories, Nostalgia Narratives, and Fake News," 399.

have the tools for reproducing inequality on the level of meaning. They powerfully create, activate, and sustain myths and characters that people can draw on.

Media as Infrastructure

Finally, the term "media" denotes not only a sphere of meanings and contentions but also a material infrastructure. The persisting digital divide in 2017 left a quarter of U.S. Americans without access to broadband internet at home, and about 20 percent without a smartphone.[39] Among those earning less than thirty-thousand dollars year, almost 30 percent do not own a smartphone to partake in the thoroughly digitized public sphere that, during the pandemic, has become ever more crucial to stay informed, engaged, connected, and—for many—employed. In many parts of central Sub-Saharan Africa, less than 10 percent of the population is connected to the mediatized world we have come to take for granted as shaping a universally human experience.[40]

In that sense, these populations are excluded from an aspect of modern life that enables participation to a fuller extent. Cut off from broadband, many are prohibited from enjoying "visual citizenship"[41] nationally and globally. This term encapsulates the idea that in order to fully inhabit a democratic society, to understand who shares society with us and how we fit in, we are highly dependent on mediated visual representations. The concept in this sense expands on Benedict Anderson's notion of nations as "imagined communities"[42] by putting the visual aspect front and center in how we jointly imagine our collective existence and coordinated activity through media. Not being able to access the latest information, however, is not only detrimental to social, cultural, and political participation but can indeed be fatal in a pandemic.[43]

---

[39] Minh Hao Nguyen et al., "Changes in Digital Communication During the COVID-19 Global Pandemic: Implications for Digital Inequality and Future Research," *Social Media + Society*, Jul.–Sep. 2020: 1–6, https://journals.sagepub.com/doi/pdf/10.1177/2056305120948255.

[40] The World Bank, "Individuals Using the Internet (% of population)," https://data.worldbank.org/indicator/IT.NET.USER.ZS.

[41] Jennifer E. Telesca, "Preface: What is Visual Citizenship?," *Humanity Journal*, Jun. 12, 2014, http://humanityjournal.org/issue4-3/preface-what-is-visual-citizenship/.

[42] Benedict Anderson, *Imagined Communities: Reflections on the Origin and Spread of Nationalism* (London: Verso, 1983).

[43] Jacqueline Wernimont, "Media Infrastructure Is and Has Always Been a Matter of Life and Death," *SSRC Items*, Apr. 15, 2021, https://items.ssrc.org/covid-19-and-the-social-sciences/mediated-crisis/media-infrastructure-is-and-has-always-been-a-matter-of-life-and-death/.

Thus, media create boundaries of belonging, not only through their cultural effects but also in a very material sense. Of course, these exclusions are interrelated, and the agency to connect and disconnect is still human in the first place. While during the pandemic we might feel that the media helped us socially connect, emotionally relieve, and cognitively orient, they also split societies and deepened patterns of exclusion. Some people were subject to new forms of discrimination as they were labelled "contagious," while others were dismissed as cognitively defunct "covidiots," and still others were altogether, for better or worse, excluded from these discourses.

Conclusion

As we have tried to show in this brief chapter, the media play a dizzying array of roles in contemporary societies. Journalists present powerful mythologies, share practical facts, and offer narratives and explanations as members of an interpretive community.[44] In successful moments, journalists' narratives and performances fuse with their intended and even unintended audiences. In less successful moments, journalists may contribute to the spread of misinformation, a deepening of division, and a reinforcement of tribal boundaries. As media are both tools for the spreading of narratives and visuals and a material, physical infrastructure, it is often hard to draw the boundaries between mediated and nonmediated communication. Arguably, there is no form of communication that is not mediated, as meanings get embodied even in facial expressions. As we engage in everyday interactions, our messages get transmitted and translated through layers of media.

During the coronavirus pandemic, professional journalists and individual social media users have played important roles in communicating to groups and individuals. They have offered mythical narratives of national resilience in the face of a "foreign" threat, providing hope and sustaining a strong will to carry through. At the same time, social media especially have also been a source of concern in their tendency to provide seemingly irrational and culturally and politically dividing reactions. Corporations in charge of infrastructures have collaborated with governments to normalize extensive surveillance regimes that tend to entrench existing social divides. Delicate analysis is required in each case of mediated interaction to consider how the media have shaped societies, communities, and individuals, and what tools are available to make their impact more valuable for everyone.

---

[44] Barbie Zelizer, "Journalists as Interpretive Communities," *Critical Studies in Mass Communication* 10 (1993): 219–37.

Contemporary Media and the Crisis of Values

Bert Olivier

> What have new media done to the communication of love? They have deepened them and given them new immediacy. But online, with an archive of messages on hand, we feel we know more than we really do about our partners. Online, we are more likely to say cruel things. Digital exchanges disinhibit when love might be better served by tact.
> —Sherry Turkle, *Reclaiming Conversation*[1]

> Western universities are in the grip of a deep malaise, and a number of them have found themselves, through some of their faculty, giving consent to—and sometimes considerably compromised by—the implementation of a financial system that, with the establishment of hyper-consumerist, drive-based and "addictogenic" society, leads to economic and political ruin on a global scale.
> —Bernard Stiegler, *States of Shock*[2]

Introduction: Axiological Equivalence

Renata Salecl, in her book on *Choice*,[3] already sounded the alarm that should have alerted one to a declining sense of value in extant society specifically (but not only) where she focuses on relationships between young people. What Salecl terms the "tyranny of choice" in the present era is the focus of her investigation. The capitalist society of today thrives on variety, and everywhere we are confronted by a baffling plethora of things, products, items, and services, including short-term sex partners or companions to choose from. While this variety of choices may be seen as a manifestation of economic and social freedom, she shows that

---

[1] Sherry Turkle, *Reclaiming Conversation: The Power of Talk in the Digital Age* (New York: Penguin Press, 2015), 206.

[2] Bernard Stiegler, *States of Shock: Stupidity and Knowledge in the 21st Century*, trans. D. Ross (Cambridge: Polity Press, 2015), 2.

[3] Renata Salecl, *Choice* (London: Profile Books, 2010).

it comes at a significant price, namely, pervasive anxiety and depression in the face of the unavoidable need to choose from the glut of options on offer. If one chooses "incorrectly," risking the scorn of fellow consumers or, worse, the possibility that one's decision may turn out calamitously, anxiety or depression may—and often does—follow.

According to Salecl, this situation has reached the point where one may justifiably talk about a "culture of anxiety." She sums it up as follows:

> How is it that in the developed world this increase in choice, through which we can supposedly customise our lives and make them perfect leads not to more satisfaction but rather to greater anxiety, and greater feelings of inadequacy and guilt? ... In today's society, which glorifies choice and the idea that choice is always in people's interests, the problem is not just the scale of choice available but the manner in which choice is represented. Life choices are described in the same terms as consumer choices: we set out to find the "right" life as we would to find the right kind of wallpaper or hair conditioner. Today's advice culture presents the search for a spouse as not all that different from the search for a car.[4]

To anyone who is aware of the essential difference between a person and a consumer object—and one might expect that this would include most people—Salecl's observation that, in contemporary culture, "the search for a spouse ... [is] not all that different from the search for a car" signals a putative equivalence that should ring alarm bells. At the same time, if this is the tendency in society, it would unavoidably influence all of those who live in it. This may be understood in terms of Jacques Lacan's insight, that one's desire is really the "Other's desire"[5]—that is, what social norms (the Other) dictate at the level of the unconscious—which, in the present context, manifests itself in the concern that one's choice of product (or sex partner, for that matter) might be judged by others as being somehow wrong or in bad taste. In other words, what one values, even tentatively—as manifested in what one chooses—is subject to the approbation or the disapproval of the Other, or society at large.

Clearly, this condition has far-reaching implications for one's sense of what is valuable. If everything is reduced to axiological equivalence by limitless, obligatory choice, it means that even one's deeply felt preference for, say, a specific person as a life partner is cast into doubt. Sometimes this potential for second-guessing may reach the ostensibly unlikely point where people may experience the unavoidable task of choosing as traumatic. Salecl enumerates some of the reasons for this perplexity: the wish to make an "ideal choice"; the fear that one's choice is

---

[4] Ibid., 3, 8-9.

[5] Jacques Lacan, "The Direction of the Treatment and the Principles of Its Power," in *Écrits: The First Complete Edition in English* (New York: W. W. Norton, 2007), 489-542, at 525.

not really free, but always already predetermined by others; the question of others' comparative opinion about one's choice; and the ethically disturbing feeling that there is no final social authority (who could preclude the need to make one's own decisions).[6]

The tyranny of choice holds sway everywhere; not even personal relationships are exempt from its negative psychological effects. Salecl's discussion of what amounts to "hooking up"—although it is subsumed under the rubric of "love choices"—exemplifies what is most conspicuous about dating today, insofar as it scrupulously steers clear of real intimacy (which is always accompanied by the risk of getting hurt) in favor of what she calls "the mechanics of contact." In her own words: "'Hook-up' culture is all about choice. We have so many options in every aspect of life that the choice of emotional attachment is not only an added burden but also an impediment to the total freedom we are meant to value. Someone who gets attached too quickly has supposedly not fully profited from that freedom."[7]

This way of viewing things helps one—particularly the young—avoid the investment of feelings, and therefore largely any possible emotional consequences, including those interpersonal ones that are arguably essential for human development and fulfillment, even if they are sometimes painful. Although this avoidance is done for the sake of "choice and control," Salecl insists, hook-up culture is (paradoxically) inseparable from uncertainty. Notwithstanding the fact of supposedly liberating young people from the burden of attachment, it encumbers individuals with something else: "insecurity, anxiety and guilt." Furthermore, regardless of the connotation of casual contact (minus emotional attachment) that accompanies hooking up, one sometimes gets emotionally involved despite one's "best" intentions. Given the norms governing relationships considered to be casual encounters, such a person is not supposed to admit such attachment to herself or himself, let alone to the person they have developed feelings for. Unsurprisingly, in such cases, emotional involvement leads to feelings of guilt, anxiety, and inadequacy which, in the context of the indispensable role of values in human lives, function as barriers to the potential mutual enrichment between individuals in a close personal relationship. To be sure, relationships sometimes flounder, creating emotional suffering, but even this is a way of discovering what is valuable in human life—it is the literary principle on which the *Bildungsroman* is based: that one becomes an emotionally and spiritually mature human being only through trials and tribulations.

In the course of answering the question why choice makes us anxious, Salecl examines the psychological mechanisms accompanying the experience of being overwhelmed by a plethora of options—for example, when buying a product such

---

[6] Salecl, *Choice*, 17.
[7] Ibid., 76.

as cheese. Feelings characteristically progress from confusion in the face of a dizzying variety of possibilities, through exasperation at oneself for one's indecisiveness, to suspicion and resentment of supposed help offered by authorities available for consultation. Such an experience illustrates, according to Salecl, "some of the reasons why overwhelming choice can increase our anxiety and feelings of inadequacy."[8] Invariably, the person in such a situation reverts to either a random choice, because of volitional paralysis when confronted by a vertigo-inducing range of alternatives, or to the banal option, triggered by an "automatic" awareness of the most advertised product. Interestingly, the central paradox of the culture of choice, as articulated by Salecl, is perhaps this:

> Choice about the organisation of society is offered and denied at the same time. Liberal democratic capitalism glorifies the idea of choice, but with the proviso that what is on offer is primarily a consumerist model of choosing. The choice of a new form of social organisation, of different ways in which society might develop in the future and especially the possibility of rejecting capitalist society as we know it all appear not to be available as choices.[9]

This suggests that there is a strong ideological element at play in the culture of choice—one that is impervious to the price human beings are paying for its putative benefits. Given the implicit equivalence of value pertaining to everything comprising the spectrum of choice in all areas—from consumer products to human beings—I would argue that the biggest price one pays is a systematic anaesthetization of one's axiological sense: the sense that some things are more valuable than others. In this respect, Salecl's work focuses on an important symptom of what is arguably a contemporary crisis in values—that is, value-awareness.

Axiological Alienation through Mediating Technology

Although the culture of choice is glorified in contemporary societies, there is clearly another side to it that suggests that choice is—paradoxically, given the negative feelings it gives rise to—overvalued. This is ironic, given that the concomitant avoidance of getting involved with another person precludes one of the primordially human preconditions for discovering what is meaningful or valuable in life, namely, intimate relationships, where one learns to value what is distinctive about another human being, and vice versa. At another level, the same irony applies to close friendships. Amplifying the axiological importance of allowing oneself to get close to another human being, instead of skipping lightly from the one

---

[8] Ibid., 15.
[9] Ibid., 149.

to the other, Sherry Turkle comments on this aspect of being human in a different —although related—context, that of the question concerning the place of technology (in the guise of robots) in humans' lives:

> I am a psychoanalytically trained psychologist. Both by temperament and profession, I place high value on relationships of intimacy and authenticity. Granting that an AI might develop its own origami of lovemaking positions, I am troubled by the idea of seeking intimacy with a machine that has no feelings, can have no feelings, and is really just a clever collection of "as if" performances, behaving as if it cared, as if it understood us. Authenticity, for me, follows from the ability to put oneself in the place of another, to relate to the other because of a shared store of human experiences: we are born, have families, and know loss and the reality of death. A robot, however sophisticated, is patently out of this loop. ... What kinds of relationships with robots are possible, or ethical? What does it mean to love a robot? ... A love relationship involves coming to savor the surprises and the rough patches of looking at the world from another's point of view, shaped by history, biology, trauma, and joy. Computers and robots do not have these experiences to share.[10]

This observation may seem to be unrelated to the question of media and values, and to be in the realm beyond extant society. Yet one should think further, particularly because of the link Turkle establishes between computers and robots—both of which are crucially dependent on electronics—and from there to smartphones, which are sophisticated computers and mediate what is available on the internet. Then Turkle's insight does not appear to be far-fetched at all. Add to this that users establish such close "relationships" with their smartphones that they evidently cannot bear being without them, and it is hard to avoid the impression of axiological alienation from those interpersonal relationships that are constitutively *human*, in favor of being quasi-pathologically attached to mediating devices and the social media that are accessed in this manner, such as Facebook and Twitter. Take Kate Pickert, for instance, who gives an account of her attachment to multiple mnemo-technical devices:

> As a working parent of a toddler, I found life in my household increasingly hectic. And like so many, I am hyper-connected. I have a personal iPhone and a BlackBerry for work, along with a desktop computer at the office and a laptop and iPad at home. It's rare that I let an hour go by without looking at a screen. Powering down the internal urge to keep in constant touch with the outside world is not easy.[11]

---

[10] Sherry Turkle, *Alone Together: Why We Expect More from Technology and Less from Each Other* (New York: Basic Books, 2011), 5-6.

[11] Kate Pickert, "The Art of Being Mindful—Finding Peace in a Stressed-Out, Digitally Dependent Culture May Just Be a Matter of Thinking Differently," *TIME*, Feb. 3, 2014, 32-38, at 34.

Turkle[12] offers confirmation of the hold that mediating technical devices seem to have on people's attention, particularly that of young children, as she discusses teachers' experiences of the apparent inability of pupils at an American school to establish "companionship" in the course of normal, face-to-face communication. To the teachers' alarm, the pupils preferred texting one another on their phones instead. The cost of this retreat into media-cyberspace, according to the teachers, was a noticeable incapacity to show empathy to fellow pupils, as well as a conspicuous inability to communicate intelligibly when addressed by teachers—one teacher described a pupil's response to a question concerning the exclusion of another from a school event as *"almost robotic."*[13]

This situation, where children seem to have lost the ability to use language in its original mode, relying instead on technically mediated exchanges, may indeed be a form of communication. But if it leads to a blunting of their affective capacities, it means that what may be potentially valuable in their relationships would forgo the all-important emotional bonding required for close friendship. It stands to reason that a culture where there is an increasing reliance on technical information-exchange would take its toll on what used to be regarded as the feelings and emotions concomitant with building interpersonal relationships. These will suffer if—as Turkle argues—conversation in three-dimensional social space were replaced by texting in that very space, in this way escaping into cyberspace, or what Manuel Castells calls the dominant spatial mode of the present era, namely "the space of flows."[14] If conversation disappears, potentially mutually rewarding interpersonal relationships would be reduced to the level of ships passing in the night, as the saying goes.

It is in this situation of hyperconnectivity and its concomitant deterioration of the human qualities of communication that Turkle promotes a return to conversation, which is directly linked to what Sigmund Freud famously called the "talking cure":

> Why a book on conversation? We're talking all the time. We text and post and chat. We may even begin to feel more at home in the world of our screens. Among family and friends, among colleagues and lovers, we turn to our phones instead of each other. We readily admit we would rather send an electronic message or mail than commit to a face-to-face meeting or a telephone call.
>
> This new mediated life has gotten us into trouble. Face-to-face conversation is the most human—and humanizing—thing we do. Fully present to one another, we learn to listen. It's where we develop the capacity for empathy. It's where we experience the

---

[12] Turkle, *Reclaiming Conversation*, 4–6.

[13] Ibid., 5.

[14] Manuel Castells, *The Rise of the Network Society*, 2nd ed. (Oxford: Wiley-Blackwell, 2010), 407–59.

joy of being heard, of being understood. And conversation advances self-reflection, the conversations with ourselves that are the cornerstone of early developments and continue throughout life.[15]

The contrast that Turkle draws here between a life lived between various screens—enabling one to communicate with others but simultaneously separating one from their embodied, conversationally accessible presence—is of crucial importance for understanding the perceptible deterioration in people's awareness of the lifelong value of interpersonal dialogue and discussion. She leaves no doubt that indispensable human capacities, such as sympathy and empathy, are cultivated in interpersonal situations. She discusses the serious questions surrounding the communicationally debilitating effects of pervasively relying on technically mediated exchanges among people, particularly the young. For present purposes what she has to say in the context of education, specifically on the question of *attention* (in a chapter aptly titled "Attentional Disarray")—an issue also explored by Bernard Stiegler (see below)—is of utmost importance in relation to the cultivation of axiological sensitization and awareness on the part of students. Referring to her students' realization that their continued texting (on their smartphones) while their fellow students were presenting their life stories, was not acceptable (itself a welcome sign that she had managed to get through to them when stressing the importance of sharing their life stories in class), she writes:

> My students became upset because, in this class, their usual split attention (looking at their phones, listening to their classmates) felt wrong. It devalued their classmates' life stories (and their own) and made them feel that they were crossing some moral line. They could imagine a day when people around you would be upset and you would still be pulled away to your phone.
> A lot is at stake in attention. Where we put it is not only how we decide what we will learn, it is how we show what we value.[16]

Turkle is right to link attention and the lack of it to ethics and to values. But she does not go far enough to penetrate to what is at stake in the continued existence of a culture where a certain kind of attention is a precondition for its flourishing. Bernard Stiegler focuses on this issue at length in the context of what he pointedly calls "the epoch of an *attention dis-economy*" (a play on what is commonly known as "the *attention economy*"—where market players compete nonstop for the attention of consumers).[17] To grasp what is at stake here, one has to recall that the formation of a specific type of attention in students has been the task of systems of

---

[15] Turkle, *Reclaiming Conversation*, 3.
[16] Ibid., 212.
[17] Stiegler, *States of Shock*, 151–52.

education going back to ancient times, and continuing until today, except that today educators seem to be losing the battle against the economic forces competing for a purchase on consumers' (including students') brain time. Stiegler reminds one that this kind of attention was originally called *logos*, and later "reason." Human beings are capable of reason, but—as one witnesses in all cultures—require education, or being educated (*Bildung*), to achieve "reason-ableness." "Disciplines" are crucial in this process of forming or shaping reason, insofar as they are the repositories of cultural knowledge or schools of thought to which individuals have contributed throughout history, and still do once they have worked through the disciplines that have shaped their attention.

For Stiegler, schools and universities play a crucial role in cultivating such culture-enlivening attention on the part of students:

> Reason is the attentional form emerging from those processes of transindividuation and that result in rational disciplines. ... Attention is always both psychic and collective: "to be attentive to" means both "to focus on" and "to attend to." As such, the formation by schools of attention also consists in educating and elevating pupils [*élèves*]; in the sense of making them civil, that is, able to consider others and capable of taking care—of oneself and of that which is *in oneself*, as of that which *is not oneself* and of that which is *not in oneself*.[18]

It is no accident that Stiegler's allusion to engendering the capacity for caring in students here resonates with Turkle's discussion of the lack of empathy on the part of young American pupils who are preoccupied with their smartphones, and of her own students' rediscovery of the ethical need to pay attention to their fellow students' presentations. After all, schools and universities comprise the spaces where teachers and professors systematically introduce students to what is valued in cultural traditions, from natural science through philosophy and the human sciences to the arts. It therefore stands to reason that this educational project presupposes the more-or-less sustained attention of students at all levels for it to succeed. This presupposition, in Stiegler's estimation, is becoming increasingly questionable: "As a result of this diseconomy of attention, it becomes increasingly difficult for schools to solicit attention from students—attention seems to be exclusively captured and depleted by an industrial apparatus designed essentially for this purpose, which is the very reason it has been named the 'attention economy.'"[19]

---

[18] Ibid., 152. Stiegler uses the term "transindividuation" to mean the transfer of knowledge critically between generations of individuals as the archivers of knowledge and constituted in the form of disciplines by such transfer. See Stiegler, *States of Shock*, 21.

[19] Ibid.

What does this have to do with axiological alienation? Attention is a prerequisite for forming diverse axiological attachments. Just how complex the current global situation is regarding value alienation becomes apparent when one considers that values—which function as values only to the degree that they are appropriated by way of attention—are qualitatively variegated, although they are all exposed to being captured by the apparatus Stiegler refers to, which is in the service of a hegemonic economic system. This qualitatively differentiated axiological spectrum means that some people value excursions into the wilderness to reconnect with nature, while others prefer the comfort of their homes to discover nature at a distance, as it were, by viewing films such as David Attenborough's *Planet Earth* series. Some music lovers prefer the virtually mathematical construction of Johann Sebastian Bach's Baroque compositions, such as his *Goldberg Variations*, while others eschew such classical music in favor of the progressive rock sounds of the band Muse, with its eclectic mix of genres and forms, including metal and rock opera. Some people and institutions promote the values of the STEM disciplines (science, technology, engineering, and mathematics), at the cost of the human sciences, while others valorize the latter ahead of the former. But all of the values inscribed in the qualitative spectrum, of which the above examples comprise a minuscule slice, are undermined, if not invalidated, by the economic system inextricably conjoined with the industrial apparatus cited by Stiegler, above.[20] The economic system, which has been alluded to implicitly by Renata Salecl as the source of the bewildering choice one faces everywhere, is neoliberal capitalism.

Slavoj Žižek writes about this system in a manner that draws attention to the experiential cognitive mechanism at the root of the present disruption of humanity's ageless axiological orientation regarding meaningful lives:

> Alain Badiou has reflected that we live in a social space which is progressively experienced as "worldless." In such a space, the only form protest can take is "meaningless" violence. ...
>
> Perhaps it is here that one of the main dangers of capitalism should be located: although it is global and encompasses the whole world, it sustains a *strictu sensu* "worldless" ideological constellation, depriving the large majority of people of any meaningful cognitive mapping. Capitalism is the first socio-economic order which *de-totalises meaning:* it is not global at the level of meaning (there is no global "capitalist world-view," no "capitalist civilisation" proper—the fundamental lesson of globalisation is precisely that capitalism can accommodate itself to all civilisations, from Christian to Hindu or Buddhist, from West to East); its global dimension can only be formulated at the level of truth-without-meaning.[21]

---

[20] See also Bernard Stiegler, *For a New Critique of Political Economy*, trans. D. Ross (Cambridge: Polity Press, 2010).

[21] Slavoj Žižek, *Violence—Six Sideways Reflections* (New York: Picador, 2008), 79–80.

Moreover, this fundamental economic liquidation of the systems of meaning that have traditionally provided a field within which human beings can orient themselves according to the spectrum of values transmitted to them by generations of parents, teachers, instructors, and professors—as mediators regarding the archives and sources of these values, including music, architecture, literature, philosophy, cinema, and the human and natural sciences—is occurring in conjunction with the use of the very media and mediating devices (foremost among them smartphones) that Turkle and Stiegler have highlighted as being instrumental in subverting common human faculties, such as empathy and attentiveness.

According to Stiegler, what is inseparable from these lamentable developments concerns schools and the university, and particularly the question of thinking, and learning to think, in this context:

> Any question concerning the university, its past, its present or its future, is bound to go back over and pose in a new way, and in this new context, the question of knowing what it means to think. To think is to participate in the production of an attentional form, and to transmit or even invent an attentional form. What must be thought today, however, and this is a trait specific to our age, is the fact that attention has become the major stake of a global economic war of unprecedented violence ... and the fact that this war is taking place in schools. And it is a war against school itself insofar as schooling is first and foremost a struggle against the destruction of attention, and in general a struggle with minds insofar as they are capable of reasoning.[22]

Anyone who has read, and understood, René Descartes's seventeenth-century text *Rules for the Direction of the Mind*,[23] which stresses the indispensable role of sustaining a line of thinking in order to connect founding mental intuitions deductively, or Martin Heidegger's *Holzwege* (translated as *Off the Beaten Track*),[24] would know what thinking entails—and it is certainly not the mental activity of exchanging truncated sentences or phrases, interspersed with a string of emojis, via smartphones. What I mean by this can be understood in the light of Heidegger's striking metaphor of *Holzwege* (woodpaths) for true thinking. Such paths are painstakingly made by woodcutters so as to avoid damaging the forest, respecting the trees and undergrowth by working meanderingly around them. The forest represents being, or reality, and the woodpaths stand for the manner in which one thinks of reality by refraining from doing any violence to its character. This

---

[22] Stiegler, *States of Shock*, 152–53.
[23] René Descartes, "Rules for the Direction of the Mind," in *The Philosophical Works of Descartes*, vol. 1, trans. E. S. Haldane and G. R. T. Ross (Cambridge: Cambridge University Press, 1911), 1–77, at 33–49.
[24] Martin Heidegger, *Off the Beaten Track*, trans. and ed. J. Young and K. Haynes (Cambridge: Cambridge University Press, 2002).

contrasts with the manner in which a highway is built through a forest by indiscriminately cutting everything down that stands in its designated way. The latter represents conventional (non-)thinking, which proceeds regardless of whether it respects the ontological character of reality, as distinct from the true thinking depicted by woodpaths. While universities have the conventional task of training or preparing students for contributing their work-share to the economy of their countries, it is not the university's *only* task to travel on the highway of work; it is precisely its duty to teach students to think against the deceptive smoothness of convention, respecting the nature of reality by exploring the forest via epistemically undulating woodpaths.

Stiegler's point, above, is precisely that the "global economic war" being waged at universities and in schools is anathema to thinking, insofar as that war imposes a conventional pattern of attention-capturing information-fragments— "whatever marketing devises," combined with "purely procedural technological knowledge"[25]—on the consciousness of smartphone-wielding consumers, including students. In other words, Stiegler argues that in the service of capitalism, smartphones and other electronic "mnemo-technical" devices appear to be colonizing human capacities, such as knowing and memory, and that this is occurring with the tacit (if uncomprehending) approval of human beings themselves.[26] Put differently—and this bears directly on the indispensable role of archiving knowledge in all its epistemological and axiological variegatedness—the "technologization" of knowledge and values has dislocated the conditions of the possibility of "transindividuation" that is indispensable for the maintenance and renewal of disciplines of all kinds—the very linguistic-rational disciplines that comprise the repository of traditional values, even if it is granted that such values are always subject to (the values of) disputation, critique, and revision. Furthermore: "this disruption has interfered with the critical faculty itself as the capacity to distinguish between knowledge, opinion and dogma."[27] In the era of "fake news" and "posttruth," his observation sounds all too familiar.

Experiencing Something as Valuable, Desire, and Fetishization

In light of the above, one might legitimately ask: apart from presupposing attention as the human capacity for concentrating on meaningful or valuable aspects of existence, what are the prerequisites for experiencing something as valuable? Earlier I alluded to Lacan's notion of desire as inextricably linked to experiencing

---

[25] Stiegler, *States of Shock*, 135–36.
[26] Stiegler, *For a New Critique of Political Economy*, 35.
[27] Stiegler, *States of Shock*, 21.

something as valuable, or, privatively speaking, desire's absence—that is, when one confronts something intensely repugnant, desire is no less implicated than when something is irresistibly desirable. This requires elaboration.

Consider that, according to Turkle's and Stiegler's understanding, the axiological landscape of contemporary young people is clearly impoverished as far as a sense of value is concerned—and I use the word "sense" advisedly, because value is not only, or primarily, a *concept* which applies to someone or something that is valued or cherished; value is *sensed*, as Kaja Silverman so perspicaciously observes in her book, significantly titled *World Spectators*, where "spectators" denotes human beings who bestow meaning and value on the world through perception or "spectating."[28] In other words, the very act of *perceiving* things in the world—visually, audially, or in a tactile manner—endows them with meaning and value. This is not difficult to understand. Who has not delighted in the sight of a flock of birds winging in miraculous unison through the evening sky, executing dynamic pirouettes in the changing light of the setting sun? Or relished the birdsong in the early morning? Our sensing these wonders of nature constitutes them, and the world they inaugurate and sustain, as meaningful and uniquely valuable. The same goes for sensorily experiencing and enjoying cultural practices and events, such as the delight we gain from seeing dancers on stage, exemplifying what beauty human movement, coordinated with music, is capable of embodying; or standing in awe, observing the improbable contours of Frank Gehry's deconstructive architectural marvel known as the Guggenheim Museum Bilbao. Compare this with the relative sensory deprivation accompanying the preoccupation with smartphone screens at which young—but not only young—people stare for disproportionate periods of time, in the process severely reducing their potential value-generating perception of the world in all its variegatedness.

In this regard, it is noteworthy that Silverman points to Heidegger's claim, in *Being and Time*, that "being-in-the-world" coincides with being human, something that instantiates the paradox that this is both a universal human state of being *and* simultaneously a thoroughly particular condition.[29] This paradox is also emphasized by psychoanalysis in terms of the singularity of human desire: *all* human beings approach the world through their unique, albeit unconscious, desire, which means that each person's desire is unrepeatably singular—it is "the metonymy of our being," as Lacan puts it[30]—and that the ethical imperative the subject

---

[28] Kaja Silverman, *World Spectators* (Stanford, CA: Stanford University Press, 2000).

[29] Ibid., 23, referencing Martin Heidegger, *Being and Time*, trans. J. Macquarrie and E. Robinson (Oxford: Basil Blackwell, 1978).

[30] Jacques Lacan, *The Ethics of Psychoanalysis*, Book 7 of *The Seminar of Jacques Lacan*, trans. D. Porter (New York: W. W. Norton, 1992), 321. See also Mari Ruti, *The Singularity of Being: Lacan and the Immortal Within* (New York: Fordham University Press, 2012).

faces is therefore to "take it up."[31] To clarify further, Silverman draws attention to Heidegger's choice of word for the individual human being, namely *Dasein* (there-being), which means that "Each human being occupies a specific *da*, or 'there.'"[32] This she understands, in psychoanalytic discourse, as an indication "that the 'there' from which each of us looks is finally semiotic; it represents the unique language of desire through which it is given to the subject to symbolize the world."

Silverman's allusion to Hannah Arendt's acknowledgement of having learned from Augustine that the *identity* of a person can be determined only by ascertaining what the object of his or her *desire* is, must be seen as highly significant in the present context. This is so, given that *either* the singularity of individuals' desire has been replaced by the general, or common, desire *for* mnemotechnical devices and what they mediate, and therefore (worse) that such humanizing desire has been extinguished by the *fetishization* of these apparatuses, *or* the devices function as "triggers," from the perspective of which the subject's unconscious desire may be "deciphered" (which instantiates the "normal" structure of desire). Overwhelmingly, evidence indicates that the former is the case—humanizing desire has been extinguished by fetishization. What would this mean in psychoanalytical terms?

According to Silverman, the implications of Heidegger's concept for a human being, *Dasein*, corroborates that the subject's "essence"—or, in psychoanalytical language, the subject's desire—has to be conceptualized "in a profoundly nonessential way."[33] In other words, Silverman's insights confirm that, what individual human subjects uniquely *are*, must somehow be understood in a decentered manner: singularizing desire is activated by something outside of the subject. Put differently, the subject may be understood by way of a fantasy relationship with what Lacan calls the *objet petit a* (object a)—the "little other object" that "triggers" the subject's singular, but unconscious, desire—for example an aroma, a painting, a melody, a certain kind of flower, or the silhouette of a mountain, which mysteriously awakens in one an unfathomable yearning for "something" (ultimately the profound, ineffable "lost object" or *das Ding*[34]). It must be emphasized that this is the normal structure of desire—where one's desire is initiated by something outside of one, or inside one in the guise of a persistent memory, which—paradoxically—refers to an external, past event. This understanding of desire also has im-

---

[31] Lacan, *The Ethics of Psychoanalysis*, 311-25; Bert Olivier, "Lacan and the Question of the Psychotherapist's Ethical Orientation," in Bert Olivier, *Philosophy and Psychoanalytic Theory: Collected Essays* (London: Peter Lang Academic Publishers, 2009), 53-89.

[32] Silverman, *World Spectators*, 23.

[33] Ibid., 24.

[34] Lacan, *The Ethics of Psychoanalysis*, 66-67; Dylan Evans, *An Introductory Dictionary of Lacanian Psychoanalysis* (London: Routledge, 1996), 207.

portant consequences for the visual aspect of identification with the images of people or of animals—for example, of a universally respected person who stands for integrity, or of a lion, which represents strength—insofar as what appears within the visual field of the subject is potentially something that influences the subject's never-ending, or intermittently repeated, series of "identifying" acts, themselves underpinned by the subject's unconscious desire. If human identity is rooted in what is "outside" the subject, in what can be desired as the "remarkable," all images encountered in the visual space before one are potentially desirable—not merely insofar as they are *images*,[35] but especially insofar as they are axiologically charged or represent something valorized in various ways, which resonates with the subject's singular desire.

Returning to the alternatives one faces at present regarding a person's singularizing desire in relation to the pervasiveness of mediating technical devices, it seems that one of two possibilities would have to be the case. If desire is activated by something outside of the subject, and (say) smartphones are considered as such triggers, then they would evoke one's desire for what the smartphone *as mediating device* represents metonymically, such as (the illusion of) perfect communication, or of access to all information, for example. This would conform to the structure of desire. If, alternatively, the above relation has been replaced by a generalized desire *for* technically mediating devices, which would lead to these devices being extinguished as metonymies for a person's desire—that is, to having their status changed from triggers of desire to fetishes—one faces a disturbing prospect. Why? To begin with, if the desire of consumers were to display a general shift from desire for commodities (such as food or a reliable motor car) as *means* to the satisfaction of a family's needs (the normal structure of desire), to one where the commodities were to be desired *as such* (for themselves), it would imply (in psychoanalytical terms) that commodities would function as fetishes, which is a distinctly unhealthy situation. Again, why?

The answer has to do with the relation between commodities and the capitalist system, on one hand, and the relation between fetishes and perversion, on the other. Commodities may be said to instantiate metonymies of the capitalist economic system, and insofar as smartphones are *commodities* (and not considered as mediating devices), this applies to them, too. On the other hand, it is significant that, as Ian Parker notes,[36] for the later Freud, perversion was tantamount to the refusal or disavowal of castration—recalling that the latter represents disempowerment or lack, which the pervert disavows, thereby committing himself or herself to a belief in the attainability of *plenum*, or fullness. *Lack*, in turn, is constit-

---

[35] Jean-Luc Nancy, *The Ground of the Image*, trans J. Fort (New York: Fordham University Press, 2005), 6.

[36] Ian Parker, *Lacanian Psychoanalysis: Revolutions in Subjectivity* (London: Routledge, 2011), 49.

utive of the human subject, insofar as it lacks "being," in Lacanian terms,[37] which means that the fetishist (committed to "lack of lack") no longer acts in conformity with the structure of desire. Instead, the fetish interposes itself between the desiring subject and what is deemed valuable in the world—which therefore recedes as value-infused "destination" of human perception or spectatorship.[38] The fetishist's world comprises fetishes (including smartphones) that effectively function as *barriers* to the world of valued entities and events. Put graphically, insofar as many, if not most, smartphone users today are predisposed toward these gadgets as fetishes—and the earlier discussion of the work of Sherry Turkle and Bernard Stiegler suggests that this is indeed the case—and *not* primarily as means to the end of communication, the users show that they not only do not value the things comprising the human world (trees, rivers, wildlife, and so on) but also are *incapable* of doing so because of their preoccupation with the gadgets (considered as fetishes) in question.

To be clear, insight into fetishistic behavior is afforded by a character named Ugolin in the film *Manon of the Spring*.[39] Ugolin becomes infatuated with the eponymous Manon, a shepherdess on his uncle's farm, and follows her around, surreptitiously acting as voyeur. He does not have the courage to tell her about his desire for her, but when she inadvertently loses a pink ribbon used to tie her hair, he takes it and sews it to one of his nipples, where it eventually causes infection. The ribbon is the fetish, a *plenum* (because it no longer *triggers* his desire for something else), to which he has redirected his desire for Manon, and the festering metaphorically indexes the abnormal character of this situation. Analogously, the obsessive preoccupation with (the ostensible plenum of) electronic communication devices, such as smartphones, today instantiates a kind of infection of life-sustaining values, in which one may read the makings of a looming—if not already existing—axiological crisis.[40]

Conclusion: The Hollowness of Influence

In this chapter, I have surveyed the axiological landscape of contemporary society through the lenses of choice (Salecl), alienation via mediating technology (Turkle and Stiegler), and desire, together with fetishization (Lacan), among other things.

---

[37] Evans, *An Introductory Dictionary of Lacanian Psychoanalysis*, 98-99.
[38] See Silverman, *World Spectators*.
[39] Claude Berri, dir., *Manon of the Spring*, film (France: Pathé Distribution, 1986).
[40] Bert Olivier, "'Passiewe nihilisme' in die huidige era," *Tydskrif vir Geesteswetenskappe* 59, no. (2019): 471-92; and Bert Olivier, *Why Nothing Seems to Matter Any More—A Philosophical Study of Our Nihilistic Age* (Baltimore, MD: Montagu House, 2020).

To bring it all together, the Polish film *Sweat*[41] requires brief scrutiny, insofar as it concentrates, in the figure of the contemporary "influencer," the loss of a quintessentially human sense of value. As a phenomenon, the influencer is inseparable from what Manuel Castells calls the "network society" of the current era; influencers are internet and social media celebrities with followers numbering in the thousands, for example on Instagram—which is the platform that features in the plot of *Sweat*. All they (have to) do is film themselves doing something or, in many cases, doing nothing, except (for the likes of American influencer Kylie Jenner) to show off their curvaceous figures, which people are willing to pay to see. Others, like the protagonist of *Sweat*, Sylwia, engage in an activity such as motivational fitness performances—mostly on camera for her fans, but occasionally in public, at a mall, where she is shown sweating profusely and intoning her quasi-ecstatic feelings in response to the crowd's adulation while working out. The film's exploration of the tension between Sylwia's high-powered, driven persona in the context of her huge fan base, on one hand, and the diametrically opposed isolation and loneliness she experiences when not engaged in some performance (sometimes to earn her living from advertisers, whose products she wears or uses in front of the camera), is arguably paradigmatic of the lives of influencers, phenomenologically speaking.

Regarding the theme of this chapter, the axiological wasteland of the present is graphically portrayed in the contrast between Sylwia performing for her followers and craving some kind of genuine connection with another human being when she is alone. She has sacrificed the value of a mutually fulfilling relationship on the altar of internet celebrity. In the process, she is alienated from other people by the audiovisual mediating technology, which disallows anything but a one-way relationship of fetishistic image-voyeurism on the part of her fans, and anaesthetizes any potential desire for an other on her part by predisposing her to focus, via smartphone selfies (for example), on her toned, suitably attired body. But when she is alone in her luxurious apartment, the film shows, with admirable sensitivity and directorial restraint, this thwarted desire, manifested in her melancholy facial features. After all, as one exchange with an old acquaintance reminds Sylwia, the point of all the possessions her fame has brought her, is to share them with another human being. That is what brings value to one's life. But arguably the near-total mediation of human lives in the present age, consummately captured by von Horn in *Sweat*, has poisoned the well of such value.

---

[41] Magnus von Horn, dir., *Sweat*, film (Poland: Lava Film, 2020).

Part Four:
Ethical Potentials and Problems in Media Communication

Why Moral Agency Is Crucial to Mainstream Cinema

James Mairata

Introduction

This chapter examines the significance of morality in mainstream feature films—specifically, the crucial role of morality in feature-film storytelling, how it was established, how it is manifested within the form, and why its importance has remained undiminished and relatively unchanged since the invention of the moving image more than a century ago. These areas are considered in two sections: the social conditions around the establishment of cinema exhibition, and the evolution of cinematic storytelling as a form. In choosing to focus on mainstream cinema, the chapter considers the default industry to be Hollywood/American feature filmmaking, as it has dominated world cinema culturally, financially, and in terms of form since the First World War.[1]

As of 2020, the world's four largest media conglomerates—all American owned—also controlled the Hollywood studios: AT&T, with TimeWarner, including HBO and Warner Bros.; Comcast, with NBC Universal Media and DreamWorks Animation; ViacomCBS, with Paramount Pictures; and the Walt Disney Company, a conglomerate in its own right. While feature films may not be the greatest source of revenue for these companies, they are evidently significant: 2019 was a record year for the American industry, with over 101 billion USD in revenue across home entertainment and domestic and international box office.[2] While the

---

[1] In 2020, Chinese box office revenue surpassed that of Hollywood for the first time, unseating more than a century of Hollywood's worldwide cinema revenue dominance. While COVID-19 severely impacted both Hollywood's film production and exhibition sectors, revenue trends from the last few years show that the Chinese industry was in any case on-course to eclipse Hollywood—the pandemic effectively accelerated the process.

[2] Rosa Escandon, "The Film Industry Made a Record-Breaking $100 Billion Last Year," *Forbes*, Mar. 12, 2020, https://www.forbes.com/sites/rosaescandon/2020/03/12/the-film-industry-made-a-record-breaking-100-billion-last-year/?sh=2c22623134cd.

Honorable mentions to Netflix and Amazon Prime. Netflix continues to grow quickly and

Chinese film industry now rivals Hollywood in terms of box-office revenue, it still lags significantly behind the worldwide reach and scope of the American industry.

Controlling the Photoplay

The Kinetoscope began to be used in 1895 in the United States and Europe to show "actualities"–short moving pictures–in Vaudeville venues and in travelling shows. In the United States, dedicated film houses known as nickelodeons,[3] showing slightly longer fiction films, began to appear in working-class, immigrant areas around 1905. The popularity of these early movie houses grew exponentially. In New York the number grew from fifty establishments in 1900 to more than four hundred eight years later, while the daily patronage rose to over two hundred thousand. Initially, the "crude peep shows"[4] were located in the working-class/immigrant areas, but their popularity ensured that they quickly spread to the middle classes and were so popular that by 1914, cinema was clearly the "first true mass amusement in American life."[5]

The low admission cost of five cents contributed to the popularity of the nickelodeon across all demographics, including among children, exacerbating the already growing concern from various reform groups over the claimed detrimental effect that the uncontrolled growth of immigration was having on Victorian middle-class values. In the early years, around half of the screened content originated from Europe,[6] which tended to emphasize Catholic values in contrast to local Protestant standards. American Victorian sexual restraint was undermined by short subjects that referenced premarital sex, adultery, and interracial relationships. Progressive reformers were concerned with the perceived undermining of "family values" and with the involvement of women, because the reformers claimed that the medium encouraged "primitive passion." The superintendent of schools for the state of Nebraska claimed that films promoted "too much familiarity between

---

will reportedly spend 17 billion USD in 2021, while Prime spent 11 billion on content in 2020.

[3] A nickel was the term for a U.S. five-cent coin, the price of admission, and *odeon* derives from the ancient Greek word for a place for musical performances–hence the word "nickelodeon."

[4] Lary May, *Screening Out the Past: The Birth of Mass Culture and the Motion Picture Industry* (New York: Oxford University Press, 1980) 3-95.

[5] Ibid., xii.

[6] Domestic production expanded quickly and by 1913 accounted for 90 percent of screened content.

boys and girls."[7] Jane Addams, editor of the social-work journal *Survey*, further contributed to the perception of the nickelodeons as degrading and immoral by claiming that they were located in "undesirable localities," where men could offer "girls certain indignities," [8] as unchaperoned women, men, and unaccompanied children mixed freely in audiences.

Not only were reformers critical of what was screened and the venues themselves, but there was also criticism of the form itself. The films depicted moving images—actual people that appeared "realistic"—and elicited emotional responses in the audience, making the form more of a "threat" than the theater or the novel. "Shown in a darkened room, its screen images penetrated the subconscious with its silent message."[9]

The criticism of nickelodeons was actually part of a wider movement against the perceived spread of vice across America's rapidly growing cities. The concerted attacks on the movie houses finally boiled over in New York City on Christmas Day, 1908, when the chief of police succumbed to pressure from a group of Protestant denominations and closed all 550 of the city's nickelodeons. Social workers, vice crusaders, and clergymen called for a public hearing on the movies, and the mayor informed all of the closed movie houses that they would have to reapply for their licenses, which would be restored only if they could prove that they had reformed their premises so that they were "morally and physically clean."[10] Following the closure of movie houses in other cities, cinema owners realized that "the suggestion of immorality was bad for business,"[11] and that it was in their best interests to cooperate with reformist groups. The National Board of Review was subsequently established, with an overwhelmingly Protestant executive and representation from organizations such as the YMCA, the Federal Council of Churches, and the New York School Board. But the review board was administered largely by the film industry, and this process of self-censorship and "regulating morality"[12] continues to this day.[13]

---

[7] May, *Screening Out the Past*, 40.
[8] Ibid., 44.
[9] Ibid., 53.
[10] Ibid., 57.
[11] Ibid., 53.
[12] Johan Andersson and Lawrence Webb, "American Cinema and Urban Change: Industry, Genre, and Politics from Nixon to Trump," *The City in American Cinema: Film and Post-industrial Culture*, ed. Johan Andersson and Lawrence Webb (London: Bloomsbury 2019), 1–42.
[13] The Motion Picture Association (MPA) includes the main film studios and Netflix, with censorship regulation the responsibility of the Classification and Ratings Administration.

At the same time, some progressive reformers argued that because cinema was a "mass" medium and reached all areas of society quickly, it could be harnessed to send out the "right" messages—essentially to promote progressive values. "[T]he power of the movie medium could bring about a secular conversion among the masses," and "cinema could spread American values through the universal language of cinema."[14] This perception found support from one of Hollywood's most famous filmmakers, D. W. Griffith.

Griffith made over three hundred films with Biograph between 1908 and 1913 and was a key innovator in the process of developing cinema from simple, unsophisticated short works to elaborate, prestigious, long-form events, as embodied famously in *Birth of a Nation* (1915), the most successful film of the silent era. Griffith apparently described himself as a "secular preacher" and claimed that he was reforming the film industry in conjunction with reforms sweeping the cities which were intended to counter gambling and "light ladies." "Griffith used his tools to manipulate the medium and show God's will surfacing in the chaos of material life."[15] The scenarios of Griffith's films tended to adhere to two main outcomes: the hero either triumphed or was ruined for not achieving an ideal standard.

Storytelling as Form

When visiting the nearest cinema, or if viewing a mainstream feature film at home or on a device, we invariably bring to our viewing a number of preconceptions, and extra- and intertextual expectations. These tend to be relatively specific: that the film will run for approximately two hours; that there will be a coherent story in the Aristotelian sense that has some kind of resolution; that it delineates specific characters, two or three of whom are given prominence in the narrative and are expected to behave in a way that makes sense and seems logical to us. More specifically, the narrative always proceeds through a chain of cause and effect, and the principal characters are goal-orientated and act for a reason—their actions are motivated. The duration of the narrative is traditionally structured into three to five acts, which involve (1) setting-up the plot and characters, with a plot device usually centered around the introduction of some kind of conflict that creates an imbalance that needs to be restored; (2) development of the plot as the protagonist undertakes some kind of journey (physical and/or psychological) while having to overcome various complications; and (3) the protagonist achieving their goal, returning their world to balance. So highly standardized is this form of storytelling that these "rules" can be found in Hollywood screenwriting

---

[14] May, *Screening Out the Past*, 53.
[15] Ibid., 74.

manuals from as early as the 1910 s[16] and have varied minimally since. The conventions are in fact so powerful within mainstream, popular cinema that if one or more of them are absent, we tend to feel dissatisfied and are likely to reflect poorly on the experience of viewing the film.

Even more persuasive is the assumption that the plot and characters will be underpinned by some kind of morality. Normally it is good versus evil, as the protagonist behaves morally and strives to right any wrong that they or the antagonist has committed or intends to commit. Related to this moral dimension is the expectation that immoral characters will not be rewarded and/or will eventually be punished for their behavior. While these conventions can be found in the overwhelming majority of mainstream cinema films, variations and exceptions are fairly common. For example, we are encouraged to find the psychotic Hannibal Lecter character in *The Silence of the Lambs* (1990) likeable, as the film ends with him still at large. Similarly, the series Dexter successfully functions around having us empathize with a protagonist who is a calculating serial killer—essentially asking us to rationalize our acceptance by portraying him as a victim of his condition, whose victims are themselves murderers. The plot of the Woody Allen film *Crimes and Misdemeanors* (1989) revolves around a respectable, married ophthalmologist who has his mistress murdered when she threatens blackmail. Initially plagued by guilt and regret, he finds the feelings eventually fading, and the film ends with him unpunished, successful, and free of any remorse. In *Three Billboards Outside Ebbing, Missouri* (2017), the film ends with the plot unresolved and the implication that the protagonist is about to commit a crime.

Just as in Griffith's films, characters in today's cinema continue to be overwhelmingly defined by their morality. Chloe Zhao, winner of the best picture and best director awards at the 2021 Academy Awards for her feature *Nomadland*, commented on the characterization in the film by recalling a phrase from her childhood: "[P]eople at birth are inherently good. Those six [words] had such a great impact on me when I was a kid. I still truly believe them today, even though it sometimes might seem the opposite is true. But I have always found goodness in the people I've met everywhere I went in the world."[17] While *Nomadland* claimed the major awards, it cannot really be categorized as mainstream; however, Zhao's invitation to direct the thoroughly mainstream Marvel superhero film *Eternals* suggests that the emphasis and significance of character morality remain crucial within mainstream cinema.

---

[16] David Bordwell, *The Way Hollywood Tells It: Story and Style in Modern Movies* (Los Angeles: University of California Press, 2006), 1–50.

[17] Gary Maddox, "At a Deeply Political and Surprising Oscars, *Nomadland* Triumphs," *The Sydney Morning Herald*, Apr. 26, 2021, https://www.smh.com.au/culture/movies/at-a-deeply-political-and-surprising-oscars-nomadland-triumphs-20210420-p57kwv.html.

The symbiotic relationship between mainstream cinema and morality dates back not only to the beginning of cinema but much earlier, to the origins of storytelling. Michelle Sugiyama argues that while the origin of storytelling remains unclear, early evidence of the correlation between storyteller bias and self-interest "suggests that storytelling originated as a means of pursuing fitness interests by manipulating other individuals' representations of their environment. Narrative is a social as well as cognitive phenomenon: storytelling is the intersection at which the study of language and the study of social exchange meet."[18] The early manifestation of storytelling as weapon already suggests the potential for the involvement of morality in both the content and practice of storytelling—directly echoing both the content of cinema and its manifestation as industry.

Sugiyama further notes that traditional storytelling was time consuming, which meant that there needed to be a good reason for individuals to be taken away from more significant tasks, such as working, securing food, and so on. In other words, storytelling entertained, but it also functioned as a kind of "social intelligence." "Storytelling can thus be seen as a transaction in which the benefit to the listener is information about his or her environment, and the benefit to the storyteller is the elicitation of behavior from the listener that serves the storyteller's fitness interests."[19] The status given to stories as social intelligence simultaneously enhanced the status of the storyteller.

Fatih Mehmet Ciğerci and Recep Yilmaz note the twenty-thousand-year-old cave paintings in Lascaux, France, and their depiction of life at that time as among the oldest known examples of storytelling.[20] Yet it is myths that represent the earliest complete form. Often heavily imbued with religious themes, myths seek to explain the fundamentals of human existence and the world—the origin of people, of death, sin, customs, socialization, education, and culture—while also serving as entertainment. At the same time, the importance of conforming and abiding by laws and religious beliefs are reinforced by the inevitable retribution that befalls any transgressors. "An important part of the process of the legends is the motivation to oppose the Supreme Being. According to this, at the beginning people lived and went in peace ... but people rebelled and this brought death."[21]

Contrary to common belief, myths are actually intended to be based on truth—often religious truths—even though they take place in a different world and time

---

[18] Michelle Scalise Sugiyama, "On the Origins of Narrative, Storyteller Bias as a Fitness-Enhancing Strategy," *Human Nature* 7, no. 4 (1996): 403–25.

[19] Ibid., 412.

[20] Recep Yılmaz and Fatih Mehmet Ciğerci, "A Brief History of Storytelling: From Primitive Dance to Digital Narration," in *Handbook of Research on Transmedia Storytelling and Narrative Strategies*, ed. Recep Ylmaz, M. Nur Erdem, and Filiz Resulolu (Hershey, PA: IGI Global, 2019), 1–14.

[21] Ibid., 4.

and often with characters and animals that possess supernatural powers.[22] Traditional storytelling, such as oral forms, were modified and reshaped as they were passed down from generation to generation. "The adaptability of a story to the needs and intent of a storyteller and an audience is vital to the nature of storytelling."[23]

Kristin Thompson and David Bordwell point out that the Hollywood film had essentially settled into its current form by around 1917. "Filmmakers came to assume that a film should guide the filmviewer's attention, making every aspect of the story on the screen as clear as possible."[24] Hollywood cinema in the silent era placed an emphasis on ensuring that the storytelling was clearly accessible. This also resulted in the development of more sophisticated characterization through enhanced character psychology and traits, as it became evident to filmmakers that audiences were better able to follow a narrative if cause and effect and goal orientation motivated and explained character action.

The move to story films, or the "photoplay," from single-reel shorts started in the United States around 1903, as audiences responded favorably to the longer films. *The Great Train Robbery* (1903) was an early example of a longer film, running for about twelve minutes and consisting of fourteen separate shots.[25] Narratives that featured a beginning, middle, and end were preferred because of the perceived enhanced level of spectacle and entertainment that they offered. Often adaptations of classic literature and historical events, the multireel films superseded the previously dominant vaudeville segments and "cheap melodrama." Crucially, the longer films enabled more complex storytelling, and along with a defined structure, they also prioritized cause and effect, because it "showed the ethical order lying at the core of the universe. ... [U]nlike the earlier one-reel 'shorts' which merely titillated the senses, the photoplay carried a moral lesson. In this, critics saw that film might become an adjunct to libraries, schools, and museums."[26] Happy endings were encouraged to better demonstrate the importance of virtuous conduct, while a tragic ending was acceptable, provided that it affected those that had practiced "bad habits."[27]

Just as D. W. Griffith had intended, the move to longer films had a number of implications. It attempted to distance cinema from its "common" nickelodeon ori-

---

[22] Kate Elson Anderson, "Storytelling," in *21ˢᵗ Century Anthropology: A Reference Handbook*, vol. 1, ed. H. James Birx (London: SAGE, 2010), 277–86.

[23] Ibid., 8.

[24] Kristin Thompson and David Bordwell, *Film History: An Introduction* (New York: McGraw Hill, 2010), 22–39.

[25] Charles Musser, *The Emergence of Cinema: The American Screen to 1907* (Los Angeles: University of California Press, 1990), 337–70.

[26] May, *Screening Out the Past*, 65.

[27] Ibid., 65.

gins and lowbrow appeal by more closely aligning the storytelling with "high" art and thereby initiating the perception of cinema as a worthy and credible art form. Most significantly, the greater complexity in the storytelling enabled the integration of moral agency, both into the scenario and into an underlying logic that served to assist audience comprehension.

In considering moral agency in storytelling, Lynne Tirrell compares the perspectives of Hume and Kant and observes that "the Humean would emphasize the way a story engages one's sympathy, while the Kantian would emphasize the way a story explores concretely the rationality of particular actions in particular situations."[28] While the implication is that their positions seem to be in opposition, in terms of mainstream cinema both are highly relevant. Hume's position is more emotive, while Kant's is based more on rationality. Yet mainstream narratives manipulate both emotive and rational processes in highly effective ways to maximize audience engagement. "To understand people, whether others or oneself, one must put their actions into the appropriate contexts and produce hypotheses about their reasons for acting."[29] A number of scholars, Meir Sternberg and David Bordwell in particular, have considered the significance of the process of hypothesis forming in relation to cognitive theory and narrative comprehension.[30] This theoretical perspective considers how the audience members actively predict what will happen next. Depending on what is occurring on-screen, they can make numerous hypotheses for any given moment. If a hypothesis is proven incorrect, then the tendency is to quickly replace this with another hypothesis. Confirmed or denied, the process of repeated hypothesis forming continues throughout a viewing and can operate at multiple levels—within a scene, within sequences, and simultaneously in considering possible outcomes across the entire film.

Hypothesis forming draws on our ability to make sense of the narrative we are watching. We create our hypotheses on the basis of information presented to us, from which we extrapolate probabilistic outcomes, but also from our own filmic experience,[31] our experience of the world, and our ability—as moral agents—to judge character, behavior, and motivated action. Yet another significant aspect of viewing cinema is that it provides us with the opportunity to "simulate" immor-

---

[28] Lynne Tirrell, "Storytelling and Moral Agency," *The Journal of Aesthetics and Art Criticism*, 48, no. 2 (1990): 115–26.

[29] Ibid., 117.

[30] David Bordwell, *Narration in the Fiction Film* (London: Routledge, 1985), 37–38.

[31] For example, our extratextual knowledge of genre and its conventions informs us that in a horror narrative, if the image is suddenly plunged into darkness, the protagonist is isolated and afraid, and the soundtrack becomes prominent, we can hypothesize with a high degree of accuracy that something is about to happen—and we will likely further hypothesize on what this might be.

ality. "The usefulness of film here lies in the way it can, not only present hypothetical scenarios to pose the 'why be moral?' question, but also chart responses offering concrete evocations of human experience to support claims about the importance of morality in our lives."[32]

Falzon notes Plato's writing on the conflict between immorality and self-interest, and Hollywood cinema often explores this conflict.[33] One timely example can be found in the film *Contagion*, released in 2011, and its depiction of the collapse of law and order after a virus devastates the world. The film experienced a surge in viewings early in 2020, following the outbreak of COVID-19. The renewed interest in the film obviously stems from the real-life parallel, but the film also generates curiosity by presenting "hypothetical scenarios" around extreme character behavior triggered by theoretical scenarios.

Conclusion

Cinema's initial, unprecedented penetration into "mass" society meant that it easily eclipsed, in terms of reach, any popular form of storytelling that had come before. The spectacular adoption of early cinema and the grand predictions of its potential to influence probably panicked some establishment figures, who felt it might erode or even usurp their authority and power. "The promiscuous mingling of genders, classes, and ethnicities in these theatres, coupled with the 'vicious' and 'vulgar' nature of the films themselves made the moving pictures a particularly visible target for those concerned with the maintenance of the cultural status quo."[34] At the same time, early cinema owners and filmmakers that had initially exploited the perceived immorality and titillation of early films now realized that they had to distance themselves from this criticism by reforming their product—in terms of both what was screened and the quality of the venue it was screened in. At first glance, it seems remarkable that this self-regulation was achieved while simultaneously still retaining cinema's popularity. The move to "quality" films, as personified by Griffith's own practice, and the decision to source famous and respectable novels and theatrical works for cinema meant that the storytelling conventions from those forms was also transplanted into cinema. Yet the achievement seems less remarkable when we consider that—as Joseph Campbell claimed —virtually all storytelling is itself derived from the concept of the so-called

---

[32] Chris Falzon, "Why Be Moral?," in *Routledge Companion to Philosophy and Film*, ed. Paisley Livingston and Carl Plantinga (New York: Routledge, 2011), 591–600.

[33] Ibid., 596.

[34] William Uricchio and Roberta E. Pearson, *Reframing Culture: The Case of the Vitagraph Quality Films* (Princeton, NJ: Princeton University Press, 1993), 3–40.

monomyth.[35] With the parameters of moral agency embedded into the very sense-making processes that audiences apply to cinema, and with the demand for mainstream cinema still growing—even if we now consume it in different ways—the status and function of morality continue to operate relatively unchanged since its initial application to cinema at the beginning of the twentieth century.

---

[35] Joseph Campbell, *The Hero with a Thousand Faces*, 2nd ed. (Princeton: Princeton University Press, 1968), 36–38.

Trolls and Bullies: A South African Case Study of Cyber-Misogyny and the Media

Lizette Rabe

> Three "estates" lie at the foundation of a just and orderly society, namely marital families, religious communities, and political authorities.
> —Martin Luther, 1483-1546[1]

> Ecquid Novi? – what is news?
> —Thomas Peucer, 1660(?)-1696[2]

> There were Three Estates in Parliament; but, in the Reporters' Gallery yonder, there sat a Fourth Estate more important far than they all.
> —Thomas Carlyle (1797-1881), quoting Edmund Burke (1729-97)[3]

Introduction

This chapter builds on the above statements, expressed over a period of time, which presume a society built on certain values and principles, but which have nevertheless failed to ensure, or secure, the rights of women. Or, more correctly, the human rights of the majority of the world's population.

The argument focuses on how women are exposed to the new phenomenon of cyber-misogyny, and specifically on how it affects and inhibits, and even incapacitates, female journalists. A South African case study of female journalists is

---

[1] Michael Welker et al., foreword to this volume.
[2] Peucer answered this question in the first dissertation on journalism, at the University of Leipzig in 1690. News was defined as "the birth and death of princes" and the "death of famous men, and the end of the notorious." See Arnold S. de Beer, Louis F. van Ryneveld, and Wadim N. Schreiner, "Leipzig: From Tobias Peucer's *De Relationibus Novellis* (1690) to *Ecquid Novi* (2000)," *Ecquid Novi* 21, no. 1 (2000): 11-4. The rest of the definition is also masculine.
[3] Lizette Rabe, *Quote Unquote–Quotations on Freedom of Speech, Journalism, the News Media and a World of Words* (Stellenbosch: SUN Media RAP, 2016), 18.

used to represent the Global South with regard to this issue, from within the field of media studies, with the focus on one high-profile example. Centering on cyberbullying as it plays out against women journalists—cyber-misogyny—I make use of the media sociological theories of media and feminism as well as media hegemony theory (MHT).

As foundational context, this chapter first discusses these theoretical points of departure, after which I address the three "value" statements above. This is followed by a contextual positioning of the (South African) mediascape, and then a case study of female journalists in South Africa, focusing on one journalist in particular, before the chapter offers some concluding observations.

Theoretical Contexts

This chapter draws on the fields of media and gender, specifically media and feminism and media hegemony theory, against the background of what is called the Fourth Industrial Revolution, or the Digital Revolution. This revolution affects the media fundamentally—both in terms of platforms on which professional mainstream news media are disseminated, and in terms of how these media are consumed.

To provide some context, Klaus Schwab, founder and executive chair of the World Economic Forum, describes the Fourth Industrial Revolution as follows:[4]

> We stand on the brink of a technological revolution that will fundamentally alter the way we live, work, and relate to one another. In its scale, scope, and complexity, the transformation will be unlike anything humankind has experienced before. We do not yet know just how it will unfold, but one thing is clear: the response to it must be integrated and comprehensive, involving all stakeholders of the global polity, from the public and private sectors to academia and civil society.

Whereas the first Industrial Revolution used water and steam to mechanize production, and the second used electricity for mass production, the third used electronics and information technology to automate production, while the fourth built on the digital revolution of the third. This fourth revolution is characterized "by a fusion of technologies that is blurring the lines between the physical, digital, and biological spheres." Three factors, namely, "velocity, scope and systems impact," indicate that the current transformations are not a prolongation of the Third Industrial Revolution but, rather, a fourth, distinct one. As Schwab explains:

---

[4] Klaus Schwab, "The Fourth Industrial Revolution: What it Means, How to Respond," World Economic Forum, 2016, https://www.weforum.org/agenda/2016/01/the-fourth-industrial-revolution-what-it-means-and-how-to-respond/.

The speed of current breakthroughs has no historical precedent. When compared with previous industrial revolutions, the Fourth is evolving at an exponential rather than a linear pace. Moreover, it is disrupting almost every industry in every country. And the breadth and depth of these changes herald the transformation of entire systems of production, management, and governance.

These factors also severely affect the rapid transformation of the news industry (or mainstream media/mass communication industry) from previous technologies. This totally new mediascape has also influenced, both positively and negatively, new ways of media praxis. The scope of this chapter does not allow delving deeper into this phenomenon, but suffice it to state that the media industry faces never-foreseen challenges to survive in terms of new business and content models.

It is at the interface of these nexuses, against the background of the value statements in the epigraphs, that this chapter contributes to new thinking on women's position in late modern pluralistic societies—as can be concluded from the case study on women in media, and why certain ingrained societal patriarchal values should be questioned.

Theoretical Frameworks

Women's subjugated position in society is accepted as a given, despite, for example, the UN's Universal Declaration of Human Rights, formulated in 1948,[5] or in South Africa's Constitution of 1996.[6] The United Nations' thirty-eight-point declaration after the Fourth World Conference on Women in Beijing, in 1994,[7] articulated numerous commitments in its "Platform for Action." The conference expressed determination to advance the goals of equality, development, and peace for all women and girl children "everywhere, in the interest of all humanity." This included ensuring "women's equal access to economic resources, including ... information [and] communication . . . as a means to further the advancement and empowerment of women and girls, including through the enhancement of their capacities to enjoy the benefits of equal access to these resources."

---

[5] Universal Declaration of Human Rights, https://www.un.org/en/about-us/universal-declaration-of-human-rights.
[6] Constitution of the Republic of South Africa No. 108 of 1996, https://www.gov.za/sites/default/files/images/a108-96.pdf.
[7] Fourth World Conference on Women, Beijing Declaration, https://www.un.org/womenwatch/daw/beijing/platform/declar.htm.

Women's role in the media has been described in various studies.[8] As this study focuses on South Africa, it is appropriate to pay homage to one of the first feminists in South Africa, the journalist and author known as MER, or Maria Rothmann, who emphasized that women's rights should be regarded as human rights and not made second class, as happened so often during her lifetime.[9] MER, who died in 1975, just days after her one-hundredth birthday, was appointed almost a century ago, in 1922, as the first "women's page editor" of the Cape Town daily, *Die Burger*.

Before advancing the argument, it is first worth noting the significance of qualitative research, the paradigm within which this project falls. I begin with the Weberian concept of *verstehen* as it is applied to media scholarship. To apply this concept as conceived by Weber more than a century ago to the digital age might seem unsuitable; compared to the digisphere, the beginning of the twentieth century might even seem prehistoric. But this concept, introduced by Weber at the first conference of the German Sociological Society in 1910, where he presented

---

[8] Linda Steiner, "Body Language—Gender in Journalism Textbooks," in *Women in Mass Communication*, ed. Pamela J. Creedon (Newbury Park, CA: SAGE, 1993), 301–16; K. Viswanath, Gerald M. Kosicki, and Pamela J. Creedon, "Women in Mass Communication Education: Progress, Problems and Prospects," in Creedon, *Women in Mass Communication*, 237–63; Liesbet van Zoonen, *Feminist Media Studies* (London: SAGE, 1994); W. J. E. Randle, "Women and Gender in the African Media," *Rhodes Journalism Review* 27 (1999): 27; George Spears, Kasia Seydegart, and Margaret Gallagher, *Who Makes the News? Global Media Monitoring Project 2000* (London: World Association for Christian Communication, 2000); Sibongile Mpofu, "Are 'Untouched Citizens' Creating their Deliberative Democracy Online? A Critical Analysis of Women's Activist Media in Zimbabwe" (PhD diss., Stellenbosch University, 2017); Bimbo L. Fafowora, "Media Construction and Representation of Women in Political Leadership Positions: A Study of Selected News Media Outlets in Nigeria" (PhD diss., Stellenbosch University, 2020); Monika Djerf-Pierre and Maria Edström, "Introduction: Comparing Gender and Media Equality across the Globe: Understanding the Qualities, Causes and Consequences," in *A Cross-National Study of the Qualities, Causes, and Consequences of Gender Equality in and through the News Media*, ed. Monika Djerf-Pierre and Maria Edström (Gothenburg: Nordicom, 2020), https://www.gu.se/en/research/comparing-gender-and-media-equality; Carolyn McGourty Supple and Elisa Lees Muñoz, "To Get More News Coverage of Women, We Need More Women Making News," https://www.evoke.org/articles/2021/april/to-get-more-news-coverage-more-women-making-news; and Luba Kassova, *The Missing Perspectives of Women in the News* (Washington, DC: International Women's Foundation, 2020), https://www.iwmf.org/missing-perspectives/.

[9] Lizette Rabe, *Rykie—'n Lewe met Woorde [Rykie—A Life with Words]* (Cape Town: Tafelberg, 2011), 46–53.

a detailed description of a survey of the press,[10] is indeed, and possibly especially, applicable to the digital media. Weber conceptualized a framework in which to ask probing questions about the sociopolitical environment. His experience as a journalist as well as a sociologist assisted him in conceptualizing the "meaning," or "understanding" (*verstehen*) of the press of the day. This notion of *verstehen* is still applicable to a postmodern, digital society, especially as it is argued in qualitative research that it is the researcher who "makes meaning" or "understanding" in terms of the "bigger picture."

Since this chapter pivots on two theoretical frameworks—first, media, gender and feminism, and, second, MHT—I present a brief overview of them here.

The construction of gender is of course rooted in feminism, which, briefly and succinctly, can simply be described as the advocacy of women's rights, on the grounds of the equality of the sexes, to emancipate women from age-old gender-based injustices.[11] Feminism strives to counter traditional hegemonic views of gender according to which power and control are in the domain of men, while women are subjugated.[12] It is not necessary here to digress into foundational arguments on the notions of gender, namely, the normative or biological determinist perspective and the constructivist perspective. Briefly, the former sees both sex and gender as biologically acquired and assumes that gender identity, sexual orientation, and gender roles are the results of nature.[13] The constructivist notion, on the other hand, argues that while sex is biologically determined, gender is "a function of interactions or performativity within the social system," as has been contended since Simone de Beauvoir's seminal *The Second Sex* (1972).[14]

Regarding women's contribution to the media, feminism per se has been studied only in the past few decades. An early feminist, and someone who can be described as one of the first women in media, British "protojournalist" Lady Mary

---

[10] Siegfried Weischenberg, "The Disenchantment and Measurement of the Media World: Weber's Universal Press Project, Its Fate and Its Legacy," *Max Weber Studies* 13, no. 2 (2013): 237–42.

[11] Julia T. Wood, *Gendered Lives: Communication, Gender and Culture*, 9th ed. (Boston: Wadsworth, Cengage Learning, 2011); Judith Butler, "Sex and Gender in Simone De Beauvoir's Second Sex," *Yale French Studies* 72 (1986): 35–49; Judith Butler, *Gender Trouble: Feminism and the Subversion of Identity*, 4th ed. (New York: Routledge, 2010).

[12] bell hooks, *Feminist Theory: From Margin to Center*, 3rd ed. (New York: Routledge, 2015); and James Watson and Anne Hill, *Dictionary of Media and Communication Studies*, 8th ed. (London: Bloomsbury, 2012).

[13] Mari Mikkola, "Feminist Perspectives on Sex and Gender," in *Stanford Encyclopedia of Philosophy*, 2017, https://plato.stanford.edu/entries/feminism-gender/.

[14] Among others, Laurel Westbrook and Kristen Schilt, "Doing Gender, Determining Gender: Transgender People, Gender Panics, and the Maintenance of the Sex/Gender/Sexuality System," *Gender and Society* 28, no. 1 (2014): 32–57.

Wortley Montagu, said in the eighteenth century about the subservient role of women in society: "Hide your learning, daughter, as if it were a physical defect."[15]

Women were of course the exception in Britain's eighteenth-century protomedia industry.[16] In America, female names were just as scarce before 1800, although research indicates they played a larger role there than in Britain.[17] At least fourteen women were publishers and printers of newspapers–the result of their becoming widows of publishers and continuing publication after their spouses' deaths.[18] In England, female empowerment by women was already evident in the nineteenth century. Women of the Langham Place group financially supported the *English Woman's Journal*, which first appeared in 1858. Male colleagues felt that marriage should be a woman's only career, stating, for example, that "It would be an excellent thing if all single women could get married as fast as they can, and the rest hold their tongues in a dignified manner."[19] In 1857, a woman who owned the Victoria Press, publisher of the *English Woman's Journal*, trained the first female printers. Male printers expressed their dissatisfaction, saying "[t]he mixing of genders in the printing works threatens the moral values and consciousness of the innocent woman and worsens the base passions of humanity."[20] Despite such protestations, there were more than five hundred female printers in the United Kingdom by the end of the nineteenth century.

One can easily infer from the above that early female "journalists" were also feminist activists who contributed to the franchise being obtained in the following century.[21] As an early woman journalist wrote in a British magazine of her time: "I ask no favours for my sex: All I ask our brethren is that they will take their feet from off our necks, and permit us to stand upright on that ground which God designed us to occupy."[22]

An early form of empowering women was introduced by Eleanor Roosevelt, spouse of the American president, who allowed only female reporters to her press

---

[15] Lizette Rabe, "Eve-olution: The Status of Female Voice in South African Media," *Ecquid Novi* 23, no 1 (2002): 152-69.

[16] Marita van der Vyver, "Die Groeiende Rol van die Vrou in die Afrikaanse Pers met Spesifieke Verwysing na *Die Burger* en die Nasionale Pers" ["The Growing Role of Women in the Afrikaans Press with Specific Reference to *Die Burger* and Nasionale Pers"] (Master's thesis, Stellenbosch University, 1987), 6.

[17] Kay Mills, *A Place in the News: From the Women's Pages to the Front Page* (New York: Columbia University Press, 1990).

[18] Van der Vyver, "Die Groeiende Rol," 10.

[19] Ibid., 23.

[20] Ibid., 27.

[21] Rabe, *Rykie–'n Lewe met Woorde*, 33-60.

[22] Van der Vyver, "Die Groeiende Rol," 31.

conferences in a bid to create more posts for women.[23] According to this source, this policy drastically altered attitudes toward women reporters: "She brought women into government and brought their ideas to bear on government." It also created job opportunities. Newspapers and news agencies were compelled to appoint at least one woman, or to retain women's posts during the Depression. The increase in the numbers of women is indicated by the following: only one American woman journalist was accredited in World War I; in World War II, more than twenty were accredited.[24] The war proved that women could fulfill any conceivable "male" position. More important, it swayed public opinion in favor of the working woman.

Various stages of feminism have developed since these early feminist writings. These have also played out in various ways in different environments. Among others, the field of gender and media studies has attempted to understand how the media influence peoples' perceptions of gender, as well as how media spaces and content can be used to overcome gender inequalities.[25] Julia Wood's findings that media representation of gender usually falls under three themes are still relevant:[26]

- the underrepresentation of women (creating the impression that men are the dominant gender);
- the portrayal of gender in stereotypical ways; and, last,
- the "normalization" of "traditional" gender roles, plus, relevant to this contribution, violence against women.

Feminist theory therefore developed from a movement focusing on the liberation of women from oppression and inequality as a result of male hegemony. As a body of scholarship, it has been adapted by scholars in different geopolitical-historical contexts for specific needs and purposes.[27]

I now touch briefly on the various stages of feminism and feminist theory, although there is no single definition of feminism.[28] It incorporates the struggle

---

[23] Mills, *A Place in the News*, 36.
[24] Van der Vyver, "Die Groeiende Rol," 106.
[25] Farhana Goga, *Towards Affirmative Action: Issues of Race and Gender in Media Organisations* (Durban: UNESCO & Cultural and Media Studies, University of Natal, 2000); Colleen Lowe-Morna, *Whose News? Whose Views? Southern African: Gender in Media Handbook* (Johannesburg: Gender Links, 2001); and Wood, *Gendered Lives*.
[26] Julia T. Wood, "Gendered Media: The Influence of Media on Views of Gender," in idem, *Gendered Lives*, https://www1.udel.edu/comm245/readings/GenderedMedia.pdf, 231–44.
[27] Mpofu, "Are 'Untouched Citizens,'" 72.
[28] Lynn Parry and Beschara Karam, "Feminist Media Theory," in *Media Studies: Institutions, Theories and Issues*, ed. Pieter J. Fourie (Lansdowne: Juta, 2001), 383.

for political and legal rights, equal opportunities, sexual autonomy, and the right to self-determination. All in all, feminism is concerned with the advancement and achievement of equal social and political rights, and the fight against sexism.[29] Feminism is seen as a major branch of theory within sociology, as it focuses on social problems, trends, and issues that are otherwise overlooked or misidentified by the historically dominant male perspective in social theory.

Since the first reflections on the position of women, feminism can be identified according to various stages, as it encapsulates "a myriad of various theoretical perspectives emanating from the complexities and specifics of the different material conditions and identities of women"; all of these are "informed by the many diverse and creative ways" in which power is contested in "private and public lives."[30] Probably the best known of these is Gayle Tuchman's 1978 study, with its now classical terminology "Symbolic Annihilation"[31] of women—also relevant to this study with its focus on cyber-misogyny "annihilating" women journalists.

First-wave feminism began in the mid-nineteenth century and continued through the early part of the twentieth century in women's liberation movements in different parts of Europe and the United States.[32] Second-wave feminism began with the publication of Betty Friedan's *Feminine Mystique* in 1963, after which scholars identified consecutive (third-wave) developments within the women's rights movement.[33] Besides third-wave feminism, there also are liberal, Marxist, and radical feminism, as well as Black or African feminism, also called womanism; all represent various perspectives in the development of the women's rights movement.[34]

A brief explanation of Black or African feminism, or womanism, will be useful. This type of feminism regards itself as distinct from Western feminisms, as it

---

[29] Watson and Hill, *Dictionary of Media and Communication Studies*, 104.
[30] Josephine Ahikire, "African Feminism in Context: Reflections on the Legitimation Battles, Victories and Reversals," *Feminist Africa* (2014): 8.
[31] Gayle Tuchman, "The Symbolic Annihilation of Women by the Mass Media," in *Culture and Politics*, ed. Lane Crothers and Charles Lockhart (New York: Palgrave Macmillan, 2000).
[32] Wood, *Gendered Lives*, 66.
[33] Such as hooks, *Feminist Theory*; Wood, *Gendered Lives*, 8th ed.
[34] Feminism has been identified in waves, which have prioritised specific social demands in different socio- and geo-political contexts. The first wave simply demanded voting rights for women, while the second wave sought to expand the legal recognition to women's equality in work. The third wave highlighted the differences between and among women, as well as women's reproductive rights. Other variants of feminism also include, *inter alia*, liberal, radical, and Marxist-socialist feminism (Mpofu, "Are 'Untouched Citizens,'" 71).

relates to the specific challenges of Black women.[35] Black or African feminism was further sectorized by womanism, which argued that traditionally, only the struggles of Western, white, middle-class women were recognized.[36] Still, as is the case for other feminisms, women struggling specifically against the social and political realities of the African continent claim no single definition of Black or African feminism, as a specific African feminism or womanism.[37] Womanism can also be defined as a feminist approach developed by African women with different lived experiences from those of their Western counterparts.[38]

Besides such "officially" demarcated waves of feminism, some authors argue that the digital era brought about a shift from third-wave to fourth-wave feminism beginning around 2008.[39] One author refers to the internet's "call-out" culture, in which sexism or misogyny can be identified.[40] The #MeToo movement and activism around what can be described as institutional sexual harassment is a clear manifestation of this fourth wave.[41] I should also note, for the record, that different genders besides the binary constructs of female/male exist and have been described.[42]

My second theoretical point of departure is MHT. Given the "normalization" of "traditional" gender roles (as manifested in the epigraphs to this chapter), the roots of MHT can be found in Antonio Gramsci's concept of cultural hegemony.[43] MHT assumes that the media entrench the ideologies of dominant classes in society (or, in this case, the dominant gender). This assumption explains the media's perpetuation of the patriarchal ideology in societies. Taking into account the summative quotations from past centuries at the beginning of this chapter, it is ironic

---

[35] Kathleen Sterling, "Black Feminist Theory in Prehistory," *Archaeologies* 11, no 1 (2015): 95.

[36] hooks, *Feminist Theory*, 43.

[37] Gwendolyn Mikell, *African Feminism: The Politics of Survival in Sub-Saharan Africa* (Philadelphia: University of Pennsylvania Press, 1997), 3.

[38] Mpofu, "Are 'Untouched Citizens,'" 74–8.

[39] Jennifer Baumgardner, "Is There a Fourth Wave? Does It Matter?" in *F'em: Goog Goo, Gaga and Some Thoughts on Balls* (New York: Seal Press, Perseus Books Group, 2011); Kira Cochrane, "The Fourth Wave of Feminism: Meet the Rebel Woman," *The Guardian*, Dec. 10, 2012, https://www.theguardian.com/world/2013/dec/10/fourth-wave-feminism-rebel-women.

[40] Ealasaid Munro, "Feminism: A Fourth Wave?" *Political insight* 9 (2013): 22–5. Available from: http://www.psa.ac.uk.

[41] #MeToo Movement, https://metoomvmt.org/.

[42] Annelize Visser, "Geslag vs Gender" ("Sex vs Gender"), *Vrye Weekblad*, Mar. 25, 2021, https://www.vryeweekblad.com/lewenstyl-en-kos/2021-03-25-geslag-vs-gender-die-abc-van-die-t-in-lgbtq/.

[43] Nico Carpentier and Bart Cammaerts, "Hegemony, Democracy, Agonism and Journalism: An Interview with Chantal Mouffe," *Journalism Studies* 7, no 6 (2006): 964–75.

that, in a digital, postmodern society, this media bias is still the case in its new manifestation of cyber-misogyny. Gramsci's conceptualization of hegemony drew upon Marxist ideology, explaining the mechanisms of power in capitalist societies, something that can also be understood from a feminist perspective, namely, that power forms the basis for male dominance and the subjugation of women, especially through social institutions like the mass media. Already in 1984, observers noted that hegemony is the "dominance of [a] certain way of life and thought and ... the way in which that dominant concept of reality is diffused throughout public as well as private dimensions of social life."[44] This certainly is also applicable to what is described as cyber-misogyny.

Of importance to this chapter is the fact that scholars maintain that the concept of hegemonic masculinity is used to "describe gender power play and hierarchy in gendered social relations within society"[45]—including, indeed, the subversion of the female gender through the promotion of patriarchal and hegemonic ideologies within media discourses.

The Three Foundational "Value" Statements

The three summative value statements cited at the beginning of this chapter are foundational to my argument, as they help to illustrate the reason why women are still the target of abuse in what is termed "late modern pluralistic societies."

The first value statement is drawn from the foreword to this project by Michael Welker et al., namely, the value statement ascribed to Protestant reformer Martin Luther.[46] The second statement concerns the role of the media in society, specifically Thomas Peucer's description of what news is, or should be.[47] The third is that there were three estates that formed the basis of society, but that a Fourth Estate, the press (today's media), was "by far" more important.[48] This statement has been attributed to Carlyle, as quoting Burke, and later attributed to both. At the time it was expressed, it referred only to men as members of that esteemed Fourth Estate.

Luther's proclamation from about five hundred years ago states that "three estates" formed the foundation of a just and orderly society, namely, "marital families, religious communities, and political authorities." This implied that "parents

---

[44] David L. Altheide, "Media Hegemony: A Failure of Perspective," *Public Opinion Quarterly* 48 (1984): 477.

[45] Connell and Messerschmidt, as cited in Fafowora, "Media Construction and Representation."

[46] Welker et al., foreword.

[47] De Beer et al., "Leipzig: From Tobias," 11.

[48] Rabe, *Quote Unquote*, 18.

in the home; pastors in the church; magistrates in the state" were, according to him, "the three authorities whom God appointed to represent divine justice and mercy in the world, to protect peace and liberty in earthly life."[49] Thus, "household, church, and state" were the three institutional pillars on which social systems of "education and schooling, charity and social welfare, economy and architecture, art and publication" were to be built.

To critique this statement is to state the obvious. Naturally, it was proclaimed from within a patriarchal, male-dominated society in which women were subjugated as minors in terms of rights. Therefore, as a value statement, it would not be acceptable as a foundation for a "just and orderly," let alone equal, society. Rather, it was precisely such patriarchal-religious statements that contributed in a major way to the subjugation of women, instead of treating them as equals.

To be fair, we must note that this description of societal order obviously did not have its origins in the statement by Luther. As Welker et al. write, there are "various classical and Christian antecedents to these early Protestant views." Later theorists have propounded various versions of the three-estates theory, also moving away from an "overtly Christian worldview," but theologians, "both Christian and Jewish," still argued from within the marital, confessional, and political covenants prescribed by their respective gods as the basis for personal and public ends. Welker et al. write that these three "contracts" have also morphed over time within social contract theory, that is, in the marital contract between husband and wife, the governmental contract between rulers and citizens and, last, the religious contract between preachers and parishioners.

From a feminist point of view, these societal orders can be faulted for the way they entrench the subjugation of women, starting with something like the marriage formulary, which in many denominations still describes the man as the head of the household, with the bride pledging to obey him. These orders have also affected the status of women for many years—and still do in some societies—leading women to be viewed as legal minors, with either their husband or their male family members as their legal guardians. As to women's role in church, in some denominations and religions women have made great strides in being treated as equals, but in others women will not experience equal treatment for many years to come.

Simply put, one can say that this first statement cannot be used as a value statement to provide a basis for a just and equal society.

Moving to the second statement, which is closer to the focus of this particular chapter, namely the media, we can see that it also excludes women. It states that "news" is the birth and death of princes or generals, or announces war and peace—all the domains of men, and of a patriarchal society.[50]

---

[49] Welker et al., foreword.
[50] Rabe, "Eve-olution," 154.

Journalism has generally been described as the rough first draft of history, and for centuries history has been written by men. No wonder academics who study gender insist that, instead of a stereotypical portrayal of women in the media, *herstory* instead of *history* should be written.[51] This definition of news implied only male practitioners, with women joining the ranks of general reporters and, specifically, political reporters, much, much later—in fact, only in the twentieth century. It therefore is no surprise that women's representation in the media has always been stereotypical. Although great strides have been made, ingrained prejudices and practices still exist, as found, for example, in South African surveys of women in the newsroom since 2006.[52] At the time of this writing, a survey conducted by the South African National Editors' Forum (SANEF), titled "Sexual Harassment and Gender Inequality in the Workplace," was underway. In its accompanying email SANEF stated that it "is deeply troubled by the lack of research into workplace harassment and gender inequality in the media." The survey was "the first step in establishing its severity."[53]

All media and gender studies have confirmed the stereotypical representation of women in the news, the logical conclusion being that a new mindset is needed in media offices before women can make significant progress as news providers *and* news subjects.[54] A new definition of news is also necessary (as opposed to Peucer's unwritten "law," which still prevails). The need for gender diversity in the media classroom is also suggested. More than three centuries after the first doctoral dissertation on "what is news," the answer is still defined in the masculine—just as Peucer answered the question at the University of Leipzig in 1690. The rest of his response contains an inherent masculinity, as he wrote of the "transition of government, the transactions of war and peace."[55]

Unfortunately, not much has changed since the last South African "Glass Ceiling" report.[56] However, what was new, and became much clearer in the latest report, was the extent to which women journalists are exposed to cyber-misogyny,

---

[51] Ibid., 153–54.

[52] Lizette Rabe, "The Glass Ceiling and Beyond—Realities, Challenges and Strategies for South African Media," SANEF AGM, East London, 2006, https://sanef.org.za/about-us/resources/; and Glenda Daniels, Tarisai Nyamweda, and Collin Nxumalo, *Glass Ceilings: Women in South African Media Houses* (Johannesburg: Gender Links, and Media and Development Diversity Agency, 2018) https://genderlinks.org.za/what-we-do/media/research/glass-ceiling-research/glass-ceilings-2018-cyber-misogyny/.

[53] SANEF, Press Release, https://www.surveymonkey.com/r/TBT8NJY (press release about the survey, emailed to author, Feb. 23, 2021).

[54] Rabe, "Eve-olution," 159–68.

[55] Ibid., 16.

[56] Daniels et al., *Glass Ceilings*.

which is the ultimate focus of this chapter, to be discussed in the case study to follow.

Third and last, the statement attributed to Burke and Carlyle, about the Fourth Estate, needs brief reflection. Commenting on Burke's remark that there were three estates of Parliament—the clergy, the nobility (or upper house), and the commons (or lower house)—Carlyle added that while they were important, the "Reporters' Gallery yonder" was "more important far than they all." These words were also the origin of the description of the press (or media) as the Fourth Estate. Yet in a society that pledges equality for all, women are still bearing the brunt of discrimination and inequality in this very important Fourth Estate and, in the digital age, are also the object of cyber-misogyny.

The question asked by Welker et al.—"What can and should ... social spheres, separately and together, do in shaping the moral character of late modern individuals who by nature, culture, and constitutional norms are free and equal in dignity and rights"[57]—cannot be answered without assessing the fate of women, and women journalists, both globally and, specifically in this case, in South Africa to garner an idea of the *un*free and *un*equal rights of women in general.

According to Welker et al., to answer the question "[w]hat are and should be the core ... functions and moral responsibilities" of each of the variety of social spheres in order to "better understand and better influence the complex interactions among individualism, the normative binding powers of these social systems, and the creativity of civil groups and institutions," one solution lies in the answer to how a society that is still patriarchal can, as a collective, ensure that women (journalists) are treated in a free and equal way. As the case study illustrates, another solution lies in not exposing women (journalists) to maltreatment in the form of cyber-misogyny. If, as a collective, we do not try to find answers to counter a still patriarchal society, there can be no question of,
- in Luther's words, a "just and equal" society or,
- in the words of Peucer, what news should consist of, up to modern digital media or,
- in the words of Burke and Carlyle, how the Fourth Estate can represent women in a just and equal way.

Therefore, as a contribution to this volume on the media and its role in late modern pluralistic societies, I present, as a case study, the following matter of cyber-misogyny and its effect, not only on the quality of journalism but on the quality of life of female journalists.

---

[57] Welker et al., foreword.

The Situation in South African Newsrooms

First, as context, it might be enlightening to give an overview of the already mentioned studies on the status of women in South African newsrooms.

In the first "Glass Ceiling" report, in 2006, the findings on discriminatory practices, structural inequalities, cultural factors, prejudices, patriarchy, and sexism were not at all surprising.[58] Female reporters said they were treated as "lesser citizens." In the words of one respondent, "There's a sense that many men do often still feel they are superior to women. No amount of workshops is going to change this ingrained sense of entitlement." Also: "Preferences and privileges enjoyed by white men" still prevail—but now the "white old boys' club seems to be replaced by a black old boys' club." Female journalists also felt they were "patronised and their opinions do not appear to be taken as seriously as those of men." These instances were often seen as innocent, but they were "subtle, like jokes made at their expense when they give their opinions, or teasing. It seems friendly and even affectionate, but it is actually demeaning."

The newsroom culture had a "distinct maleness" and a "culture of maledom." "Institutionalised discrimination" was also a factor. As one respondent said, it was "[i]nteresting that these are the levels where skills are not the only requirement, but also the ability to fit in and perpetuate that establishment. In newspapers, women are rarely accepted at the upper levels of the organisation." Family responsibilities were "treated with distrust," which meant that female journalists had to work "twice as hard."

The survey found that a new definition of news and news practices was necessary. In fact, there was a need to reinvent, redefine, renew, and reimagine news for a postcolonial, postapartheid society. One respondent said that what was needed was "broader, deeper, constant debate as to what constitutes news, and what sort of social reality affects/underpins news events, news production and the social responsibility of news purveyors—as monitors/watchdogs/reporters." Another: "Thirty years ago my fate and that of others was decided by a clique of men in power, often while they networked in the pub! Nothing has changed." Yet another said that she regularly saw "relatively junior women staffers asked (half-jokingly, maybe ...?) to get tea; referred to as 'girls', and, if not exactly sexually harassed, then certainly expected to participate in banter that many might find undermining." In 2006, it was stressed that an audit was necessary on how many women were on which levels in media houses, as well as a study on sexual harassment in media houses.

Following the release of the 2006 report, Ferial Haffajee, as chair of SANEF and, at the time, editor of the *Mail & Guardian*, said at the meeting of the International Women's Media Foundation, about a week later, that her newspaper might

---

[58] Rabe, "The Glass Ceiling."

"exist in a cocoon," as it took "so easily" to her as a woman editor because female leadership "is in its DNA." However, she was shocked "by the results of our research into a glass ceiling in the media industry."[59] The survey painted "a picture of an industry stuck in the dark ages—which in South Africa is pre-1994"—consisted of "cosy boys clubs" and "frustrated senior female journalists for whom the promise of freedom is not arriving." Only about 40 of the 150 members of SANEF took part in the survey and, "as Lizette Rabe[,] who co-ordinated the study[,] acerbically noted, it's taken SANEF THREE YEARS TO GET THE STUDY DONE" [Haffajee's capitalization].

Haffajee added: "It presents a scary picture." There was an "intrinsic maleness of newsrooms and ingrained sense of entitlement," with men who "don't see the issue as important." She referred to the SANEF annual general meeting, where, "as this research was presented, an esteemed colleague blustered: never mind about that, when are we going to tackle female domination of the magazine industry?" And another one: "Do we really have to give women four months maternity leave? It's ridiculous. Why do I have to pay a premium for female skills."

The report also noted that women complained that senior female journalists "took on the perceptions and prejudices of their male colleagues in order to win acceptance." There was no "emotional commitment" to equity; it was rather viewed "as another box to tick." A "backlash" was also reported:

> Men affirming each other. In the ribald and irreverent atmosphere that is the newsroom, it's become a topic of jibe and cynicism. The golf course and the pub remain the main sites of doing business, making contacts. To play the game, you've got to imbibe this culture. So, women are frustrated because the workplace is still not delivering an atmosphere of empowerment.

Haffajee said SANEF needs to lead by "popularising this research to our industry": "We must take it into newsrooms, talk about it and show that non-sexism is a right of equal value to nonracialism." With the research limited in scope, being based only on SANEF membership, it means an "industry-wide audit" is needed "so we really know what's happening."

Since 2006, two more Glass Ceiling studies have been executed—in 2009 and 2018.[60] The latest shows that challenges for women in the South African media are becoming less about numbers and more about "underlying sexism in the me-

---

[59] Ferial Haffajee, "Is She Man Enough?," Glass Ceiling address, Jul. 17, 2006, PDF version of address in possession of author.

[60] Daniels et al., *Glass Ceilings*.

dia, with new threats like cyber-misogyny emerging."[61] This survey found dramatic shifts in the race and gender composition of media houses since the first survey in 2006. Black men comprise half of top media managers, while the proportion of Black women in top media management has increased fivefold, but is still 20 percent lower than Black men. With new media forms "sweeping across the landscape," South Africa "fits into the global media pattern of traumatic job losses, random and messy digitisation processes, a huge downturn in advertising revenue and a decline in sales and circulation." Unfortunately, only three out of the fifty-nine media houses that participated in the 2018 study gave data on wages. This adds to "general perceptions [that] suggest a growing gender wage gap as a result of fewer senior and top managers, and a growing throng of junior cadets running the social media platforms of media houses."

The study also explicitly indicated a "new threat against women," namely cyber-misogyny. It included "some of the ugliest forms of sexism being used to try and silence media women." But, the report stated, "the media is operating in a climate of the #MeToo movement globally and the #Totalshutdown movement nationally," which has increased women's assertiveness about sexism and patriarchal domination. Although sexual harassment is "a daily reality" for women in the media, mitigating it "is not prioritised."

Indeed, the first-hand account by Haffajee, not only former SANEF chair but one of South Africa's most influential journalists and the main focus of the case study, is "chilling testimony to one of the ugliest emerging forms of gender violence in the media." The report also states that cyber-misogyny "may just be emerging, but like the speed of the social media that spawned it, is guaranteed to spiral out of control if not addressed seriously."

It needs to be stated that South African female journalists are not the only female journalists to experience cyber-misogyny, as can be seen from countless academic studies and reports in the mass media.[62]

---

[61] Gender Links for Equality and Justice, *Glass Ceilings: Women in South African Media Houses* (2018), https://genderlinks.org.za/what-we-do/media/research/glass-ceiling-research/glass-ceilings-2018-cyber-misogyny/.

[62] Debbie Ging and Eugenia Siapera, "Special Issue on Online Misogyny," *Feminist Media Studies* 18, no. 4 (2018), https://www.tandfonline.com/doi/full/10.1080/14680777.2018.1447345; "New Research: Online Attacks on Women Journalists Lead to 'Real World' Violence," https://www.dw.com/en/new-research-online-attacks-on-women-journalists-lead-to-real-world-violence/a-55712872; Ylva Rodny-Gumede, "Cyber Attacks on Female Journalists Threaten Everyone," *Mail & Guardian*, Mar. 6, 2019, *https://mg.co.za/article/2019-03-06-cyberattacks-on-female-journalists-threaten-everyone/*; and Conor Friedersdorf, "When Misogynist Trolls Make Journalism Miserable for Women," *The Atlantic*, Jan. 7, 2014, https://www.theatlantic.com/politics/archive/2014/01/when-misogynist-

Cyber-Misogyny: A South African Case Study

Before presenting the case study, I first describe briefly what a case study entails. According to Johann Mouton,[63] a case study is usually qualitative in nature; it is also inductive and has no hypothesis, but rather some "general ideas" or "expectations" that act to guide the empirical research. Although there are similarities to other qualitative research approaches, the major difference can be found in the definition and delimitation of the "case," focus, or study.[64] For this chapter, the case involves the experiences of senior female journalists in the South African media environment, with a specific focus on Ferial Haffajee. Though it can be seen as a small case, it can provide an understanding, in terms of the concept *verstehen*, of a larger situation or similar phenomenon regarding not only the issue of South African female journalists and cyber-misogyny, but also a global situation affecting women in general. The following discussion focuses mostly on the experiences of Haffajee although reference is also made to other female journalists and their experiences of cyber-misogyny.[65]

After the South African national elections in May 2019, Angela Quintal, Africa program coordinator for the Committee to Protect Journalists (CPJ), wrote that, in the lead-up to the elections, journalists cited online harassment and threats as the biggest challenge to their work.[66] As a journalist herself, she referred to how she was prevented from covering the preelection violence in 1994 by her editor, who stopped her from covering the so-called Shell House Massacre. This was when African National Congress (ANC) security guards opened fire on members of the Inkatha Freedom Party (IFP), killing more fifty people. She quit, refusing "to witness South Africa's first democratic election from behind a desk."

A quarter of a century later, Quintal returned to Johannesburg for the sixth democratic elections on May 8, 2019, as an international observer for the Electoral Commission (EC). Whereas there had been a risk of physical violence in the 1990 s, journalists in 2019 had to contend with online harassment, cyber-bully-

---

trolls-make-journalism-miserable-for-women/282862/; "Sexism's Toll on Journalism," https://rsf.org/sites/default/files/sexisms_toll_on_journalism.pdf.

[63] Johann Mouton, *How to Succeed in Your Master's and Doctoral Studies* (Pretoria: Van Schaik, 2001): 149–50.

[64] Sharan B. Merriam and Elizabeth J. Tisdell, *Qualitative Research: A Guide to Design and Implementation* (San Francisco: Jossey-Bass, 2016), 38.

[65] The following is mainly based on Lizette Rabe, *A Luta Continua–A History of Media Freedom in South Africa* (Stellenbosch: African Sun Media, 2020).

[66] Angela Quintal, "Discredited, Threatened, Attacked: Challenges of Covering South Africa's Election in the Digital Age," Committee to Protect Journalists, Jul. 1, 2019, https://cpj.org/blog/2019/07/south-africa-election-journalists-online-harassment-threats-doxx.php.

ing, and toxic social media, especially facing fear and uncertainty about whether the digital threats would turn into physical attacks.

Ranjeni Munusamy, at the time associate editor at Tiso Blackstar, publisher of the *Sunday Times*, *Sowetan*, and *Business Day*, had covered the political violence in KwaZulu-Natal in the 1990 s, and said that those making the threats did not know what it was like "to live in a war zone and did not witness people being killed because some or other politician declared them as an enemy." They were using "inflammatory language to fire up their constituencies, but seem not to realise that words have direct consequences."

In 2019, Munusamy was one of five journalists who swore an affidavit in SANEF's case against the Economic Freedom Fighters (EFF) following "a barrage of [online] threats against journalists from the party's leaders and supporters." SANEF requested the Equality Court to prohibit the EFF from "using any platform, including social media, to intimidate, harass, threaten or assault journalists." Munusamy's affidavit, as well as those of the other journalists, detailed the threats and how they were affected, both personally and professionally.

Quintal wrote that "given the heightened rhetoric and vitriol in the election, the legal stalemate left journalists feeling vulnerable, while politicians and party supporters appeared emboldened." Some journalists tried to downplay the threats, insisting they were not "cry-babies," and that colleagues elsewhere in Africa "had it far worse." Younger journalists, "in particular," said harassment and intimidation were "normal."

But, wrote Quintal, the bigger issue was social media platforms spreading disinformation "to discredit, threaten, and harass the press." While social media were "weaponised," journalists were singled out for verbal abuse at rallies or in party statements. The EFF was not alone in harassing journalists, but had the biggest impact. Their main target, as "public enemy number one," was journalists. In the end, Munusamy did not cover their rallies and avoided writing about the party, even considering "getting out of journalism" to "get away from the fire." According to Quintal, the press "battled the threats alone." It did not get support from the EC, nor from Chapter 9 state institutions like the Commission for Gender Equality and the South African Human Rights Council. And the "police weren't much help either."

It is not a coincidence that the following cases all concern women journalists. Foremost among them is Haffajee, recipient of CPJ's 2014 International Press Freedom Award, who said that it appeared that the EFF enjoyed "virtual impunity."[67] Seven cases laid against the EFF in 2018—"its year of violence"—have

---

[67] Ferial Haffajee, "An Army of Trolls Marches on in Mindless Violence—And Nobody Is Stopping Them," *Daily Maverick*, Mar. 7, 2019 https://www.dailymaverick.co.za/article/2019-03-07-an-army-of-trolls-marches-on-in-mindless-violence-and-nobody-is-stopping-them/.

become "virtually cold cases." Haffajee was concerned how cyber-bullying affected journalists. If anyone "would know about harassment, trolling, bot armies and cyber-hate," it was Haffajee.[68] After already having been harassed a number of years earlier for publishing the infamous Muhammad cartoons, she had to take legal action against (the now defunct) Bell Pottinger PR company for defamation and breach of privacy after being harassed (along with two other editors) as part of a disinformation campaign. She was "singled out" by the EFF and labelled publicly, together with other senior journalists, as the "Ramaphosa Defence Force" because of their "supposed bias" toward President Cyril Ramaphosa. In an interview with Quintal, Haffajee said she "continues to report critically," but that there were times that she "definitely censored" herself.

Haffajee was also concerned about the effect on younger journalists and how cyber-bullying affected journalists' mental health, adding that she did not "trust the system to protect us." This was emphasized by then *Sunday Times* political reporter Qaanitah Hunter, who tweeted less than a month before the elections in 2019 about the effect of threats: "Being a journalist is terrible for your mental health ... simply because no one speaks about the effect of this on our lives." She was sent an image of a gun from a mobile phone number used by an official of the ANC's Women's League. The official later apologized, but denied being the sender. Hunter experienced "automatic trolling" after every "big story about the internal dynamics of the ruling party." This campaign to discredit her included a picture of her with a caption stating, "this is what a liar looks like."

Hunter was also body-shamed. After one such incident she tweeted, "And then ANC comrades zoom o[sic] to my picture and body shame me on their whatsapp groups. I'm done. Taking a mental health break. Sometimes that thick skin gets withered."[69] Hunter received overwhelming public support.[70] Three weeks later, she won SANEF's Nat Nakasa Award for Courageous Journalism. Awards judge and veteran journalist Joe Thloloe said that her courage was "displayed in revealing her own anxieties, in writing and talking and sharing her fears about mental health, in warning us all to find equilibrium in the demanding and volatile jobs we do."

Radio and TV journalist Karima Brown, who tragically died from COVID-19, was "doxed" by EFF leader Julius Malema during the 2019 election campaign (doxing is publishing the private documents of an individual). After the doxing by Malema there was "an onslaught of graphic messages on social media," both through voice and WhatsApp messages, "many threatening rape and murder."

---

[68] Quintal, "Discredited, Threatened, Attacked."
[69] Qaanitah Hunter, Twitter account, https://twitter.com/QaanitahHunter/status/1134874308210253824, Jun. 1, 2019.
[70] Quintal, "Discredited, Threatened, Attacked."

She laid a charge of harassment with the police. Because the Electoral Code of Conduct was in force, she also complained to the EC.

The EC "dragged its feet," and Brown brought a case in the Johannesburg High Court, arguing that Malema and the EFF had contravened the electoral code. Quintal sat in the public gallery and watched as the EFF lawyer "attacked Brown, her journalism, and her credibility." While judgment was reserved until after the elections, the cyber-hate continued.

During the same time, Malema "turned to his 2,4 million Twitter followers" to focus on *Daily Maverick* investigative reporter Pauli van Wyk. While not mentioning van Wyk or her publication, those who commented took Malema's tweet to refer to her. His tweet was viewed as incitement, including the "apparent reference" to the 1838 massacre of Boers by Zulu King Dingane. It read: "We are still cruising nicely, bana ba baloi (children of wizards) are not happy. Go for kill[,] fighters, hit hard."

Almost a month after the election the Johannesburg High Court[71] ruled that Malema and the EFF had violated the Electoral Code of Conduct, and they were ordered to pay Brown's legal costs. Their conduct had the effect of jeopardizing free and fair elections "by fostering a chilling effect on robust media reporting."[72] However, Malema was not ordered to apologize on Twitter or pay a fine. Instead, the judge said Brown's "strident and political tone" had "fuelled the flames of discord." Still, it remained a victory for Brown and journalism, setting "an important precedent that could stand to offer South African journalists some protection."

Not only female journalists were harassed; so were male journalists.[73] SANEF, concerned about the "ongoing attacks, harassment and intimidation" of journalists, issued statements on the harassment and arrest of journalists on two consecutive days.[74] The editors' forum reiterated the media's important role and said that there were several channels for recourse for grievances. Later that same month, however, SANEF again had to condemn the harassment of journalists, referring to a "number of incidents" that happened that very week, from intimidation to bullying.[75] It also noted "with grave concern" the SABC's (South African Broadcasting Corporation) statement on "death threats" its journalists received after covering various stories, including on alleged corruption, as well as "political and corporate bullying" directed at its journalists.

---

[71] "South African court rules Malema, EFF violated Electoral Code of Conduct in Karima Brown doxing incident," Committee to Protect Journalists, Jun. 6, 2019, https://cpj.org/2019/06/south-african-court-rules-malema-eff-violated-elec/.

[72] Quintal, "Discredited, Threatened, Attacked."

[73] "SANEF Condemns Harassment of Journalists," SANEF Statement, Jul. 10, 2019.

[74] "SANEF Condemns Harassment and Arrest of Journalists in Durban," SANEF Statement, Jul. 11, 2019.

[75] "SANEF Condemns Harassment of Journalists," SANEF Statement, Jul. 26, 2019.

In terms of the global picture, UNESCO noted that journalism "is one of the most dangerous professions in the world"; ninety-four journalists and other media workers were killed in 2018.[76] According to Reporters Without Borders' (RSF) World Press Index, there was "a growing trend of hatred" against journalists, culminating in increased violence. Freedom House stated that the media was "under attack," and part of this assault came from elected leaders who should instead have been the "ardent defenders of media freedom."[77] UNESCO's director for freedom of expression and media development, Guy Berger, noted several instances of "mobilisation of mobs" at rallies and online, creating an environment in which journalists "are treated as liars and trouble causers who deserve the ill treatment they receive."[78]

Haffajee wrote about her experience after having been targeted by political trolls and bots on social media for several years, and how these platforms were a rising threat to media freedom.[79] On cyber-misogyny, as a trend targeting women in particular, she wrote that "naming it makes it no less painful, as I have found." Also:

> Every morning, I pick up my phone and check WhatsApp messages. Then, I open my Twitter feed. "Bitch!" reads a response to something I've posted or written or reported. I block. "Cunt," reads another. Block. "Racist, go back home," says another.

"I will smack you so hard, you won't know your name," I type. And then block.

According to Haffajee, online abuse "has become so commonplace that blocking is part of the daily routine now."[80] However, "just occasionally, you have to fight back." She referred to Donald Trump's message to four U.S. congresswomen "to go back to where they came from," which "ignit[ed] a fusillade of stories from

---

[76] "Number of Journalists Killed on the Job Rises in 2018," *Aljazeera*, Dec. 31, 2018, https://www.aljazeera.com/news/2018/12/number-journalists-killed-job-2018-rises-181231021858196.html; "Multi-Stakeholder Consultation on Strengthening the Implementation of the UN Plan of Action on the Safety of Journalists and the Issue of Impunity," UNESCO, Aug. 16, 2017, https://en.unesco.org/sites/default/files/report_-_multistakeholder_consultation.pdf.

[77] "Democracy in Retreat," Freedom House, 2019, https://freedomhouse.org/report/freedom-world/2019/democracy-retreat.

[78] Guy Berger, "UNESCO's Safety of Journalists' Agenda: What Impact?" *Australia Journalism Review* 40, no. 2 (2018): 29–39.

[79] Ferial Haffajee, "Twitter and the Rest of Social Media Are a Rising Threat to Media Freedom and I Am Part of Their Roadkill," *Daily Maverick*, Aug. 6, 2019, https://www.dailymaverick.co.za/article/2019-08-06-twitter-and-the-rest-of-social-media-are-a-rising-threat-to-media-freedom-and-i-am-part-of-their-roadkill.

[80] Ibid.

people who had been told so." This made Haffajee think about writing about "the black digital Trumps in South Africa" who instructed her to "Go home" and "Go back to India if you don't like it here."

Haffajee's next trauma was caused by a fellow (male) journalist. It happened in July 2019, when he started "his infamous thread numbering and naming a group of journalists," calling them the "Cabal." They were "part of a narrative of disinformation"–while he himself "deliberately misled ... the public." She muted him on Twitter because "the deluge of responses was too abusive to cope with." But it had "real-life consequences." She literally felt it shortly afterward, at the Zondo Commission. She sat near the back in a crowd accompanying Jacob Zuma to give testimony. During tea-time, somebody started "stage-whispering" the word "cabal." Then it was picked up, and "soon it was repeated." And "then they laughed. It stuck to me like spat venom." Haffajee remembered that she still was not sure whether she did quality journalism that week, as she kept hearing "cabal," "cabal," "cabal," And: "I've worked hard for 29 years as a journalist to not be part of any cabal, so the whispers cut to the heart of me."

Haffajee said the internet's powerful social media platforms hosted among the "worst forms of violence against journalists." It not only became "a battlefield" for violence against female journalists but, in fact, made them "roadkill." UNESCO and other advocates saw it as a rising threat to media freedom, as women journalists were particularly targeted in cyber-bullying. Haffajee experienced it physically: "I realise that when reporting, I walk with a stoop now, bent from the world as if to protect myself. It's not like me. At news events, like EFF media conferences, I make myself small and will ask questions in a way that sounds to me, as I reflect, almost obsequious. It's definitely not like me."

Haffajee decided not to be part of SANEF's 2019 case against the EFF–"not because I don't identify with it or support it with my full heart." It rather was a need that "the spotlight should turn away because the insults sear at me" and because she had started to "imbibe the insults and opprobrium, to cut my cloth to fit the words flung with abandon and to begin to second-guess myself." She read "with disbelief" Malema's response to her decision– namely, "a high-five" from him for not being one of the journalists in the case. She was "lauded" for "still going to EFF press conferences"–some journalists do not "because it's a risk"–and for "engaging as an equal." Haffajee's reaction: "I am no equal. I am a roadkill."

The SANEF case followed Malema's speech in November 2018 outside the building in which the Zondo Commission sat, "when he outdid even himself in the rhetoric of hate." In his "wide-ranging speech" he named the "Ramaphosa Defence Force"–publisher Palesa Morudu, editor Max du Preez, activist academic Nomboniso Gasa, legal scholar Pierre de Vos, journalist Ranjeni Munusamy, and Haffajee. She remembered that she was the only journalist at the rally that day, "and so got special treatment." Malema addressed her directly: "Ferial with all her skills as a former editor[,] why are you not asking Pravin [Gordhan, a cabinet minister] if he has an account outside South Africa. Ferial never asks, instead, she attacks [the] EFF." Then Malema "told his supporters to write down" all their names and to attend to them "decisively everywhere you see them." In the "world of trolling armies," it was "an instruction to attack, either online or even 'IRW' (in the real world)."

Haffajee recalled: "But then something happened that made Malema pull back." The crowd around her "started growling," despite "at least two lines of police officers" as security for the precinct around the commission. Malema saw what was happening and, "being the brilliant (perhaps Machiavellian) politician he is, he changed the tune." He then said his supporters must "engage with them from a civilised point of view" and "must never be violent with them"—suddenly warning against harming those he had named, straight after telling them to "attend to them decisively."

In its defense, the EFF said "that political speech is often only rhetorical and that Malema cautioned his supporters." But they also argued that journalists cannot be given special protection under the Constitution because "it could open the floodgates for other groups, such as politicians, to claim similar treatment." Again, it was argued that such special protection would harm Section 16 of the Constitution, which enshrines free expression. Haffajee said it was a clever argument "and one that resonated with journalists." She said she did not want to curtail free speech, "but neither do I want to feel so permanently nervous." Haffajee was not sure that "the battle against online violence" would be won in the courts, but the "powerful social media platforms"—Twitter, Facebook, WhatsApp and Google—had to do more "to prevent technology being weaponised."

In another instance, Malema, on the instruction of Twitter, had to take down a tweet in which he clipped a WhatsApp message from Karima Brown, including her phone number. At a press conference he said he only agreed to delete the message because "I need that thing [Twitter]."

Haffajee: "Malema is a general and Twitter is his army of 2.4 million followers." He was not unique in using social platforms, as "trolling armies are now used around the world by politicians to grow or protect or gain power." There were many examples, she wrote, mostly targeting female journalists. Social media have made democracies more democratic "by giving people a voice, by making sure the media is more accountable." The media is also "not the only platform in town" anymore, because everyone "with a smartphone or a data point is their own media," thereby "smashing media monopolies." But it also spews threats severe enough "to make the life of journalists so dangerous that they quit." Or it could result in the election of authoritarian regimes, "or political change so seismic that it turns the clock backwards."

Haffajee is a veteran of being targeted precisely because she practises courageous journalism. As editor of *City Press*, she published a review of an exhibition of artist Brett Murray. Part of the exhibition was a controversial painting, *The Spear*, depicting then president Jacob Zuma as Lenin, "but with his penis exposed in a piece that referenced the parable of the *Naked Emperor*, the cautionary tale of what happens to leaders whose followers are too scared to tell them the truth." Murray, an activist artist whose first works date from the Struggle, "hadn't stopped resisting, especially as the governing ANC descended into corruption."

The review caused one of "the first Twitter storms," with Haffajee the target "as the hive of hate swarmed." Ten years later, Haffajee said she had forgotten "most of the hate," but some stuck. She said the contents of the tweets made her "feel ill," although she did not "know the words yet to explain why." There was more to come: "There was mayhem. I was scared. People knew where I lived. We didn't have the language to describe digital misinformation or disinformation."

Haffajee regarded Twitter as a platform to "micro-report, to live blog, to carve an opinion in the constraints of 140 characters"—"a liberating tool and a democratising one." Indeed: "I enjoyed Twitter. Until it turned on me."

Another example of how Haffajee became a target of cyber-misogyny happened a day "after publishing an essay that took me months to report and which had been done with due care and consideration." Haffajee opened her social media "to find distorted images of myself as a gargoyle and a mad elf staring back at me." Alarmed, she scrolled through images "of myself jumping out at me."

The topic of her reportage was an in-depth study of state capture as "sophisticated corruption where policy and positions across the state are commandeered by powerful patronage networks." In this case, the patrons were the Gupta family, who, as Indian immigrants, befriended Zuma "and then proceeded to enrich themselves spectacularly."

Haffajee had heard "that a group of journalists who had written about the Guptas were under surveillance and were a target, but I had given it little thought." But she was one of them. "The images bombarded Twitter for weeks." After the first distortions of her image, "they morphed into images of more destructive hate." Among other images, her face was photoshopped onto a "barely clothed dancer," onto a "busty cheerleader wearing a barely-there costume," onto a dog being walked by Johann Rupert (the "face" of so-called white monopoly capital), and onto a cow being milked by him. A dog, a cow, a prostitute: "the nasty purveyors of online hate could not get more stereotypically sexist."

It became clear that Bell Pottinger designed the campaign in the same way it had designed "black ops" in countries such as Iraq, using "click farms and designers in India from where the Guptas ran some operations." Haffajee and others sued Bell Pottinger, "or its insurance company, as the PR giant went bankrupt."

"I'm roadkill, not an equal of Malema's and other trolling armies, because they have impacted on me," Haffajee wrote. The images of her, the words of a journalist colleague who turned on her, and Malema's trolling army "fill me with shame." She has asked herself "so many times how this digital misogyny impacted as hard as it did, shaming me and causing me to hide the images and to hide from them and to feel like I had to explain them." She still lacks an answer, "except that I have realised that when hate comes to you packaged and delivered on to your phone and into your palm, it gets into you."

The "designers and purveyors of cyber-misogyny" use online attacks to silence journalists, and it is part of Haffajee's routine now to spend part of each day blocking hate. She even experienced a man so incensed by what she tweeted "that he sent me a direct message in which he said I deserved a bullet to my head." He did not even "bother to hide his identity." She reported it to Twitter. Eventually, she got through "to the bots who take reports" and he was blocked—"but only for a time," as there "is no life sentence for making death threats against women on Twitter." Haffajee said that, while social media executives "flood the free media conference circuit" and "speak the language of ending cyber-hate and online misogyny," the situation is so severe that UNESCO has recognized the trend as a rising threat to free expression.

Despite social media executives' assurances of fighting online misogyny, Haffajee's experience was the opposite. Trying to report such incidents, she found "Twitter's chatbots, which field first line reporting, to be singularly unhelpful." Attempting to report such messages and attacks, "most times I get a bot (or a poorly paid and poorly trained casual worker in one of their outsourced customer complaints teams) which or whom, in essence, tells me I have to put up and shut up when called 'bitch', 'cunt', 'witch' or any of the casually flung epithets that come at us day after day." The response would be that they do "not violate Twitter rules," followed by the advice "to block or to mute the hate." It's the "digital equivalent of telling women journalists ... to go and cover easier beats than investigative and political journalism that do not generate hate." Something that, "I guess, is just what the online merchants of hate want—to get us off the beat."

Besides SANEF and the five journalists requesting the court to interdict Malema and the EFF "from intimidating, harassing, threatening or assaulting any journalist,"[81] it also asked to interdict Malema and the EFF from publishing the personal information of journalists, as well as preventing Malema and his party "from openly or tacitly endorsing such actions by its supporters or followers."

SANEF argued that Malema and the EFF had created a "toxic environment" for journalists. Malema's statements "need to be accepted at face value" because "words have consequences." His statements amounted to "a call to violence," even starting "long before he declared that journalists should be treated as politicians." SANEF stated that, in effect, Malema said that if journalists "don't write what he likes they [the EFF] will continue to call them out." This meant "journalists will be

---

[81] Pieter du Toit, "Malema, the EFF and a History of Violence," News24, Aug. 5, 2019, https://www.news24.com/news24/analysis/analysis-malema-the-eff-and-a-history-of-violence-20190805.

fair game and the abuse and harassment will continue, because they are regarded as politicians."

Malema asserted that neither he nor the EFF could be held responsible for the actions of supporters or followers, but this defense was rejected by SANEF. The EFF also did not "dissuade their supporters from making threats and harassing journalists." The EFF said that journalists themselves were complicit in the creation of the "toxicity" because of their bias towards them. It was clear that the SANEF case could become "a seminal issue in the evolving case law on what constitutes hate speech," how "the murky world of social media and politics intersect," and whether political leaders can be held accountable for their supporters' actions.

Meanwhile, the Press Council of South Africa, at its annual general meeting in August 2019, warned that violent threats through social media "are intended to undermine media freedom," and that "aggrieved members of the public and politicians should use existing channels to lodge complaints."[82] Mahlatse Mahlase, at the time SANEF chair, said the organization noted and welcomed the public debate in the wake of the court case.[83] She believed the discussion would strengthen and improve "our national discourse on the importance of media freedom and freedom of expression."[84]

A male journalist, Max du Preez—one of the applicants in the case—had also been physically threatened at the Zondo Commission, and three days after Malema's speech, another female journalist, Ranjeni Munusamy, was harassed at a shopping mall. Her affidavit stated:

> At approximately 18:00 on that day, I visited a shopping centre near my house. I go there often on my way home from work. I do not wish to disclose the precise location because I do not want a repetition of what happened on the day. While shopping, I noticed three men looking at me. As I walked past them, they repeatedly called my surname in a mocking tone. I tried to ignore them, walking past them quickly. The men were waiting for me at the entrance of the shop when I left. As I passed them they hissed at me and shouted my name. ... As a consequence, I am wary of going out to public places.

SANEF argued that these physical and "online threats, abuse, harassment and hatred levelled at the applicants" were a direct result of Malema's speech. Their complaint was "not to stifle criticism of the media and journalists," but because

---

[82] "Press Council of South Africa Annual General Meeting," SANEF Statement, Sep. 6, 2019.
[83] Mahlatse Mahlase, "Letter from Our Chairperson, SANEF and Five Others v EFF and Another—Setting the Record Straight," SANEF Statement, Sep. 14, 2019.
[84] The full set of court papers is available at https://sanef.org.za/sanef-vs-eff-court-papers-2/.

the comments "by the EFF, Malema and Malema's purported supporters go beyond fair criticism of the media" and, in fact, constitute hate speech under the Equality Act.

In one of many SANEF statements since then, the watchdog body had to state its "deep concern" regarding the "increased trend of death threats and social media harassment of journalists."[85] The consequent self-censorship by journalists deprives "society of information and further affects press freedom"—besides directly affecting the UN's "human rights-based efforts to promote peace, security, and sustainable development."

Conclusion

The point of departure of this chapter was that, although certain values of a fair, just, and equal society regarding gender have been enshrined in statements by various influential personalities over centuries, they have not ensured a fair, just, and equal society for women. After discussing these value statements and various other elements relating to this study, including the theoretical points of departure, this chapter attempted to elucidate women's experienced reality by referring to the general position of women in society, using a specific case study to highlight the position of women journalists in a postmodern, digital age. By showcasing how women journalists experience cyber-bullying, specifically cyber-misogyny, the chapter demonstrates that women are still subjugated in terms of a patriarchal, male chauvinistic society. This case study is meant to showcase the general experience of women, representing not only South Africa and the Global South but women globally and in general. Women are still not only sidelined but subjugated in various environments, despite declarations, constitutions, and other policy documents that are supposed to guarantee a fair, just, and equal society. It is on the interface of these nexuses, and against the background of cyber-misogyny, that this chapter wishes to call for a new thinking regarding the position of women (and other genders) with regard to their position in late modern pluralistic societies.

---

[85] "SANEF Concerned About the Ongoing Escalation in Death Threats & Harassment of Journalists on Social Media," SANEF Statement, Jan. 28, 2020.

"Attitude" Can Damage Attitude When Journalists Abuse Their Power

Bodo Hombach

On January 28, 2016, at the invitation of WDR intendant Tom Buhrow, I spoke to the executives of that public-broadcasting institution and stayed for a discussion afterwards. At that time, I had left—after ten years of service—as managing director at the WAZ Media Group and devoted myself to my foundation and university work.

Circumstances change quickly. I don't distance myself from any line of the old, unabridged text, but the fact that a White House spokeswoman wanted to advance "alternative facts," that fake news has become part of everyday digital life, that sympathy clicks have a price list, that intentional journalism is becoming fashionable, and that a "documentary film" that has important scenes faked by actors is to be defended with the words that these scenes are "more authentic than reality"—all of this I could not have imagined six years ago. I would have found harsher words than what follows.

Keynote Address to WDR Executives, on January 28, 2016

This is a delightfully unexpected gathering suggested by your intendant. In this industry, one is not safe from surprises. Here am I—a former manager of the classic paper media, after ten years of overseeing processes of restructuring—to address the assembled executives of the publicly funded Westdeutschen Rundfunk. This is marked in red in my calendar! Thank you for the invitation and for the hour of your life.

Twenty years ago, I would have been amazed at your hospitality. In the meantime, the dual system [of old-style media and digital media] has settled in. All the prophecies of doom for the book and news industries were overworked. Competition, however, invigorates, is meant to last, and keeps things fresh. It would be threatening for both sides to become confusingly similar to each other.

You may know the story of the two lion hunters: before the hunt, one puts on sneakers. "Why?" the other asks him—"do you think you'll be faster than the lion?" "No," says the first, "but faster than you!"

There is division of labor. All media genres face common opportunities and risks. That commonality connects us. I have nothing to proclaim here. Especially not from a high horse. I want to think out loud, almost as a soliloquy.

Public broadcasting in our country is a cultural institution. It has saved journalism from degenerating as it has in other countries. News is a commodity, but not only that. Market laws have their meaning, but not everywhere. Audiences are to be taken seriously, more seriously than they often take themselves.

We are experiencing a broad economization of societies. A media company or broadcaster cannot escape this. Yet one doesn't have to submit to it. In fact, you are not allowed to. You are obligated by law and fees to apply the standard of the common good to what you do. Even if you sometimes do the same thing as private media companies—for example save money—you do it differently because for different reasons. The market's cold revenge for declining acceptance does not directly hurt those in public service.

I speak to you with high esteem, though by no means in submissive bowing. My esteem does not come from a reluctance to bite those who are better off. It comes from the high standards you postulate for yourselves. That is why every citizen may measure you by these standards:

- responsibility for the general good;
- independence of reporting;
- democratic fairness, and doing justice to opinions you do not share;
- putting aside personal attitudes and views in order to provide customers with an accurate picture of the world in a truthful and reality-oriented manner;
- sensitive perception of social impulses;
- committing to enlightenment and resisting any attempt at manipulation;
- maintaining respectful views and forms;
- being open to experimentation and innovation;
- transparency of internal decision-making processes;
- fiduciary, economical, and sustainable use of allocated resources; and
- a high level of professionalism in all areas.

This is a proud catalog. I would bet that this or a similar list of attitudes and postures can be found as a "corporate identity" in the editor's statute and in every self-commitment of your management. With concrete and honest soul searching, you will also find similar standards in real life. But a certain attitude can lead to damage of these professional attitudes and postures when journalists abuse their power—when they themselves want to make policy instead of coolly reporting "to the heart," analyzing, weighing, adding nothing and concealing nothing.

The "Fourth Estate" derives its legitimacy not from a democratic vote but from the professional quality of its work. Perhaps there is such a thing as absolute truth and objectivity, but it is not accessible to us. However, it can be approached, and one must want to do so. Restless patience helps, also openness to trial and error and the tireless willingness to let one's own theses fail against reality through a libidinous relationship to self-criticism. Not to disturb one's own thesis by real research or to underpin it by staging is a grave journalistic sin. Self-exaggeration is always self-deprecation.

Searching for reality and shining a light on it is a difficult undertaking in times of organized spin-doctoring as an accepted method of political communication, the transformation of arguments into slogans, the evaporation of the center to the radical fringes. Now, in the digital revolution, nothing is spared—especially not the media world. For better or for worse, unlimited possibilities grew, but also impossibilities:
- the total unleashing of communication to naive anarchy;
- the thresholdless mobility of devices;
- the direct access to a gigantic offering of information (and disinformation);
- the virtual parallel worlds and the technical abolition of forgetting.

A net holds things together, but nets also catch things.[1] All this in the struggle to capture a resource that can no longer be significantly increased: people's lifetime and attention. All this also in the struggle for power and influence. In the protection of anonymity, hatred ferments and seethes, breaking through thin veneers of decency.

Karl Popper once described in a brilliant, precisely condensed way:

> We are still at the beginning, but we are already experiencing the dissolution of the classic milieus. A creeping brutalization of society. The devaluation of basic values. The loss of informational self-determination. The fragility of the civilizational superstructure. The defamation of important achievements of the Enlightenment. Vagrant violence. The immediate proximity of seemingly distant conflicts. The disintegration of the European idea and the relapse into nationalistic particularism. We also experience the relapse into autocratic systems with a perverted press as a stirrup holder. We are experiencing the asynchrony of effort and effect, occasion and consequence.

Those who act are criticized. Those who do not act are punished by life. Grandma's motto—"He who does nothing makes no mistakes"—is life-threatening when adaptation becomes necessary. In this context, how does a large media company prepare itself? How does it position itself? What does it want to achieve or prevent? Is it capable of reacting flexibly, dynamically, creatively, or does it sink into the melancholy

---

[1] In German: "Ein Netz fängt auf, aber auch ein."

of organisms that have exceeded the limits of their growth? Will it end up like the dinosaurs, who could only sadly carry their own weight in a pool of water—until a merciful asteroid redeemed them from themselves.

I don't want to prophesy a doom that could also be prevented with effort. It is not enough just to flip a switch. External problems have inner-system properties and consequences. Our situation requires a circuit board with many potentiometers, capacitors, resistors, and sensors. "Cold" solder joints, reversed poles, and feedback are dangerous. (I used to be a telecommunication engineer. That background sometimes runs away with me.)

A modern company is like a clever chess game. The decisive factor is not the quantity of pieces on the board but the intelligence of their interplay in a network of the shortest possible paths and transparent processes. Such a system does not have an immediate solution. But it has the resilience to tackle problems quickly and to work on them patiently. It can react strategically, build up counterpressure, and act in an adapted manner. It can save when necessary and spend without breaking the bank. It can motivate people to get moving. It can recognize undesirable developments at an early stage. It can even admit mistakes publicly and learn from them.

In short, a modern company needs leadership. Good leadership shapes things before the constraints become overwhelming. Many were startled by the cries of "lying press," often shouted out by people who greedily believe every lie if it confirms their prejudices. The suspicion that media reality has little to do with the real one now has force.

Yet serious journalism always asks about the blind spots of one's own perception. Radio, television, and newspapers are mass media. They cannot despise the masses. They must understand them. Mass media have an effect and broadcast into the group or individual society. This cannot be explained with expressions like "dumbasses" and "mobs" alone. There are those who lie to us through exaggeration, through unrestrained scandalizing, through overexposure here and fading away there.

The serious journalist thinks twice before writing once. Serious journalists are not animators of a constant culture of excitement. They criticize politicians without ridiculing them. In the deafening noise of the internet's shitstorms or candy storms, journalists provide reasoned orientation. They convince through the relevance of their topics, the thoroughness of their research, and the balance of their judgment. They keep their distance from events and persons. They report without becoming cynical. Journalists do not have a mandate, but a mission. Hans Joachim Friedrichs put it in a nutshell. His dictum that a journalist should not get involved with any cause is taken to heart by too few people today.

For me, the promise of journalism was a promise not to be manipulated. The current rampant, intentional journalism we see in Germany will end up becoming what is so prevalent in America. Certainly, professional ethics are always ideal-istic and have their flaws and stains in reality. But if journalists abandon the claim to objectivity, faithfulness to facts, neutrality, and the search for truth, then unrestraint becomes widespread.

The disinhibited person hears, sees, and reports only what he knows in advance will have an effect on opinion. The blood barrier to propaganda becomes porous. We hardly have any primary experience. For better or worse, we are dependent on secondary experience. Media that paint a realistic picture of our world are indispensable. They are too important to be left to themselves. Media are not an event for society, but one of society. The very impression that one is being coerced into "speaking well" or even "thinking well" instead of being convinced triggers resistance. It opens the floodgates for populists.

I rarely hear the question, "What if everyone does it?" as a Kantian categorical imperative. The categorical imperative of the media society is, "What if it gets out?" Power and the powerful fear nothing so much as the publication of what they do not want the public to know. This watchdog function of the media disciplines and enables democratic coexistence.

The role of quality media is constitutive for our democracy. I am prepared to think big of journalists. I wouldn't mind if they thought big of themselves. But they must do their job properly. We know the importance of controlling internal processes. There was once a TV series called "Glass House." It was a talk show hosted by Westdeutscher Rundfunk that gave to TV journalists responsible for programming opportunities for self-critical reflection and discussion. Something like that would be sympathetic and sovereign at the same time.

Let me offer a few remarks on my professional experience with good managers. They don't define themselves by fights over rank and territory. They have a sign on their office door that says, "Please disturb!" A leader:
- does not want victory, but solutions;
- doesn't mix logical levels (a conversation about plays is different from one about rules of the game);
- approaches employees, doesn't lash out at them;
- fights complexity that so readily masquerades as complexity;[2]
- can explain decisions and take responsibility;
- at the height of success, already has the next one in the drawer.

Good managers constantly interfere in their own affairs. Basically, they have only one project: pleasurable learning—against laziness of thought, persistence, and bad habits. First of all their own, then also those of the employees.

A media company lives from its creatives. You can't produce them on an assembly line. They develop through stimulation and challenge with simultaneous support. No one dares to take big leaps on spongy ground.

---

[2] In German: "bekämpft Kompliziertheit, die sich so gern als Komplexität tarnt."

Speaking of habits. American psychologist Wendy Wood found that we perform half of our activities in the same roles, rooms, or places over and over again—sometimes with fatal consequences. After a certain time, we are no longer guided by our goals, but only by habits and their rituals: the office, the outer office, the colleagues, the cafeteria, the daily meeting. I have experienced this myself. It is worthwhile to occasionally change place and task. It changes your perspective. It's like the saving escape button from the endless loop. "The beginning is always already half." This phrase from Aristotle belongs on every bulletin board.

Times do what they always do: they change. That makes it difficult sometimes, but always interesting. The right question is, have I increased the set of possibilities? If so, one then has a better chance to prevail. This allows a return to calm deliberation.

Erich Kästner had a clever quatrain for this:

Good advice for Damocles:
Look scrutinizingly heavenward!
The closeness of the possible damage lies not in the sharpness of the sword,
but in the thickness of the thread.

The "thick thread" of public broadcasting is not the fee cushion but the ability to tend the fire, not the ashes. If you occasionally fail at that, then please do it on a big task, not in shallow waters.

I started with lions and will end with this: A lion hunter came home from safari exhausted. He had shot nothing. His friend scoffed gloatingly, "What's the point of all this effort for not one lion?" The hunter raised his finger meaningfully, "With lions ... with lions, not one is already very much!"

Contributors

Nick Couldry is Professor of Media, Communications, and Social Theory at the London School of Economics and Political Theory.

Katrin Gülden Le Maire, based in Paris, is an independent researcher, theologian, and management consultant for strategy and communications.

Bodo Hombach is a German politician, former publishing executive, and advocate for freedom of the press and high journalistic standards.

James Mairata is Lecturer in Television Production at Charles Sturt University, in Australia.

Bert Olivier is Honorary Professor of Philosophy at the University of the Free States, Bloemfontein, South Africa.

Stephen Pickard, a retired Anglican bishop, is Adjunct Professor of Theology at the Australian Centre for Christianity and Culture, Charles Sturt University, Australia.

Lizette Rabe is Professor and Head of the Department of Journalism at Stellenbosch University, South Africa.

Julia Sonnevend is Associate Professor of Sociology and Communications and Director of Undergraduate Studies in Sociology at the New School for Social Research, New York City.

Olivia Steiert is a PhD student in the Sociology Department at the New School for Social Research, New York City.

Contributors

Günter Thomas is Chair of Ethics and Fundamental Theology at Bochum University, German.

Matthias Vollbracht is Head of Corporate Analysis and Research at Media Tenor International.

Jürgen von Hagen is Professor of Economics and Director of the Institute for International Economic Policy at the University of Bonn.

Michael Welker is Senior Professor of Systematic Theology and Director of the FIIT–Research Center for International and Interdisciplinary Theology at the Ruprecht Karl University of Heidelberg.

John Witte Jr. is the Robert W. Woodruff Professor of Law, McDonald Distinguished Professor of Religion, and Director of the Center for the Study of Law and Religion at Emory University.

www.ingramcontent.com/pod-product-compliance
Lightning Source LLC
Chambersburg PA
CBHW070326230426
43663CB00011B/2229